Female Identity Formation
and Response to Intimate Violence

Female Identity Formation
and Response to Intimate Violence

A Case Study of Domestic Violence in Kenya

ANNE KIOME-GATOBU

PICKWICK *Publications* · Eugene, Oregon

FEMALE IDENTITY FORMATION AND RESPONSE TO INTIMATE VIOLENCE
A Case Study of Domestic Violence in Kenya

Pickwick Publications
An Imprint of Wipf and Stock Publishers
199 W. 8th Ave., Suite 3
Eugene, OR 97401

www.wipfandstock.com

ISBN 13: 978-1-61097-343-4

Cataloging-in-Publication data:

Kiome-Gatobu, Anne.

    Female identity formation and response to intimate violence : a case study of
domestic violence in Kenya / Anne Kiome-Gatobu.

    xii + 222 p.; 23 cm—Includes bibliographical references and index.

    ISBN 13: 978-1-61097-343-4

    1. Violence. 2. Women—crimes against. 3. Sex role. 4. Sex role—Social aspects—
Kenya. 5. Women—Violence against—Kenya. I. Title.

HV6626.23.K4 G39 2013

Manufactured in the USA.

For all the women who took the vulnerable risk
of "washing their dirty linen in public" so that
"their daughters may have a more fulfilled life."

Contents

Tables and Diagrams

Acknowledgments

This project has literally taken the hands, minds and physical effort of many in the African spirit of "I am because you are." (John Mbiti)

I make mention of the following few for their special roles:

For all the women who took the vulnerable risk of "washing their dirty linen in public" so that "their daughters may have a more fulfilled life."

For my parents Hellen and Stephen Kiome and grandpa M'Rarama who instilled in me ideologies that broadened my sense of self beyond the cultural encapsulation.

For my husband Haron, and children Mutethia, Nabii and Munene who have persevered, yet supported my efforts to have this book completed.

For my book advisors: Dr. L Graham, Dr. S. Dixon and Dr. E. King, for their guidance, patience and input in the process of my book writing.

For Peggy Blocker, Elizabeth Anderson, Stella Nyanzi, and Aureol Moore in having the grace to read and re-read and keep me encouraged in the writing process.

Last but not least, for the African Gender Institute Faculty at University of Cape Town (with a special mention of Dr. Saddiya Shaikh and Dr. Jane Bennett) and the Rockefeller Foundation, whose scholarship enabled my 3-month sabbatical to put this project together.

Section I

Situating Research in Context and Theory

1

Introduction

The Peculiar Case of Female Response to Male Intimate Violence

INTRODUCTION

Ever wondered why most female survivors of violence will continually remain in abusive relationships? Even in instances when the survivor physically severs or leaves a relationship, she is anguished by the initiative of severance, and depleted of her self worth and identity. The demeanor with which most female[1] survivors[2] of intimate violence in marital relationships carry themselves is particularly puzzling and is the subject of my inquisition into female identity formation. These survivors go about their daily lives optimally maintaining their roles as mothers, wives, and employees, despite their experiences of constant (and in many cases, brutal) violence. Should a survivor have any physical bruises from beatings, she will cheerfully explain them as resulting from an accidental event not in any way connected to her ordeal. In many cases she will even excuse her spouse for his brutality (Hinga 1994, 119). Her composed behavior appears to support the mythology in which intimate violence is perceived as an accepted fate for women in marital relationships.[3] From the dominant perception in the society, she is not a clinical concern, is not traumatized, and must, therefore, be in a state of contentment and be accepting of the violence.

Contrary to such popular mythology, I argue that the survivor's composed demeanor and "normal functionality" comprise a necessary façade that functions to maintain her identity and, therefore, value in societies that formulates the woman's "identity" through her reproductive and marriage roles. I employ the terms "identity" and "sense of self" to delineate how persons negotiate the process of finding one's place and coming to an

---

1. The term "female" is used interchangeably with the terms "girl" and "woman" (denoting childhood and adulthood for female respectively). I use the term female to refer to the psycho-biological-cultural reality whose initial sex of assignment is based upon observation of biological factors that constitutes one to be female as opposed to male, at birth. The term, therefore, includes the conglomerate of perceptions that renders one to be received and nurtured as an infant female, related to as a female girl, and integrated into adulthood with expectations of being a woman within specific social, cultural and religious contexts. There is clearly no singular woman. The term is used to describe structural and perceptual differences between male and female. It is used generally while recognizing the diversity of experiences, particularities and realities of individual women and their different social locations. As such, while some women may champion discriminative aspects of their social cultural and religious locations, there are those who have struggled, and continue to struggle with, and subtly or strongly denounce them. The reality is that no woman is statically fixed on either end of the spectrum. My reference to a woman (female, girl), however, takes a viewpoint that whether one falls on either end of the spectrum, the familial, communal and societal eye treats her and relates to her as a biologically configured female, socially located in her context, and that this has an effect on her sense of self, a central concept in this book.

2. Use of the term "survivors" instead of "victims" allows the voice and praxis of the women I interviewed to direct the language and terms used to describe their experiences.

3. This perception is very well expressed by Hilda Mawanda from the Coalition on Violence Against Women (COVAW), who states that, "People have become desensitized to it [wife beating]. Beating your wife has become an accepted part of the society" (*Time.com*, 153, 18 [1999, May 10]).

understanding of oneself as an individual within the community. In using the terms identity and sense of self, I consider Erik Erikson's and Heinz Kohut's description of the terms respectively, and how each approximates my understanding of the formation of identity. To illustrate social, cultural, and religious influence on female identity formation I use Kenya as a case study context, and relate Kenyan female self and identity formation in particular to the views of Erikson and Kohut, utilizing qualitative research with female survivors of violence in Kenya.

Central to Erikson's meaning of the term "identity" is the fulfillment or belonging found in what he describes as letting go of the safe hold on childhood and reaching out to adulthood. The quality of this process depends on the "reliability of those he must let go of and reception of those receiving him" (1964, 89). Erikson calls this period in human development the "natural period of uprootedness in human life: Adolescence" (1964, 89). He also recognizes that the sense of identity, although negotiated in adolescence and adulthood, is nurtured very early in life. He states, "The self-images cultivated during *all the childhood stages* thus gradually prepare the sense of identity, beginning with the earliest mutual recognition of and by another face . . ." (1964, 94).

For Erikson, successful identity formation depends on successful resolution of each epigenetic crisis, which serves as a building block to the next. He looks at the epigenetic process as a series of steps towards identity, offering the example of a child who learns to walk and then keeps repeating this newly acquired action in a responsive socio-cultural space, noting that this drive has implications for the child's future (1963, 235). Erikson states that,

> . . . the internalization of a particular version of "one who can walk" is one of the many steps in child development which (through the coincident experience of physical mastery and of cultural meaning, of functional pleasure and social prestige) contribute on each step to a more realistic self esteem. This self esteem grows to be a conviction that one is learning effective steps towards a tangible future and is developing into a defined self within the social reality. (1965, 235)

He further states that children cannot gain such esteem from empty praise. It must be confirmed by "consistent recognition of real accomplishment" (235).

Erikson views identity as the individuation that makes one stand unique in personality and yet whole, in the sameness and continuity achieved by the approximation of the inner drives and the outer social approval or confirmation of these drives. Hence, as Erikson states, the child "learns to suppress some of his willfulness for the reward of feeling at one with the will of those around him" (1964, 102). Building upon Erikson's view of social approval I expand "identity" to include strong and integral influences of the very early stages of the child, which, I argue, shape the child's psychic formation, and therefore choices, and opportunities open to the formation of identity. I, however, expand this way of looking at identity formation, arguing that in most cultures, the formation of female identity is not pivotal at just one particular period in adolescence but has been in the making from infancy, and indeed is closely guided by the formation of a female sense of self.

I base my view on the observation that in the majority of collective cultures, (even those that consider themselves as individualized cultures), the individual finds his/her identity by finding a place for the self within the whole, namely, the community. The self within the whole is therefore not so much a case of individual self-discovery and subsequent recognition and approval by society but rather a coming into being that actually happens within the whole, and therefore with aspects of the whole being integral in this process. Being a part of the whole in collective communities for instance, means participating and meeting societal expectations, and is integral to attaining identity and a sense of self as a person. Identity emerges from the need to belong to a community or society. The aspects of society that nurture the child's sense of how to develop an identity as one who belongs appropriately in a community are internalized from the very early stage of infancy and continue to unfold through the structural development of the psyche.

In my argument, the internalization of "one who can walk" is loaded with gender messages of, for instance, who can "walk" in what gendered ways; how well does one demonstrate potential for maternal care; what is one's potential for being a good cook; what beauty features is one endowed with; and so on. The defining of a self within the community and "growing towards a tangible future" emerges from a gendered conviction through which the girl has been esteemed for years. Hence, I go beyond Erikson's argument in his epigenetic cycle, which sees developmental success at earlier stages as providing important steps of growth resulting finally in successful identity formation. Each successive stage internalizes gendered aspects of development into the defining of the self, an argument that resonates with Erikson's statement that true identity "depends on the support which the young individual receives from the collective sense of identity characterizing the social groups significant to him: his class, his nation, his culture" (1964, 93). To class, nation, and culture I add, for a female, her gender and the cultural definitions which give her a sense of belonging as a gendered being within that culture. Any real value and accomplishment by the female is gauged by the collective sense of identity as a female defined in terms of wifely and maternal roles.

In addition to "identity" as a core construct for development, it is also critical to explore the concept, "sense of self," as a part of the psychological analysis. Though, as stated earlier, identity formation for the female needs to be understood in a broader sense that addresses the question of how one's individuality and continuity fit within the communal sense of wholeness, I find it necessary to discuss these internal dynamics that influence the formation of a female identity using the work of Heinz Kohut regarding the formation of a cohesive self. The psychic formation of a sense of self along idealized imagos as conceived by Heinz Kohut anchors the foundation on which she later forms her identity as interpreted by Erikson. For female identity development, I argue that these idealized images on which her identity is anchored are *gender roles* and the idealized *male figures (concept)*.

It is my view that the formation of identity for the female is reliant on the psychological formation of a sense of self. The sense of self in turn has pre-consciously been formed through internalization of social messages aligned to society's pre-conceived definition of what it means to be a female. Development of the sense of self is a function of the internalized social, cultural, and religious influences on the individual's aspirations to identify with and attain wholeness in the society. In other words, aspects of identity formation of females may be traced to the social, cultural, and religious environment which nurtures the developing child and engenders a sense of self in that child. This environment shapes gender role expectations, the need to belong, and the high value placed on marriage and association of the female with the male, all of which affect self worth and sense of self.

I further argue that these societally based gender role demands on the female psyche are so strong that she psychologically organizes her formation of identity by crystallizing the process on the central aspects of being mother and wife. These demands are internalized at a very early age so that they shape the thinking, desires, aspirations, and hence initiatives taken by the females. The aspects of being mother and wife are central to her sense of being a person who belongs—a person of worth within the community. They are central to her inner sense of self, as well to her psycho-social identity in the culture.

Through my case study of the Kenyan context, I posit that for the female the concepts of "self" in Kohut and "identity" in Erikson indeed overlap. In collective culture the formation of identity, is anchored in a sense of belongingness and has its foundational blocks in the development of a sense of self. I make this statement even though noting that Kohut clearly claims that his idea of self is not the same as Erikson's idea of identity. Although the two concepts have some commonalities, Kohut treats the self as an unconscious psychological structure that can have social roles added later. Acting on those roles successfully usually confirms the cohesive self, which, according to Kohut forms at a very early age and may be unavailable to us except in psychological analysis. This development of the self relates to what Kohut means when he says (in one of the crucial footnotes) that self is unconscious while identity is not. He states,

> It is difficult to find an appropriate place in psychoanalysis for the concept of "identity" . . . since, amphibiologically, it is equal-ly applicable in social and individual psychology. (1978, 443)

The concept of "identity," according to Kohut, does not belong to psychoanalysis, which is more concerned with the unconscious processes and formation of psychic .structures. It belongs instead to the psycho-social domain or the pre-conscious and conscious interaction between the psyche and the outer social roles on which a person builds his/her individuality (1978, 443). In this regard, the editor's comments in the same footnote continue:

> Contrast Kohut's attempt here to retain the term "identity" as a psychoanalytic concept with his later separate delineations of "self" from "identity" and the recognition that "identity" refers to conscious and preconscious configurations and thus deals with "psychological surface." (1978, 443)

The editor refers the reader to yet another note, which quotes a letter of Kohut in 1975 in which he says:

> I see the concepts of *self* and *identity* as clearly different. The self is a depth-psychological concept and refers to the core of per-sonality made up of various constituents in the interplay with the child's earliest self-objects. It contains (1) the basic layers of the personality from which emanate the strivings for power and success; furthermore (2) its central idealized goals; and then, in addition, (3) the basic talents and skills that mediate between ambitions and ideals—all attached to the sense of being a unit in time and space, a recipient of impressions, and initiator of

actions. Identity, on the other hand, is the point of convergence between the developed self (as it is constituted in late adolescence and early adulthood) and the sociocultural position of the individual.

This differentiation is to my mind very fruitful. Some individuals are, for example, characterized by a strong, firm, well-defined self that was acquired early in life—but their identity is, due to later circumstances, quite diffuse. I believe that the personality of certain types of psychoanalysts belongs to such a pattern. The diffuseness of the identity permits empathy with many different types of people—yet the firm self protects against fragmentation. There are other people whose organization is the very opposite: a weak self but a strong, perhaps overly strong, a rigid identity. These are individuals whose cohesion is maintained by an intensely experienced social role, an intensely experienced ethnic or religious sense of belonging, etc. And these are people who, when their identity is taken from them (e.g., when they move from one culture to another, such as from the village to the city) will psychologically disintegrate. And there are, finally still others whose firm but not rigid identity rests on a firmly established self. (Kohut, 1978, 471–72)

According to Kohut's perspective, then, self per se does not incorporate social roles, although they might appear to some extent as content associated with the mirroring of the Grandiose self or the idealized parent imago. When this claim is viewed from a collective perspective, however, I argue that social roles, especially female-gendered social roles, are persistently presented in our daily general rearing, so much so that they become internalized in our psyche at a very early age. In this way, they are incorporated into the formation of the unconscious sense of self, as interpreted by Kohut, and eventually influence female identity formation, as interpreted by Erikson. This identity formation in turn has a considerable influence on a female survivors' response to intimate violence, as in the intimate violence in adult marriage relationships. This response is both affected by, and affects, their sense of self.

The adverse psychological effects of the trauma of violence, although often hidden, contradict the mythologies held about survivors of intimate violence. This claim of Wundt: that a phenomenon or experience such as intimate violence becomes a subjective or apprehended experience interacting with the psychic structure of the person involved, is thus confirmed clearly (Wundt, 1998: 109). Given these considerations, it is important to engage an interdisciplinary approach that takes into account the socio-cultural and religious contexts of the individuals. Likewise, the psychological development of an individual, in order to understand the female's self-formation and how this has influenced the female's attitudes to intimate violence must be factored in. An important prerequisite to understanding the formation of an individual identity for both men and women is familiarization with religious and ancestral beliefs held by the people with regard to life, the individual, and his/her place in the community.[4] Although the individual can maintain an internal self-coherence, she also has to appropriate particular-gendered social obligations. These are demanded of her, and communicated from a very early age, if she is to fulfill the identity expected of her as a female.

Although marriage and childbirth in most Kenyan communities are perceived as a communal obligation of both the man and the woman, (as will be discussed in greater depth in Chapter 2), the customs that regulate these expectations are gendered and can be discriminative against females. They are integrally aligned with identity formation demands on the female, and in many societies she may find herself psychologically needing to fulfill these roles as a way to acquire a sense of belonging. These, I hypothesize, may lead, for many females, to an identity development and self-formation that is organized more around obligations than it is on personal endowments.[5] These belief systems form the basis from which the survivor of violence is nurtured, comes into being and develops a self, a view of the other and a worldview[6] in which she is a player.

In the case of many African societies, the advent of mainline religions like Christianity cannot be ignored. Christianity and other mainline religions enter a setting where African traditional religion had been rooted for centuries. Christianity, with its Jewish roots and Western patriarchy,

---

4. The discussion of the Kenyan context presented in chapter two is to be viewed as a case study that demonstrates these theorizations. "Kenyan context" or "community" is used to describe the various collective social cultural and religious contexts. Kenya is very diverse with more than forty ethnic groups all reflecting different cultural and religious traditions. We cannot speak of a homogeneous culture of the whole country and it is not possible to identify commonalities with finality. Given such diversity, any discussions that refer to Kenyan context and understandings refer to affinities and parallel experiences identified through my research and experience, and that call for more explicit recognition and interpretation.

5. Erikson recognizes this fact in his statement that, "the woman, in many ways, has kept her place within the typologies and cosmologies which men have had the exclusive opportunity to cultivate and idolize" (Erikson 1968, 262).

6. The concept of "worldview" is used in Clifford Geertz's definition as a "picture of the way things in sheer actuality are, their concepts of nature, of self, of society." See (Geertz 1973, 127).

served to legitimize coinciding existing social patriarchal arrangements that worked to shape the people's patterns of perceptions. If one were to view Christianity as a culture in the sense of a 'worldview,' then theological tensions between the two perspectives of Christianity and cultural traditions become clear, tensions often arising in the day-to-day endeavor of making meaning of life's experiences,. This in turn has an impact on child rearing practices, on the development of the self, and on identity formation for individuals within the communities, both urban and rural. The subsequent effects on those who have embraced new religions like Christianity and Islam have their own powerful influences on the formation of the self for people in their respective social locations. Outcomes, and the appropriation of such influences as of religion, of cultural traditions, and of gendered pressures are the focus of this book, with particular reference to female self-formation and its effects on responses to relational traumatic situations especially intimate violence.

Specifically, I am exploring how social, cultural, and religious contexts and their influences on the psyche and formation of self can help us better understand the female's response to intimate violence. What is it that makes the well-known cycle of violence[7] so predictable with respect to women choosing to remain in violent relationships? Why is it that the female, in collective cultures especially, does not fit well within the framework of the characteristics of the theoretical intimate violence survivor as elucidated by literature of the West, especially with regard to her high functionalism? A section of the book is dedicated to a general literature review to enable the reader to understand the difference in response and personality traits of the Kenyan survivor of violence. I have sought to explore these questions by interviewing women in, or who have experienced, intimate violence in marital relationships. The objective of these interviews was to gain insight into their psychic formation of a self, the hidden costs of trauma, and, therefore, the female response to intimate violence.

I chose Kenya as a context for my research for several reasons: First, I am an insider and have experienced the context since my formative years. Second, the various socio-cultural and religious traditions of people groups in Kenya offer the richness needed to demonstrate the formative influence of socio-cultural and religious contexts in the formation of identity and sense of self. The demonstrative richness is enhanced by

7. The cycle of violence, one of the most popular micro-theories of battering based on Leonore Walker's clinical observations in the late 1970s, is discussed in greater detail in the literature review section in this chapter.

the great influence of deep religious Christianity whose tenets come into constant conflict with traditional cultural religious aspects that are markers for identity formation and sense of self. My research in Kenya should therefore be considered as a case study of a contextual sort that may be referenced in conceptualizing psycho-religious themes that will pertain to many other global cultures.

Third, by choosing to do my research in Kenya I demonstrate the inadequacy of the present arguments, claims, and intervention strategies regarding intimate violence in Kenya which are shaped by literature largely conceptualized and investigated from the perspectives of Western concepts. Such Western concepts presume that identity and the sense of self-formation from a very individualistic perspective. Although some of the literature on intimate violence in Kenya points to the social, cultural and religious context in which violence takes place, it does not account for the way this context psychologically shapes the survivor and informs her understanding of, and ultimate response to, intimate violence.[8] My hope then is to account for the contextual psychological influence on the survivors' identity and sense of self which I believe is correlated to their response to violence. Although this work is informed generally by intimate violence literature from both Africa and the West, it does not seek to compare survivors in Kenya with those in the West. The intent is to be in conversation with multi-context and multidisciplinary scholarship, including many eminent psychologists like Heinz Kohut (1971, 1978), Carl Rogers (1961, 1963), Donald Winnicott (1953, 1966), Daniel McIntosh(1997), Crystal Park and Kenneth Pargament (1997) and Ana-Maria Rizzuto (1979); and theologians including John Mbiti (1969, 1975, 1991), Teresa Hinga (1992, 1994), Larry Graham (1992) Mercy Amba Oduyoye (1992, 2001) and Anne Naisimiyu-Wasike(1994), among others. Specifically, Kohut's postulations regarding the formation of a self are critically discussed and, where necessary, aspects of his theory are reworked and reformulated to be an adequate investigative lens for the Kenyan context. The major cornerstones of Kohut's theory are, however, held intact. Modifications of Kohut's theory that pertain to the Kenyan context are introduced into the theory as a conditional voice, thereby not only expanding Kohut's theory for applicability in a collective context, but also pointing to possible implications beyond what Kohut has theorized. By conditional voice I maintain that if certain modified aspects of Kohut's

---

8. See for example works by Hinga (1994) and Nasimiyu-Wasike (1994) who have attempted to contextualize intimate violence to the Kenyan traditions and cultures.

theory hold in Kenya, then the interpretation will have social, cultural, and religious consequences.

Ana-Maria Rizzuto's (1979) work on how one's development of a God image through years of human development influences one's own self-formation has also been extensively engaged. I have used constructs from these frameworks to conceptualize the understandings expressed by the survivors of violence. These are concepts which not only challenge but also transform these theoretical frameworks, emerging from the narratives and experiences of the women by giving them a voice from the women's experience.

I have critically considered emerging concepts, themes, and patterns of the survivors' thinking. I have engaged survivors in dialogue with psychological and religious theoretical formulations. From this engagement I have proposed principles by which one can build interpretive models which show an understanding of survivors of intimate violence, models leading to improved context-based intervention strategies.

My core proposal for investigation is that the seemingly composed demeanor and functionality of the female survivor of intimate violence in collective societies is an adaptation that enables her to retain her socially-prescribed identity, roles, and self-understanding thereof, (a position from which she views self and the other) which therefore, affects her responses to intimate violence. Such adaptation may curtail optimal development of a cohesive self in relation.[9] Although the survivor of intimate violence appears to be optimally productive in the eyes of the society, her functionality may indeed be viewed from another perspective as a self-righting tendency.[10] I posit that this tendency emanates from the development of a self that is centered on her contextual understanding of her social roles as "identity" rather than an optimal integration of a self in relation. The

9. The term "cohesive self" is used in this study with reference to Heinz Kohut's (1971) self-psychology theory of the development cycle of a human being. It is the ultimate stage of human development where the two psychic structures of the idealized parent imago and the grandiose self are integrated through life experiences and relations to others from infancy through adulthood. See also Ornstein (1978). In this work, however, the argument will be made that conceptions of cohesiveness in a collective society are fundamentally different from that which Kohut may have envisioned in his theory. As will be demonstrated, fulfillment and therefore self-cohesiveness in the Kenyan context, for instance, is found through relation with the extended community and the natural and ancestral world, as well as with the spiritual dimension; hence the term "cohesive self in relation."

10. The term "self-righting tendency" is used to refer to a concept that arises from the phenomenon of resilience, where one continues to thrive despite the obstacles of adverse circumstances. See Feshbach et al. (1996, 162).

danger I discern in this adaptation is that the energies and accomplishments emerging from a well-integrated self in relation would be largely unavailable to her, although they might improve her situation, expand her achievements and capacities, and contribute to her society if she could more thoroughly integrate the drive for achievement.

Key questions that emerge from this position and which form the framework of discussions herein include: How does the female in Kenya form a sense of self, given her socio-cultural and religious context? How does the survivor of violence in Kenya understand intimate violence from her subjective viewpoint and her place in the community? What effect do the sense of self and understandings held on intimate violence have on the survivor's response to violence in their own lives? In what ways have the survivors negotiated the tension between holding a sense of self and the trauma of violence? In other words, I discuss the understandings survivors form about the violence they experience, how their sense of self has influenced these understandings and the interaction of these understandings and sense of self in their range of response to violence.

The understandings that female survivors of intimate violence hold about the violence they experience, and the range of their possible responses to it provide insight into their operating self. These understandings serve as an insight not only to the phenomenon of violence, but also to the survivor's "inner experience"[11] in subjective interaction with the outer world, the interaction with which the survivor of violence needs to be understood. The understandings held by survivors are the expressive and observable phenomena. I analyze the emerging concepts and the survivors' patterns of thinking from a psycho-social and religious perspective as a basis for gaining insight into their inner operative life. In this analysis, I have utilized data that is available to the consciousness of the survivors to help approximate their inner thought and feeling processes as they engage the phenomenon of violence. This use is in agreement with phenomenology as a research method as discussed by Moustakas (1994, 45). Citing Moustakas (1994, 57), Creswell states that "establishing the truth of things" begins with the researcher's perception. One must reflect, first, on the meaning of the experience for oneself; then, one must turn outward, to those being interviewed, and establish "inter-subjective validity," the testing out of this understanding with other persons through a back-and-forth social interaction (Creswell 1998, 207). The women who form the focus of this study are between ages 18 and 50, educated females, (grade 5

11. In view of Wundt's conception of psychology as a "science of the mind" or "inner experience." See Wundt 1998, 108.

and higher), in marital relationships (or previous marital relationships), ,
in the urban setting of Nairobi. These education and age brackets in Kenya
constitute groups that are currently identified with the dynamism and
initiative of questioning traditional social systems. These are also groups
which are grappling with the frictional tensions between traditionally held
customs and Western influences. The choice of Nairobi provides a context
of diverse ethnic groups while at the same time limiting the geographi-
cal variances of the rural settings. Conducting the study in Nairobi also
provided a good point of comparison for further studies to see the extent
to which people from the same ethnic groups hold the same or different
perspectives when living in the rural areas.

The scope of this work is therefore to 1) analyze the phenomenon of
intimate violence against women utilizing the social-cultural and religious
context of Kenya as a case study; 2) critically engage theoretical psycho-
social and religious analysis of female survivors of violence with greater
emphasis on their identity or self-formation; 3) analyze my findings of
the range of experiences of the women survivors in conversation with
psycho-religious theories of the formation of self-cohesion; 4) postulate
a theoretical framework for understanding intimate violence survivors—a
framework that has been informed by the praxis of women; and 5) draw
possible implications of the study that will provide an interpretive model
for more effective interventions with survivors of violence.

By taking into consideration psycho-social and contextual self-
formation and identity issues, the study initiates an important approach,
embedded in contexts, to advance our understanding of survivors' views
and responses to violence. The study provides invaluable information that
forms a basis from which to develop strategies for intervention with families in crisis and to address the issue of violence from its roots in social,
cultural and religious dynamics. It stresses the need to develop effective
methods of intervention informed by expressed understandings of the
survivor, as well as her social-cultural and religious context.

The study highlights, in general, areas in the *orienting systems*[12]
that can be isolated (and then transformed) than can effectively impact
our interventions in intimate violence. These include (but are not limited to,) "maturational pressures," gender-discriminative policies, gender-
discriminative traditions, and gender-discriminative religious values that

---

12. "Orienting systems" is a word coined to capture the integrated aggregate of all
that is within the context, some of which is tangible and some which may not be well
articulated. It speaks to the social, cultural, moral, ethical, and religious systems that
influence our worldviews and the formation of our mental schemas.

influence the development of psychic structures of the infant through latency and eventually to the sense of self. All these are implications that will be systematically developed throughout the body of the discussions, and the analysis of the research. My derived findings explain the observed incongruence between the survivors of violence and the expected trauma and post traumatic stress disorder (PTSD) effects, and reveal implications that first led to my inquiry in this area. My claims add to important aspects to the empirical evidence that strongly shows that children and youth growing up in violent families repeat the cycle they have accepted as normal (Gelles et al., 1993).

The study also reveals interesting perceptions regarding self-formation and its connection with the female response to intimate violence. In considering these perceptions several areas of inquiry are engaged, including the mental processes and worldviews that initially may not be obvious, but that influence the survivors' response to the violence phenomenon. For instance, does it make a difference to the growing child that distinctly different treatments, engagements, and expectations exist for the male and the female, especially by close caregivers? Does this differential encounter affect in any way the development of the child into adulthood, including her drive for achievement, self-fulfillment and the possibility of redirected energy? What important implications could a more-extended family care-giving system present for the child's development? Do all these aspects of the context affect the content and structure of her moral agency and the power with which this agency directs her daily life decisions? Does the context influence her development of a God representation as well as her relationship with such a Deity image? If these areas of development are affected by social and cultural religious influences, what implications do such effects offer to knowledge regarding intimate violence and the appropriation of such trauma by the individual who is subjected to it? In the varying responses, is there human agency in their inner processes as observed from the survivors, as they make meaning of the violence? Can religion and/or culture, (both of which have been historically perceived as perpetrating agents), be playing a role as a transforming agency in her perception and therefore her response to violence? How would insight in these areas contribute towards development of more effective intervention strategies? These are all pertinent areas of interest that are navigated in the course of this book. The study forms a basis for more extensive research on the variations of literacy, rural context, ethnicity, and religious orientation as independent variables affecting the survivor's response. More broadly, it provides a framework for investigations of intimate violence in other cultures—a framework that results from its objective of drawing implications of theoretical formulations for understanding survivors of violence through interpretive methods that take into account the relation between psychological factors and the socio-cultural and religious customs of a people.

One of the powerful reflections I have made since conducting the research and through my data analysis period concerns my reluctance to "leave" the field. Intimate violence is a sensitive subject that I, as a researcher and pastoral counselor, already have strong opinions about. I was consciously aware of pitfalls related to the emotional reactions I felt, like suppressing evidence, selecting certain theoretical conclusions to the exclusion of other influencing aspects, minimizing countervailing views, and tracking ideas that are not central to my thesis. I pursued accountability through ongoing consultations with participants and by maintaining a trail that tracked my research and coding/categorization processes. I was held accountable to my postulations through collegial presentations and by refining the work at the University of Cape Town where I took my sabbatical to write this work.

My hope is that this book will provide insight to academicians, educators, policy makers, and development workers, encouraging them to engage their communities and initiate transformation. Those caught in violent relationships, and parents nurturing young children may benefit greatly from this information and perhaps seek professional help -

OUTLINE OF CHAPTERS

I have divided the book into two sections. The first section situates the study in context and in a psycho-social theoretical framework. The second section engages the survivor's narratives to conceptualize the findings of the study, while postulating the role of religion as a transformative agency. In the latter part of this section I make recommendations for critical points of intervention and an effective model for transformations.

In *Chapter Two*, I present a brief synopsis of the general characteristics of intimate violence, paying attention to the occurrence of violence, and the cycles of violence. This brings the reader up to date with empirically conceptualized themes regarding intimate violence in general.

In *Chapter Three,* I expose the reader the contextual case study of Kenya by exploring the social, cultural and religious context in which the phenomenon of intimate violence against women has been nurtured and perpetuated.

In *Chapter Four,* I critically examine, from a theoretical standpoint, the identity formation and functionality of the intimate violence survivor. Based on a critical analysis of psycho-social theories with socio-cultural and religious context, I have argued for, and reformulated, a theoretical framework for how the female survivor of violence needs to be understood in terms of her identity and sense of self-formation.

In *Chapter Five,* I seek to grasp and conceptualize from a psycho-social perspective, the understandings expressed by the survivors of violence about intimate violence they experience. Emerging concepts and patterns of thinking have been categorized in this chapter. Issues of repression and denial, coping, and attribution have also been considered from psychological literature, and intimate violence literature including coping, battered women syndrome and PTSD.

In *Chapter Six,* I conceptualize the survivor's patterns of thinking from religious perspectives. By analytically integrating psycho-religious and theological literature, I demonstrate the powerful influence of religion in the transformation of identity and sense of self and therefore the response to intimate violence.

In *Chapter Seven,* I critically examine the emerging concepts discussed in Chapters 4 and 5 in dialogue with psycho-religious theoretical formulations to advance an integrative theory and propositions that help us gain a better understanding of the survivors and their responses to intimate violence.

Chapter Eight revisits questions raised in the introductory chapter as in summary form. I also examine implications of the study and propose areas for further research.

2

Intimate Violence

Nuts and Bolts of the Trauma

In this section, I review the general literature on intimate violence as a background for a clearer understanding of intimate violence and survivor response.

DEFINITION OF INTIMATE VIOLENCE

The way violence is defined by any culture has important implications for determining the prevalence of violence in the community. In her book *Intimate violence and Control,* Jan Stets states that intimate violence refers to "physical force used by a man against a woman in a heterosexual relationship that results in physical pain, injury or both" (Stets 1988, 1). The Center for Prevention of Intimate violence has a more general definition of intimate violence as "mistreatment of one family member by another" (Ogawa 1995, 11). In an attempt to reconcile these two definitions I use the term *intimate violence* to encompass violence against women by men who may not necessarily be in marital relationship with the woman, but who are in an intimate relationship. Such violence occurs on a continuum and may range from mild abuse, which entails pushing, grabbing, shoving, slapping or banging of doors, to more severe abuse that includes choking, kicking, beating and weapon use (Stets 1998, 3). Inclusion of non-physical forms of violence widens the spectrum of intimate violence to include psychological and emotional injury. Ginny NiCarthy, in her article, "Building Self-esteem: Overcoming Barriers to Recovery," points out that psychological and emotional injury may be more damaging to the survivor than physical injury (NiCarthy 1995, 99). Leonore Walker identifies eight areas that are standard in the assessment of psychological violence: 1) victim isolation; 2) induced and controlling weakness (e.g., rationed food or sleep); 3) obsessiveness and controlling possessiveness; 4) lethal and vague threats to self, family and friends; 5) public humiliation; 6) *forceful*[1] drug or alcohol administration; 7) distorted states of consciousness; and 8) occasional but controlled indulgence (Walker 1984, 28). For the purpose of narrowing the analysis, I specifically focus on physically inflicted violence by a male to a female partner, though most of these aspects are present in the narratives of the female survivors interviewed in Kenya.

There seems to be general agreement in all societies that violence directed at women by men is more prevalent than that directed at men by women. The Center for Prevention of Intimate violence states that in over 95% of intimate violence assaults in the U.S., the man is the perpetrator. In most cultures it seems that men have been given a historical and legal right to batter women (Ogawa 1995, 18). One of the existing myths that surrounds intimate violence is that men who batter do so because they cannot control their temper or, in other words, they have "poor impulse control." However, as the Center for Prevention of Intimate violence put it so well, the same men who batter their wives do not seem to have a similar level of problem controlling their tempers against other people they interact with—it is only the women in their lives. It seems that they are able to control themselves well enough to pick the safest targets (Ogawa 1995, 21).

OCCURRENCE OF INTIMATE VIOLENCE

Intimate violence is under-reported worldwide because it occurs in the privacy of the home or within intimate relationships. Only those survivors who need community services are willing to report the intimate violence to the appropriate agencies. In the U.S., for instance, it was not until the 1970s that intimate violence became a public concern (Stets 1998, 3), when the women's movement challenged the patriarchal order and women's second-class status. Many middle and upper class women have unreported incidents, although some particular demographics like income level, race,

---

1. The term forceful is my own addition.

religion and location are more associated with intimate violence. In situations where the society does not have a recourse for the survivors of violence, or where the practice has become normalized, the highest percentage goes completely unreported, irrespective of the economic demographic.

Two main factors relate to the occurrence of intimate violence in adulthood. The first is one's childhood background. Gelles et al. (1993) point to the cultivation of violence cycles from a person's very early stages of life:

> Violence cannot be prevented as long as we are taught that it is appropriate to hit the people we love. Physical punishment of children is perhaps the most effective means of teaching violence. (Gelles et al. 1993, 20)

It is therefore a well-known fact that witnessing intimate violence at a very early age pre-disposes the child to later accept violence as a way of life. In this regard the *Women and Law* publication states:

> The witnessing of violence by both girls and boys has been a contributory factor in the perpetuation of violence against women. Boys exposed to their father's acts of battery tend to internalize this behavior and in turn act it out on their wives when they get married. Girls on the other hand learn to accept violence as a way of life and do not challenge it. (*Women and Law in South African Trust*, 2001, 9)

Researchers have reported that parents who received physical abuse but who do not continue the cycle are parents who have received social support during their childhood or adulthood (Milner and Crouch 1993, 39). Similarly, Walker (1984) asserts that early social influences on women facilitate a psychological condition called "learned helplessness," a term mainly associated with behaviorist psychologist Martin Seligman (1990). This concept supports the theory that "intra-family violence is learned behavior that is passed down from one generation to the next" (Walker 1984, 2). Walker provides a clear illustration of how such a cycle perpetuates violence through generations for both males and females:

> Reinforcement of violence as strategy occurs at all levels in our society. It is particularly evident in some of child raising practices. When we teach children that it is appropriate to hit them for disciplinary purposes, we also teach them that people who love them the most have the right to physically hurt them if they do something wrong. It should not be a surprise then that men say they have a right to physically hit the women they love if they do something wrong. The women accept such minor abuse

in the name of discipline. However, unlike most cases of child discipline, physically punishing an adult woman rapidly escalates into violent abuse. (1984, 37)

The kind of cycle discussed above is one that rotates from victimization in childhood to perpetration in adulthood.

The second general factor relating to intimate violence is personality, which includes the interactive process of the couple involved in the violence. This personality factor is greatly influenced by beliefs in traditional gender roles; in most societies the male is groomed to be aggressive and dominant, while the female is passive and submissive. Many researchers in this area report that most battered women have low self-esteem, believe in traditional sex-roles, accept responsibility for being battered and believe that no one can help them except themselves, and that this help requires adjusting to the demands of the batterer. In this regard, Mary Alice Saunders-Robinson states:

After many episodes of battering, a woman may come to believe the lie repeated by her battering partner who says, "This is your fault. Your behavior is causing me to lose control!" Wanting her relationship to work, the woman believes that if she tries harder and is more loving, the abuse will never happen again . . . (Saunders-Robinson 1995, 136)

Some of these beliefs by the survivors contribute to their not leaving the abusive relationship. More significant, however, are the realities of financial dependence on the batterer, the lack of a better place to go to, concern for what will happen to the children, religious beliefs, and social stigma in her decisions to stay put. In the Kenyan context, I found that while the above factors may be contributing to the woman's remaining in an abusive relationship, other psychological factors related to the sense of self might be more fundamental than financial dependence and physical concern for the children.

According to Walker, traditional attitudes towards gender roles are also named as contributing to the occurrence of intimate violence. She states:

The socialization process of assigning male and female sex role behavior is also seen as contributing to violence against women. It is suggested that battered women are more rigidly socialized into female sex role stereotypes. (Walker 1984, 2)

However, in Walker's sample of 403 women, 81% of the women self-reported attitudes that were liberal while the batterers and their fathers were reported to have held very traditional attitudes. This implies, according to Walker, that the women perceived the family members as being more traditional than they were themselves (Walker 1984, 18). It would be expected that the majority of Kenyan women would hold less liberal attitudes towards gender roles because of their socialization, as is discussed in Chapter 3. Indeed, this is a fundamental argument in my discussions regarding the resultant sense of self due to gender role socialization. In turn such sense of self has implications for response to violence.

Forced sexual activities and other sadomasochistic activities are more likely to be associated with battering than with non-battering relationships. In many cases this has the effect of making sex unpleasant for many women in abusive relationships. In Walker's sample, 85% of battered women reported that sex was unpleasant as compared to 29% of the non-battered women (Walker 1984, 48). This difference would be an important factor to follow up in the Kenyan context, where traditionally sex was aimed at procreation rather than for recreation, especially on the part of the women. My hypothesis would be that even though Kenyan women did not ultimately aim at enjoyment in sex, in abusive relationships sex would be even more humiliating and therefore unappealing to women survivors of violence. The major question, if this hypothesis is true, would be what holds women in abusive relationships if they receive the double dose of physical violence and forced sexual activity, not to mention psychological stress? Although beyond the scope of this book, the answer to this question strengthens my argument that the psychological hold of traditional gender roles is integral to self-formation and therefore integral in the response to violence.

THE CYCLE OF INTIMATE VIOLENCE

Intimate violence is not a daily occurrence, but over time repeats itself in cycles with distinctive phases (Stets 1998, 4). The cycle begins with the couple relating happily, progresses to a time of tension building, followed by explosion of violence, which eventually resolves into a calm and loving phase. This cycle of violence is one of the most popular micro-theories of battering, and is based on Walker's (1979) clinical observations. Gondolf (1993) summarizes the cycle well when he states:

> The cycle of violence is implicitly derived from frustration-aggression hypothesis that one becomes increasingly aggressive as one is frustrated. The theory is fundamentally an emotion driven escalation model of violence. Tensions gradually mount until they explode in a violent incident. After the emotional release provided by the violent incident, a period of apologies, promises and forgiveness begins. Tensions gradually rise again, however, and the cycle repeats itself. (Gondolf 1993, 239)

Even though the pattern does not exhibit temporal regularity, the clarity of the pattern enables the survivors to know when a beating is coming. There seems to be consistent research findings documenting the phases through which the violence develops. Generally three phases are described: Before inception of the first phase, the couple is in what may be experienced as a normal and desirable calmness for family life. Phase 1 is referred to as the tension building phase; Phase 2 is called the explosion or violent phase, and Phase 3 is referred to as the honeymoon and reconciliation phase. These phases are not constant in duration, yet they provide a clear indication that the violence is not random. Many theories of intimate violence make the argument that female survivors use their knowledge of the phases to tell when violence is in the air, so they can avoid it in different ways as a means of buying time. Others, in anticipation of the honeymoon phase, actually prefer to trigger it so they can get it over and done with.

Phase one, the tension phase, begins with the woman's expectations of more direct aggression by the male. Most women will put up with this phase because it is usually better than the actual beating and because in some ways they have control and a voice. However, to the male, the woman's passivity validates his behavior. His justification is that since she is not reacting, she must know that she deserves the tension. To the woman, the aggression also validates her behavior, especially when she reacts in subtle "passive aggression." Both validations tend to escalate the tensional aggression. During this first phase, isolated incidents of battering may occur, including psychological and verbal abuse. The batterer may be aware of his inappropriate behavior, responding by increased possessiveness and controlling behavior in the fear that she may leave. At this point in the cycle, the abuser views himself as a victim of the woman's nagging behavior. Over many repetitions of this phase of the cycle, the batterer systematically isolates the survivor from others. Walker refers to this process as social isolation and states that it occurs both as part of and result of violence (Walker 1984, 28).

Phase two is the actual physical violence stage. Discussing this second phase Blau et al. (1993), state "emotions erupt into violent actions such as threatening, hitting, slapping, choking, throwing and sexual assault" (Blau et al. 1993, 210). The survivor usually has no control over the happenings. She may respond by tolerating the violence, knowing it is only for a short while. Anything, however trivial, can trigger this phase. The expressed violence is the outlet of the pressure that has been building over time during the tension period.

In Phase three of the cycle, reconciliation, the batterer is usually apologetic and may be very earnest. He may even believe that he will never batter again. However, he nevertheless avoids taking responsibility, finding external explanations for his behavior, including being frustrated or stressed at work, being drunk, or being pushed to that point of violence by the survivor. More often than not, the perpetrator may try to deal with the incident by shifting responsibility to the woman, suggesting ways that she can change so that he is not angered to the point of violence, and in fact, this justification by the male will normally make the survivor feel responsible for his actions. She will usually believe his allegations even though she does not accept the beating. She will usually translate his remorsefulness as deep love, thereby characterizing the violence as isolated incidents that will eventually pass away. Although remorse is the most common reaction of perpetrators in the third phase, studies show that some people do not show any signs of remorse after they have perpetrated violence on their spouses. Gondolf (1993) discusses this position in the following passage:

> In Walker's subsequent research on battered women, she found a substantial portion of her sample reporting an absence of the so-called apologetic/forgiveness or "honeymoon" phase. Similarly the typologies of men who batter reveal a type of batterer who is violent sporadically in a pattern that approximates the cycle of violence." (Gondolf 1993, 240, citing L. Walker (1983)

A mixture of the two reactions is common and may work to manipulate the survivor's mind so that she focuses on the desirable behavior of the batterer, thereby not only justifying his violent action but also taking responsibility for it. Even in the absence of apologies and begging for forgiveness, then, the phase still has the characteristics of a honeymoon period because everything goes back to normal without felt tensions.

My research implies that the cycle of violence is not as clear for the Kenyan female survivor of violence. The sporadic nature of violent situations, in many cases occurring at very short intervals ranging from a couple of days to a week, does not allow for a full cycle to take place. Furthermore, the cultural beliefs about the practice of wife beating, (which have been embedded in the society and in some cases perpetrated by the women themselves), diminish the necessity of a honeymoon period and thereby negate the third phase.

The periods between occurrences get shorter and they increase in frequency and severity as the cycle repeats. The longer the cycle stays unbroken, the more the couple becomes adversely dependent on each other. The woman's emotional involvement with the man increases her dependency on his controlling factors. She becomes dependent on him and, through secrecy and as a result of controlling threats he may be making, conspires in alliance with him. However, her attempts to make sense of the situation create psychological pressure, and a mounting depression eventually emerges, since she is not able to change the situation. Some of this pressure may regularly be released on other members of the family, especially children. Some women may eventually leave the relationship while others may explode in volatile ways, like plotting to kill the perpetrator or committing suicide. This would usually happen after a considerable period of repeated violence so that the woman comes to believe that the third phase will never materialize to permanency.

At this point however, frustration and depression will have become so great that the ability to think rationally is lost. For most survivors, the perception is that their circumstances offer very few acceptable alternatives. A woman perceives that she must either resign herself to living with the violence, escape from the situation, commit suicide or kill (harm) the perpetrator. Her perception of the man at this point may be that he is inhuman. This prolonged cycle has a life of its own, and I refer to it as the "cyclone of violence" similar to the "tornado effect."[2] The previously docile-appearing woman is capable of committing the culminating crime given her prolonged subjection to violence.

EFFECTS OF AND INTERVENTION IN INTIMATE VIOLENCE

Much has been written regarding the nature and characteristics of prolonged violence. Notable are implications for the Battered Women Syndrome and Post traumatic Stress Disorder (PTSD). Literature that has

---

2. The term "tornado effect" and its figurative presentation are borrowed from Michael Eltz, used during the course "Family Violence," University of Denver, June 20, 1998.

been generated in these two areas and especially the Battered Women Syndrome is aimed at contributing to defense litigation cases against women who end up killing their husbands in violent relationships. Research in this area demonstrates that women who eventually commit homicide do so under great psychological distress from prolonged periods of violence, and do so in self-defense. Walker's research has important insights for the Battered Women Syndrome. She states:

> Occasionally the violence between the man and woman escalates out of control and someone dies. Most of the time it is the woman; her batterer either kills her or she commits suicide as a result of his abusive behavior. Sometimes they both die; he kills her then he kills himself. And in a similar number of cases, the woman strikes back with a deadly blow and kills the batterer.... However, today it is more likely that the women who kill men are doing so in self-defense after a period of having been the victim of his violence. (Walker 1984, 38)

Walker points to a number of factors that lead to this state of lethality: 1) most women believe that no one takes them seriously, especially since the batterer is usually perceived by those outside of the family as loving and responsible; 2) many will kill in attempts to protect their children from violence or sexual abuse; 3) many believed that he would/could actually kill her given the opportunity and have lived with such fear; 4) others knew by observable changes in the man's physical or mental state that this time he would really kill them; and 5) for some of the women, their violence is a desperate attempt to keep the man from gaining control of their minds (Walker 1984, 38–41). She goes on to name factors that the create high risk of homicide, including:

- Presence of children in the home –especially when involved in the abuse.
- Occurrence of threats by the batterer to kill either the victim or someone else. Usually the women will try to hide any friendships they might have in fear that the friends will be in danger.
- Presence of weapons in the home.
- Threats of retaliation made by the batterer. Phrases such as "If I can't have you, no one will"; "If you leave, I'll find you wherever you go"; "Just do that and you'll see how mean I can really be"; as well as threats of bodily mutilation such as cutting up her face, sewing up her vagina, breaking her kneecaps and knocking her unconscious, all of which

serve to terrify the women and confirm their fears of receiving lethal blows (Walker 1984, 42).

- Greater isolation meant greater risk of lethality.

- Presence of a man's excessive jealousy. Jealously is the predominant reason given by men who kill their wives.

- Alcohol and drug abuse. There is no clear relationship between alcohol intoxication and battering. However, excessive drinking usually characterizes those relationships that end in fatality (Walker 1984, 43).

- Severity and frequency of the abuse escalated over time.

The above factors are important in assessing the risk of lethality by the survivors. In Walker's sample, battered women realized their potential lethality, even though they often doubted it would ever really happen. Half said they could never think of killing him while the other half "said they possibly could kill him" (Walker 1984, 39).

In Kenya, there have been isolated cases reported in the news where a woman has retaliated in violence against her male spouse. My assertion is that cultural and religious traditions have a great influence in checking this tornado effect in the psychic balance of women in abusive relationships. Implications of coping strategies that draw from both the cultural and religious traditions have more to do with this balance.[3] In discussing the influence of the culture on the cycle of intimate violence in Kenya, I wish to make clear that I am discussing intimate violence by men against women. This is not to mean that there is absolutely no violence of women against men, but that such violence is very minimal because of the traditional cultural gender roles that continue to inform the status of women in Kenya. In this regard, Kibwana states:

> Women do unleash violence against men but this is a lesser extent than male violence against women. Women are also violent per se. Such violence must also be addressed in our bid for development of a society in which gender-based violence is controlled. (Kibwana 1996, 174)

Hence, my recognition of greater and systematic violence addressed to the women by the men has implications for situating my research on female survivors of intimate violence.

---

3. Deeper discussion of these notions is treated in Chapters 4 and 5, which deal with the findings from the research and the coping skills employed by the women.

One of the major pointers to Post traumatic Stress Disorder in survivors of intimate violence is Walker's assertion that most women who killed their abusers have little recollection of the event other than an intense focus on their own survival. Even where it can be said that the woman's defenses against denial of her anger at being abused are unraveling, she does not seem to have conscious awareness of those feelings. Research on PTSD points to repression of the traumatic events, appropriation and processing through cognitive schema, and reappraisal of the traumatic events by controlling the flow of memorable parts of the event. With regard to intimate violence, PTSD research and literature is a very current ongoing discourse. In this book, literature on PTSD has mainly been utilized to engage coping and meaning-making theories with particular reference to psycho-religious dimensions.

Furthermore, social, cultural and individual psychic balances affect the symptoms of PTSD. These effects cannot be generalized to every cultural context especially with regard to intimate violence. Joseph et al. (1997) propose the need for an integrative approach to establish the diagnosis for PTSD, stating that "survivors of different events may have different symptoms; some survivors will be more affected than others, and some will remain affected for considerably longer than others" (Joseph et al. 1997, 69). These researchers name five theoretical paradigms that help in understanding PTSD, namely emotional processing, conditioning theory, learned helplessness, information processing and social-cognitive perspectives. Some of these will be highlighted in my discussion on the findings of my study for their applicability in Kenya. It is important to state that social cultural, and religious factors have contributed to downplaying or altering the presentation of PTSD's symptoms in the survivor. However, I believe that many survivors of intimate violence in Kenya do have varying degrees of PTSD, and that this may in many ways explain the normalcy of their functionality. In other words, if the literature on PTSD were to be directly applied to assess its prevalence among the survivors of violence in Kenya, most likely the bigger percentage of the survivor population would be diagnosed as PTSD-free.

I point out in my interrogation of the data areas that I perceived PTSD symptoms to be blurred by the overpowering need to maintain the social identity and sense of self. While social cultural factors and the nature of intimacy in intimate violence may in some ways explain the altered symptoms, I introduce the notion of a social culturally manipulated sense of self, and the influence of religion, as major determinants in clouding the clarity of PTSD symptoms in Kenyan survivors of violence. The attempt to establish indicators of PTSD among this sampling would require a longitudinal study over an extended period of time, which is beyond the scope of this book. The task here was to explore contextual social, cultural, religious and traditional gendered factors in the formation of a self, and, accordingly, how such self is likely to respond to intimate violence. These aspects, I believe, are largely lacking in the literature on the battered women syndrome, PTSD, and theories regarding the cycle of violence.

Even though very few intimate violence cases have been statistically documented in Kenya, intimate violence is definitely a significant problem. In her article "Violence against Women: A Challenge to the Church," Teresia Hinga perceives violence as an issue that requires attention because it is escalating. She states:

> One of the most urgent moral questions of our time pertains to the ever conspicuous and escalating violence and abuse against women and children. Almost daily there are reported cases of incidents of terror meted out against women. (Hinga 1994, 117)

Also, during a seminar organized by the women's desk of the National Council of Churches of Kenya in 1993, it was reported that:

> Even though there is general pervasiveness of violence in our society, violence against women and girls in particular has escalated. This is evident in the frequency of reports, which we read in local newspapers and hear and see through electronic media. Such reports have increased in number, even though many cases go unreported due to the structural hindrance and fear experienced by women and girls. (Bula and Lunda 1993, 1)

Reporting of a marked increase in Domestic Violence cases, a program manager at the Gender Violence recovery Center in Nairobi Women's Hospital stated that they saw an increase from 299 in 2004 to 412 in 2007 (Voice of America, March 5, 2010). In a similar report by the IRIN (a service of the UN office for the coordination of Humanitarian Affairs) police cases of Sexual violence were said to be 2,800 in 2004, an increase of about 500 from 2003. Such reports of increase in Domestic Violence in its various forms may not necessarily mean that more women are being beaten than they used to be. It might be a reflection of a society where women are beginning to question the right of their spouse to beat them and therefore, are more readily willing to come forth in reporting. There is however, no doubt about the prevalence of intimate violence against women in Kenya.

The social cultural and religious context of intimate violence in Kenya and how it unfolds in intimate relationships, are explored in detail in Chapter 3. Its effects on the understandings, self-formation and worldview of the female survivors of violence in Kenya is the gist of the field research findings discussed in depth in Chapters 4 and 5. The study was conducted in Nairobi, a multi-lingual and cultural hub of Kenya. The twenty-three participants should be viewed as a source of qualitative data that provide merely a slice of the greater picture. Important findings emerge that lay the groundwork for theories to be tested in further research within the broader population.

3

The Orienting System

Socio-Cultural and Religious Contextual Influence on Female Identity Formation —A Case Study of Kenya

In this chapter I offer a general exploration of the socio-cultural and religious contexts of Kenya, as a case study. I make the claim that context has an enormous influence on the formation of identity and a sense of self, and that such influence is also gender-distinctive in its appropriation. While I acknowledge that Kenya is so widely varied in its social, cultural and religious traditions that no one perspective can be fully representative of the whole of Kenya, I have striven to capture aspects that could be generalized to the various Kenyan cultural contexts by using both Kenyan and general African resources, as well as my own insight into the context. I specifically trace traditional claims that are relevant to gender relations in Kenya today but which may *not* necessarily apply to every post-modern individual, yet, which I believe continue to influence our society in very tangible ways. Many times such influence is so deeply ingrained that it creates a psychological conflict within individuals who find themselves pulled between polarized traditional beliefs and Western influence. I would not be surprised if certain groups of people therefore, cannot relate to some specific lines of thought presented here, especially when we acknowledge that Kenya is a rapidly, socially-developing country, caught between traditional mores, values and beliefs, and Western religious and post-modern modes of thinking.

In my discussion of Kenya's social, cultural and religious beliefs and traditions, I have made the case that the distinction between religious and cultural aspects is very fragile. Religion, (both modern traditions and especially African traditional religions), permeates the lives of the people so thoroughly that a meaningful distinction cannot be made between that which is religious and that which is cultural. The interconnection of religious and cultural aspects of the context strengthen arguments set forth regarding the under-girding influence of socio-cultural and religious influence on the formation of a self within the Kenyan context. It is therefore crucial for the reader to appreciate the sacredness with which these mores, virtues, beliefs and values are held (which the outsider would consider cultural issues). These sacred mores, virtues, beliefs, and values lay the foundation and exert a strong influence on the ongoing identification of a female child, within the community who is in the process of self-formation. The synthesis between religion and culture and its due influence on self-formation rather than the distinction between religious and socio-cultural aspects, is the focus in this chapter.

African traditional religious and cultural beliefs, (which in many ways continue to be prevalent in the lives of the people), are a good entry point into the understanding of life in Kenyan societies. Each human being is born into a particular cultural context or established pattern of life. From this point on, members of a community are inclined to follow the patterns of the culture set before them by those who are already participants of the community. Culture, like humans, is organic, not static. Even as culture influences the individual's worldview, it too is simultaneously challenged and is reformulated and reproduced by the individual and other factors. Culture influences not only the physical aspects of the person, including way of dressing, food eaten and mannerisms, but also the patterns of thinking of the individual, including institution of morals, beliefs, values and general patterns of perception or worldview. Therefore, when discussing the cultural aspects in Kenya, the emphasis is not on homogeneity, but rather upon diverse worldviews within which dominant beliefs and perceptions find expression.

I begin with a general discussion which is pertinent to my thesis regarding the beliefs and traditions about life and the place of the individual in the community. Fundamental concepts regarding marriage and childbirth, (which in the Kenyan communities are integral in defining the place of the individual), will be briefly treated also. I will then engage these beliefs with ideas about the identity formation of the female in Kenya with particular attention to her gender roles and how these unfold, defining her social and economic status. I will describe the role that religion plays for the Kenyan female in gaining such status.

UNDERSTANDINGS OF LIFE, INDIVIDUAL AND COMMUNITY

Kenyan understandings of life, the individual and community, and their intricate complexity compounded with religious and ancestral beliefs, are important prerequisites to understanding the formation of an individual identity for both men and women. These factors form the basis from which a self comes into being, views itself, and therefore acts.

In *The Individual and Community in African Traditional Religions,* Theo Sundermeier discusses adequately the concept of life in African communities. He states that everything, including humans, plants and animals, as well as the surroundings, share life. Life is passed on from parents to children. Every generation is only a link in a long, never-ending chain of life. He states that the concept of continuity and unity in the African understanding of life is a comfort—the African knows that one is part of a life that has always flowed in his or her family. For this reason, no one individual's values can be above the collective value of life. The individual is simply a recipient of life and has a duty to pass it on (Sundermeier 1998, 15).[1]

John Mbiti, an African philosopher, captures very well the requirements of identity formation for an individual within the Kenyan society. Although Mbiti writes for Africa as a whole, the fact that he is Kenyan and cites many Kenyan communities, puts him right on target in his discussion of identity formation in the Kenyan society in general. Discussing the place of the individual in a community-oriented society, Mbiti states that

> the individual does not and cannot exist alone except corporately. He owes his existence to other people including those of the past generations and his contemporaries. He is simply a part of the whole. The community must therefore make, create or produce the individual. (Mbiti 1969, 108)

Echoing Mbiti, Sundermeier states that individuals exist only insofar as they are members of a group. Leaving the mainstream endangers the

---

1. See also Mbiti, who states that childlessness is in effect "the death of the unborn and a diminishing of the family as a whole" (Mbiti 1969, 107).

person and those following in lineage (Sundermeier 1998, 18). In the face of a calamity, a misfortune, illness or even a bad harvest, people search for signs of discord in the community and try to find out who is responsible. In effect, curses spoken over those not willing to be part of the whole exert a prevalent and influencing religio-cultural belief. The communal orientation in Kenya therefore deeply influences the behavior, thinking and livelihood of individuals in significant ways.

MARRIAGE AND CHILDBIRTH IN KENYA

Marriage in traditional Kenyan societies was, and still is, an important social and religious institution that provides fulfillment in the life of an individual:

> It [marriage] provides a socially recognized paired relationship that is relatively permanent, the stability of which is supported by many social institutions. It is within a successful marriage that an individual finds his or her material, sexual and psychological needs most effectively satisfied. (Bahemuka 1992, 119)

Marriage in the African setting is not an affair between two people. It involves the larger family and indeed the community. This view emanates from the view that "the person does not exist all by himself: he exists because of the existence of other people" (Mbiti 1991, 108). Mbiti asserts that marriage is a sacred relationship established as a binding covenant. The importance of marriage may be underlined by Mbiti's assertion that it is the pivotal point of, or a center of, human life in an African understanding. Thus varying customs govern different societies with respect to who one could or could not marry, the husband and wife relationship, death of a partner, children within the relationship, separation, divorce, and inheritance, to name a few (Mbiti 1991, 107).

According to Mbiti, marriage was the meeting point of those that have already departed, the living, and those yet to be born. Because of the importance of marriage in African life, the obligation to get married is strong, as may be reflected in Mbiti's statement:

> Marriage fulfills the obligation, the duty and the custom that every normal person should get married and bear children. This is believed to go back to the very beginning of human life. Failure to get married is like committing a crime against traditional beliefs and practices. (Mbiti 1991, 110)

In Mbiti's words, the "supreme purpose of marriage according to African peoples was to bear children, to build a family, to extend life and to hand down a torch of human existence" (Mbiti 1991, 110).

Bahemuka echoes similar sentiments:

> Every African marriage called for procreation. There was no marriage in the African sense unless the fruit of that marriage could be seen. It was the duty of every couple in that society to reproduce and to contribute to society by giving it new members. The parents were biologically reproduced in their children; they contributed to perpetuating the chain of humanity. Marriage and procreation were therefore seen as unity, a unity that attempted to recapture, even if partly, humanity's lost gift of immortality. (Bahemuka 1992, 120)

Thus, if one did not participate in marriage, there was a sense of being cut off from community life, from partaking in human existence. Bahemuka's statement above; ". . . to recapture, even if partly, humanity's lost gift of immortality" renders a cultural belief sacred. The belief's coincidence with the Christian story of creation and the fall of humankind (and the consequent loss of immortality,) will work to relegate marriage, a traditionally sacred cultural expectation, the status of a Christian sacred mandate. Mbiti names other aspects that gave marriage a social and sacred position and hence status for the individual being: the uniting link of life, bringing up families and building kinships, remembrance of parents after death, creation of good personal qualities and the fulfillment achieved through marriage (Mbiti 1991, 110–12).

The importance of marriage may be well captured in the description of various types of marriages expounded by Bahemuka (1992). They show the lengths to which society went to cater to anomalies that would hinder an individual from fully participating in the marriage institution. For instance, *ghost marriages* were arranged as an intervention to cater to a young man who may have died before getting married. In this case the woman is married into a family and assumes the name of the deceased son, but can have children with another male (usually an older brother) in the home. *Child marriages* ensured that before a man who fathered a son in old age died, the son would have children to remember him (Bahemuka 1992, 122). Other types of multiple marriages (like polygyny,) served such social and economic needs as producing a labor force, catering to widows, and achieving or maintaining social status. Bahemuka states that polygyny in the African societies was "a unit of both consumption and production, as well as a sign of wealth" (Bahemuka 1992, 124).

In some societies like the Meru, polygyny provided room for participation in marriage for outcast women such as *ngirani*,[2] who traditionally could not be married as a first wife. Beliefs surrounding such traditions revolved around a curse connected to death (assuming a religious dimension) that would befall the man who married such a woman. While beliefs like these seem far-fetched to a modern Kenyan, it is interesting to note that they are very powerful in the minds of young people even today, when they must make a marriage partner decision. I am reminded of a young Christian man, a contemporary of mine, who was very much in love with a young woman and had made public his intention to marry her, until he found out that she was a *ngirani*, then his mind was changed. His was a classic example of how Christianity, (which preaches equality and the absorption of traditional beliefs that were found discriminative and contrary to Christianity) has not necessarily erased the deep cultural beliefs that have a traditionally sacred dimension. These concepts deeply permeate the lives of the people.

Beliefs regarding the cycle of life are indicative of the importance of marriage and childbirth among many Kenyan communities. For instance, among the Meru of Kenya, to whom I belong, a newborn child is said to be born as a certain other person within the family. The patrilineal side of the family gets to be named first depending on the gendered order of births. Our first son for instance is born as my husband's father, while our second son is born as my father. (If the second born had been a girl then she would have been named after my husband's mother to fulfill the patrilineal side.) Their grandfathers literally continue their lives through these grandsons. It is such an important belief that the names given to the newborns are derived from the behaviors of the one he/she is born as. For instance, our first son is called *Mutethia*, meaning a helper, because his grandfather was a great helper in the community. Our second son is called *Muthomi*, meaning a scholar because of my father's emphasis on education both for himself and for the family. Our third son is called *Munene*, meaning king, or leader, because my husband's brother was a civil leader for many years. Such naming is not a simple matter for the parents to decide, but a communal (extended family) decision. I remember I had some "fancy" name that I wanted to call my first son, but it was not acceptable to the extended family because it did not reflect his grandfather. In my

2. Not much is known of how a woman became *ngirani* except that it ran through the family lineage. Some hearsay has it that a family with very beautiful women was pronounced *ngirani* to give an opportunity to the older men to marry such women so as not to compete with the younger men.

"naïve, progressive" thinking I made a fuss about it, pointing to my right as the mother of the boy, until the significance of the belief and its implications on the boy's life as he grew was explained to me. The name takes the role of being a constant challenge to the child growing in the community to measure up to the desirable characteristics of his/ her namesake family member. If the child inherited a name of undesirable character, then the child's challenge is to change his/her name in his/her generation. The child therefore knows that through his/her name, he/she is bound to the larger community and must make every effort to act responsibly towards it. The name in this way becomes the continuity of a lifetime development of a personality and identity within the community. The belief regarding the continuity of life, which persists even today, was so pervasive that people went to great lengths to ensure that children were born to continue the lineage. Commenting on "woman to woman"[3] marriage in traditional Africa, Bahemuka states:

> It was through such unions [woman to woman marriage] that Africans showed explicitly that they were at pains to try to perpetuate the family's name and that society continuity was paramount. (Bahemuku 1992, 123)

The birth of a child is therefore considered a great blessing both to the family and the larger community. Children, according to Mbiti, are seen as "buds of hope and expectation" (Mbiti 1969, 107). Childlessness is a great tragedy. It is in effect "the death of the unborn and a diminishing of the family as a whole" (Mbiti 1969, 107). Indeed, the society goes to great lengths to ensure that people of childbearing age get married and have children.

According to Mbiti, marriage is a "profound religious act by means of which young people accept that they have to become bearers of children and their community give approval to that step" (Mbiti 1991, 104). Marriage and childbirth therefore are the focus of "human existence" and are in practice not an individual choice but a communal obligation of the individual (Mbiti 1991, 106). Marriage is not just a physical act, but has in it a sacred dimension through which the African understanding of the universe and human life may be perceived. The importance of marriage and childbearing for both men and women is explicit in Mbiti's assertions below:

3   Woman to woman marriage refers to the social arrangement where a wife who could not bear a son designated a certain girl to become the wife of the son she could not bear. The idea was to see the name of her son "who was born socially but not biologically." See Bahemuka (1992).

> Therefore marriage is looked upon as a sacred duty, which every
> person must perform. Failure to do so means in effect stopping
> the flow of life through the individual, and hence diminishing
> mankind upon earth. Anything that deliberately goes towards
> the destruction or obstruction of human life is evil and wicked.
> . . . Marriage is the meeting point of the three layers of human
> life according to African religion. These are the departed, the
> living and those to be born. The departed come into the picture
> because they are the roots on whom the living stand. The living
> are the link between death and life. Those to be born are the
> buds in the loins of the living and marriage makes it possible for
> them to germinate and sprout . . . (Mbiti 1991, 104)

Much has been written regarding the outmoding of many of these practices
in modern Kenya, especially the urban areas. Polygyny is one of the most
contested of these social institutions, having proponents that strongly call
for its reconsideration and opponents who show it to be a declining institution. Of importance to note is the fact that, despite the trend towards
modernity and Westernization, the mode of thinking and worldview of
many people in Kenya continue to be affected by cultural traditions that
pervade their daily life. Traditional worldviews strongly co-exist with
tangible social changes taking place due to influences of foreign culture,
religion, formal education, industrialization and modern technology.

One may argue that social change and Western influence have affected and altered all these traditional beliefs and views regarding marriage
and childbirth. I submit that the changes that have been effected are relative and have not negated the core beliefs held by many Kenyans. In other
words, there is a continuity of traditional beliefs in spite of the apparent
social cultural changes. Even where an individual subjective belief may
have been altered, continued communal beliefs may have strong bearing
on the perception and sense of the individual. In many cases inner conflicts
result with respect to areas of life that are integral to the sense of self of the
individual involved.

Some notable areas where major changes may be observed regarding these Western influences and Christianity, (yet which demonstrate the
strong traditional ties to identity formation) concern the marriage institution: Today's marriage, for instance, is in many cases based on mutual
attraction, which in turn changes its focus from procreation to companion-
ship and love. However, the importance of procreation is still a strong factor
in the definition of a successful marriage. While a woman may not simply
be divorced for infertility today, the centrality of procreation may justify,

if only in the eyes of the society, a man's promiscuous behavior or acquisition of a second wife. The conflict between these prevailing worldviews, and especially the advent of Christianity, which I believe presents the most important social change in marriage, is discussed in greater detail in the section on female identity formation in Kenya. First, however, a description of African religiosity is in order, to set the stage from which religious engagement by the survivors of intimate violence in Kenya is premised.

DESCRIPTIVE CHARACTERISTICS OF AFRICAN RELIGIOSITY

John Mbiti, writing from an African traditional religious perspective, states that to be African is to be religious (1991, 108). Mbiti describes religion as a pervasive reality in the lives of people in the African context—a lens through which the African seeks to comprehend, both intellectually and spiritually, the world and his/her place in it. He views religion as an intricate weaving of all aspects of being human: "religion is found in all areas of human life" (Mbiti 1991, 10). It permeates all spheres of African life, making no distinctions between what is cultural, political, or religious, they all interrelate. Hence, anything that cannot be logically explained is relegated to a theological mystical realm. This has been the African way of being in traditional Africa. As Mbiti states, the African view of the universe is profoundly religious (Mbiti, 1975, 32).

Africans who have embraced Christianity and other world religions have similarly appropriated, and even integrated, indigenous African religious beliefs and ideologies so that they permeate the thinking, reasoning, and worldview of individuals and communities. For a majority of people, religion, whether Christianity, or other religious traditions, including Kenya's own traditional beliefs, acts as both a guide and a compass for one's life. . Our very being—the way we think about things and the ideologies we hold about ourselves, about others, and about our place in the cosmos—has religious dimensions.

When I reflect on Mbiti's assertion that to be African is to be religious (1991, 108), I, as someone with psychological training, am aware that African religiosity also has an inner reality that finds expression through external and observable practices and symbolisms. Consistent with Mbiti's perspective that religion permeates all spheres of life, the practice of religious rites and expectations in individual behavior expresses a socially-engendered inner belief in the existence of a Deity. Yet the practice of religion has a reciprocal effect. The constant and regular observance of cultural religious practices also serves to confirm, develop, and strengthen that inner reality. Being thus pervasive, religion in human complexity and daily reality calls on most Africans to be in constant engagement with religious ideologies and theological reformulations within the communal context and individual experience.

In considering aspects that characterize African religiosity and religious influence in the African's life, I begin with Mbiti's statement that "to be an African [human] in the traditional setting is to be truly religious" (Mbiti 1991, 108). This statement raises, then, the counter-question: what makes one "human" in the African setting? Of utmost importance is the concept that to be human is to be part of the whole, and wholeness comes through participation in community rites, celebrations, and ceremonies. A person becomes complete as he/she integrates into the community through rites of passage. For the African person being religious means being both aware of and in respectful relation to those in the spirit world and to the Divine, since these are interpreted and mediated through the cultural context in which persons live. In many parts of Africa, being in communication with a Deity entails active participation in communal rites, both those that speak to the family and those that pay respect to the Deity. The relationship is not necessarily a personal communication with a Deity; in many cases, participation requires a middle person, either a diviner or a "living dead" who had some connection to the family lineage (Mbiti, 1970, 108). Age and respect commanded in the community put one in a better position to be in such communion with the Divine.

Also important is the need to keep good relations with other humans, the inanimate, and the environment through virtues and mores that are developed as part of the community moral system. Excessive deviation from such morality and a general incompatibility with others in the community evokes a disciplinary action from the community, stemming from fear that an individual's rebellion and misconduct could cause the wrath of the Divine to descend upon the family or the larger community.

Religion guides the morals, attitudes, relations, and actions of each individual within the community. In the development of virtues and vices in traditional Africa, the importance is not whether they are "legal" or politically right. What is important is the betterment of the community and that the morals and virtues guide the relations between families and others. Most prohibitions in this sense would be regarded as taboos, thereby creating a sense of mandate from a higher authority than the mortal. Ancestors, who continue to live amongst the people, are taken to be parts of this harmonizing system, and in this way render profoundly sacred what is accepted within the community and what is expected, influencing the individual's guiding principles of what is morally right. It is this synthesized religiousness in many African settings that brings out the cultural sentiment of putting community first, before one's self, underscored in Mbiti's statement that "I am because we are and since we are, therefore I am" (Mbiti 1975, 108). This notion of individual moral responsibility to the larger community is believed to emanate from the belief in the higher authority of the ancestral presence within the community, and authority which guides and harmonizes all, pointing to the synthesis of most cultural aspects of the society with religiousness. For many African theologians like John Mbiti, therefore, religion is the intricate lifeline that holds communities together and gives individuals within those communities a sense of belonging, and a sense of self.

A fundamental characteristic of African religiosity is that the distinction between what is religious and what is cultural is not significant. It is very important to see how characteristics of African religiosity are intertwined with cultural traditions and mores, because this intertwining strongly influences how Christianity and other external religious traditions have been appropriated and therefore this intertwining has a significant influence in the formation of the self. Behavior is also shaped by the experiences of the person, and sometimes religious and cultural practices cannot be separated: what is religious is cultural and what is cultural is sanctioned as religious. Religion, in all its symbolic representations, is not a static factor in a person's life. Our ongoing epistemological development through life's experiences is in constant engagement with our religiosity. It calls for reshaping, renegotiating, repressing, rekindling and transforming integral symbolism and therefore it impacts our comprehension of life experiences.

FEMALE IDENTITY FORMATION IN KENYA

Identity and self-formation[4] of a woman in Kenya are primarily a function of her reproductive role (as a mother) as well as her married role (as a wife). These inform her view of the self and the other's view of her own self. The dominant Euro-centric sense of one's identity is a connotation of

4. The notion of self-formation (and in some ways identity formation) is central to the thesis of this book because of the perception of the self as an agency for behavioral patterns and transformation. This notion has been discussed in detail in the introductory chapter.

one's differentiation, potentiality and active role in the society (in terms of careers, position and influence),[5] yet the Kenyan woman's role as a giver and provider of continued life are the most important factors in her identity and social achievements. As Sundermeier (1998) discusses, both she and the man are simply recipients of life, the most important thing in most African communities, and they have a duty to pass it on.

A critical interrogation may reveal the imbalance between males and females concerning these critical aspects of marriage and childbirth which have previously been discussed. These customs were supposed to create a sense of self in the community.

I have already mentioned polygyny and the notion of labor force, wealth, and status that the man commanded by having more than one wife. The concept of continuity of one's name is again a strong patriarchal concept in that the name that needed to be maintained was a son's (male) name. Hence the *woman-to-woman* marriage that both Mbiti (1991) and Bahemuka (1992) discuss is an attempt to have a son if the traditionally-married wife was either barren or had not borne a male child. *Ghost marriages,* described earlier, served the purpose of perpetuating the family name in the case of a son who died before he was married. For the most part, then, the customs held as important were really developed to serve the importance of the male lineage continuity in the society.

The customs that have evolved through the centuries to enable the fulfillment of the obligation to marry and have children reflect a differential status accorded to the woman and the man. First, the woman's status in society is determined by her ability to *be* in a marriage and to reproduce. This is essentially different for the man. Although the man continues to have the parenting role as a father, this is not intimately tied to his identity in the society. He will have the social status as a full member of the community by fulfilling the obligation to marry and father a child. In contrast, the woman's role in both these aspects does not end with the fact that she has gotten married and has successfully borne a child. She must continue to maintain these roles through her later adult life. This designates her as the primary responsible person in the union for rearing and bringing up her children as well as holding together her marriage, since she would be the loser in the case of a divorce or separation, if only in terms of loss of identity. Following this line of thought, then, bearing children and leaving them or not providing for them as expected, is tantamount to not having the children.

---

5. See Feshbach et al. (1996, 300).

In reality, in most societies in Kenya, the children are believed to belong to the husband's family, despite the fact that he is less involved in their rearing, except in disciplinary matters. In those communities where children go home with their mother in the case of a divorce, the customary custody is actually in the hands of the uncle or another significant male in her family. They are never really the woman's children. Although writing for the Zimbabwean context, Alice Armstrong's statement regarding the position of a woman and her children in marriage is very applicable in the Kenyan context. She states:

> In traditional law (and in Western Law), marriage gave the husband exclusive sexual rights over the wife and her reproductive capacities. In traditional law, this right lasted forever since, at the level of ideology, a woman remained married to a man and his family not only throughout his life but even after death. The children born during the marriage were considered his, and belonging to his family line. (Armstrong 1998, 15)

Given this understanding, Armstrong discusses, from her research, how many of her respondents cited the children's welfare as the reason for not leaving their abusive relationships.

It should also be noted that the practical aspects of reproduction and the marriage roles are not uniform for men and women in fulfillment of this sacred responsibility. The woman's obligation to marry and have children is tied to her identity as a mature human being in the society although the man has a similar responsibility. His obligation is not tied to his sense of self. A pregnant woman automatically gains a special place in the society, however, the infertile woman is of no value to the society. Mbiti is once again very explicit in this regard when he states:

> Unhappy is the woman who fails to get children for, whatever qualities she might possess, her failure to bear children is worse than committing genocide: she has become the dead end of human life, not only for the genealogical line but also for herself. When she dies there will be nobody of her own immediate blood to 'remember' her in the eyes of the society. . . . Her husband may remedy the situation a bit, by raising children with another wife; but the childless wife bears a scar, which nothing can erase. She will suffer for this, her own relatives will suffer for this; and it will be an irreparable humiliation for which there is no source of comfort in traditional life. (Mbiti 1991, 110)

Although Mbiti's Africanization has been contested with regard to the place of the infertile woman because of the present day alternatives of social reproduction including adoption and fosterage, he speaks to the gist of dominant traditional position of most Kenyan communities. The stigma of the childless woman carries a life-long scar and can be felt in the society even today. While adoption and fosterage may save her society face, it does not heal the *genocidal scar* that is ingrained in her psyche and that continues to haunt her perception of how the community views and speaks of her. In communities where the option of *woman-to-woman* marriage is available, this option gives the wife some remedy, but even *woman-to-woman* marriage leaves the scar of not being a biological mother. She has no way to fully remedy her identity and social status if she has no children of her own or with her husband. Indeed her barrenness is the single most accepted cause for divorce (Mbiti 1991, 160).

The fate of the impotent man is a much better one. Before it is even decided that he is the fault of a childless marriage, he will have married a couple of other wives who must also suffer the humiliation of not having children. Once it is established that he is the fault for childlessness, he can still fully remedy the position by having another man father children with his wife or wives on his behalf (Mbiti 1991, 145).

Furthermore, the strong influence of religion on the cultural and traditional mores and values cannot be ignored. Cultural and traditional religious observances went hand in hand in an integrated way. The African, Mbiti asserts, is profoundly a religious being whose religion permeates all functions of life. For many Africans a fine line divides traditions or beliefs considered cultural and those considered religious. Religion can be found in all sectors of the African mind. Addressing the place of religion in the African's life, Sundermeier states that "life is most important in Africa… preserving life is the real purpose of any religious activity" (Sundermeier 1998, 14). For many Kenyans, life has no coincidences. They seek to comprehend and explain aspects of life religiously (Mbiti 1969; 1991).

Orientation towards incoming religious beliefs of various traditions that do not necessarily complement the traditional cultural religious beliefs further creates difficulty for identity formation. Increasingly, considerable religious influence from outside Kenya appears through missionary work, trade contacts, the influx of immigrants from various parts of the world and, especially today, the flood of ideologies through the Internet. For instance, Christianity was embraced and continues to be contextualized through engagement and appropriation of both Christian and African traditional values and mores. Hence to many adherents, Christianity is not just a system of rituals to be followed, but also a real life engagement with a Divine that must make sense to their realities. Indeed, for many African Christians, their desire to embrace Christian beliefs in life situations has been the greatest point of inner conflict with regard to concepts that were pronounced heathen by the previous missionaries, but which, in the African tradition (and therefore religion), were deep-seated beliefs.

In his book *Pastoral Care From a Third World Perspective: A Pastoral Theology of Care from an Urban Contemporary Shona in Zimbabwe*, Mucherera clearly postulates the psychological tragedies wrought by inner conflict produced by the tension between ingrained traditional beliefs and the social and religious change brought about by industrialization and the advent of Christianity in African societies. He argues that in the quest to find one's identity within the society, individuals converted to Christianity to find themselves straddled in inner psychological destabilization which he calls 'hybridity.' He posits that to be an effective counselor to individuals and families in these cultures, one must have an integrative awareness of the dual cultures at play in the lives of the people (Mucherera, 2001). Mucherera's work beautifully captures and advances my claim that identity formation in a collective culture like Africa, is not a function of the Western modality of achievement and fulfillment. Even for doctrine-grounded African Christians, the sense of self founded on socio-cultural and religious norms that somehow assume a sacred dimension is ingrained.

Marriage, and the issue of polygyny, when perceived from the dual perspectives of Christianity and the African traditional religions, has been an area of great contention. Most families in the present day, for instance, are moving away from polygyny for various reasons, including the Christian convictions of monogamy, economic constraints for raising larger families, female empowerment, and redirected focus of marriage from procreation to mutual attraction. At the same time, however, others use the African traditional notion to justify their maintenance of mistresses on the side. In fact some people have performed traditional rites to engage in a second marriage, since the church would not recognize such a marriage. Either way the modern multiple marriage has further lowered the social status of women, even though some would argue that the procurement of a second or third wife through traditional recognition would serve to secure the woman who is marrying as a second wife. Bahemuka highlights this:

> This means that polygamy cannot be used as a status symbol. It is because of this that the practice of serial and consequential polygyny is becoming common. A man marries one wife legally, and lives with several mistresses at the same time. After a while he divorces the wife and marries one of the mistresses. Although the mistresses may be treated better than the wife, they do not achieve the status of a wife. (Bahemuku 1992, 129)

Serial and sequential polygyny, therefore, is a two edged sword for women because both the divorced wife and the mistress lose. The first wife has low status as a divorcee while the married mistress cannot attain the full status of a wife. Furthermore, the fact that marriage today is increasingly based on mutual attraction has implications for hurts and pains that many women go through when their husbands begin getting involved with other women in intimate relationships. This aspect may not have been very prevalent in traditional polygyny marriages.

Christianity, as introduced to the African people, was not bereft of its Jewish and Western baggage of patriarchy. It served to justify and consecrate the sociological arrangements it found within the African traditional religions that coincided with its own values. In the example given above, Christianity has been used to justify polygyny with citations from the Old Testament. In many ways, interpretations of the Bible have only been contextualized to the point that they are serving patriarchal ends. Hence "Christian values," as interpreted from patriarchal perspectives regarding marriage relationships and the status of women, even in the institutional church and priesthood, are in many ways gender insensitive. Kariuki notes that Christianity socialized the woman to believe that she is inferior to the man. He cites Max Weber's beliefs that "religious ideas serve to legitimize existing social arrangements" (Kariuki, 2003, 8), and also notes that although the book of Proverbs speaks of the woman as a "source of great wisdom" the Proverbs' overall effect is "clearly that women have a subordinate position" (Kariuki 2003, 9). Biblical scriptures are invoked in various forms during the Christian marriage rite as a resource to offer guidance for a "good marriage." Most common are passages in Genesis about the creation of woman from the man's rib and therefore as a helper (which in many interpretations connotes subordination), as well as passages about the man being the head of his family and general submission of woman to man in marriage relationships (Gen 2:21–23, Eph 3:21–24 and 1 Cor 11:

7–9).[6] All these passages combine to reinforce the place of the woman in the traditional marriage relationship.

Marriage, whether under traditional or Western law, gave the man both conjugal and proprietary rights over his wife. It is interesting to note that many aspects of traditional law are still observed in conjunction with Christianity. Bride price is yet another good example of the ingrained continuity of cultural traditions synchronized with western Christianity because it coincides with the Jewish cultural practice of dowry. It is one aspect of traditional marriage that has continued to hold a special place even in Christian marriages. In most of the Kenyan cultures, bride price was viewed as an appreciation to the girl's family by the man's family for the gift of an additional family member. The man was not expected to come up with the bride price by himself, as marriage was a family affair. Thus, the woman married into the family and not just an individual, a view that has both negative and positive connotations.

On the negative side, bride price gave proprietary rights of the woman to the family such that where the woman lived on family land with other extended family members, many of the women had to live with violence and mistreatment from a larger section of the family-in-law. Armstrong highlights the problem that this can pose in a manner relevant to the Kenyan situation, noting that

> a woman was married by the husband's whole family. The family referred to her as 'our wife.' They paid bride price for her. She had certain duties towards them as well as towards her husband. They have a responsibility towards her, but also the power to control her actions to some extent. The right of the husband to control his wife may be extended to his whole family. (Armstrong 1998, 19)

Elsewhere she states,

> Although women are traditionally said to join their husband's family through marriage, today women are also expected to contribute to the support of the extended family. This means there is a three-way conflict between the needs of the woman's extended family, the man's extended family and the couple themselves and their children. (Armstrong 1998, 18)

---

6. The role of religion and its influence on domestic violence is dealt with depth in Chapter 5.

A second, seemingly positive aspect concerns the responsibilities that the man's family has towards the woman to provide for her in case of the husband's death. However, this expectation is vulnerable to abuse. In some of the African communities, customary law requires the woman to be inherited by the brother as a way of ensuring such provision for her and her children, through Levirate marriages. In these circumstances, the woman is obliged to give all marital services to the new husband (brother-in-law), including sexual relations, and to submit to him just as if he were her husband.

A third enormous ill of the practice of the bride price is its connotation of marriage as being parallel to the purchase of goods. Such a concept emanates from the language used and its corresponding symbolism. Speaking to the effects of bride price in marriage, Hinga states:

> The language used to describe what a man does when he takes a woman as a wife is in the *Gikuyu* language for example, the language of the market place. Such an act of taking a wife is described as *kugurana* or *kugura muka*. The same word *kugura* is used to refer to the acquisition of commodities like sugar or goats. When a person's daughter becomes pregnant outside of marriage, it will be said that *mburi ya ngania niroinirwo kuguru*, that is to say "somebody has broken the leg of X's sheep." Again the language reflects a woman as a commodity analogous to sheep. (Hinga 1994, 125)

Such language connotes that a woman becomes a man's property at marriage. She is no longer in the hands and custody of her father (and never her mother) but now of her husband. The word in Meru, Embu and Gikuyu referring to her husband from this point on is *Mwene*, meaning "owner." Nasimiyu-Wasike points out the effects of such language in the concept of marriage:

> Some of our men think that the herd of cattle, goats and sheep that they pay as bride wealth for their wives gives them the right to beat their wives at will. They believe they own the wives and have a right to control them. (Nasimiyu-Wasike 1994, 110)

Apparently, many people have manipulated the bride price to suit selfish ends. It has been regarded as a purchase price. The price is sometimes demanded in large amounts of money which, when not paid in full, can cause undue tensions. Bride price has also adversely affected the humanness and sense of self-worth of many women because of the subjective standards used to base the bride price on an evaluation of her education and beauty.

The issue of divorce is another sensitive one in the Kenyan context. Whether viewed from the Christian perspective or the African traditional perspective, the belief is that marriage is a life covenant. Writing about Christian marriage, Bahemuka states that

> in Christianity, marriage comes to be viewed as a divine gift requiring those who receive it to establish a lasting union. The union is called the "unity of flesh" and forms the basis for the understanding of sexual life in Christianity. (Bahemuku 1992, 126)

Given that a similar understanding of marriage as a lifelong institution was held in traditional Kenya, one can appreciate the source of emotional and inner conflict that may be associated with even the mere thought of divorce by a woman whose marriage is robbing her of her livelihood, as in the case of violence. It also has implications for creating dilemmas in the counseling and guidance that a priest (pastor) would give to a woman who sought his/her help.[7] Many pastoral caregivers, for instance, have been known to ask a woman who seeks their help regarding abusive relationships what she did to the man to warrant such a beating. One may wonder how clearly such a pastoral caregiver in the Kenyan situation distinguishes between cultural beliefs that he/she has grown with and the Christian virtues he/she may be upholding in a counseling situation with a woman in violence. However much the pastoral caregiver may not approve of the violence, does such a question hint that there may be situations that can justify violence? What is the foundation of such justification in terms of culture and religion? How does such a caregiver continue to show care to the woman in accordance to his/her religious call and yet honor the instilled beliefs of a woman's need to be submissive to the husband? (Wifely submission to a husband is a coinciding factor both in Christian religion and traditional cultures.) Would the caregiver successfully address the issue by citing the Bible or by calling a council of relatives or elders into the situation?

It is apparent that, of the traditional values, numerous aspects have survived and are actually being championed by many African theologians. The issue of contextualizing Christianity for instance is currently on the table as a heated discourse in many theological gatherings and literature. Proponents of this position have argued for seeking a genuine African

7. See Gatobu (2003) for a more detailed discussion regarding the pastoral response to the survivor of domestic violence.

theology, but one that is grounded in scriptural texts, with the rationale that God does not want us to leave our culture because God and Christ are above culture. We are therefore to understand Christ through our context in order to find the meaning and the relevance of Christianity in our life. While I too would love to adopt this view because of my convictions concerning the immeasurable value of many of the African virtues and beliefs and the whole notion of contextualization which I actually argue for in this book, I am hesitant to do so recognizing the insensitivity to justice and gender issues with which some of these values are being championed. My major critique in this regard is in the vulnerability of idealizing cultural "values" at the expense of the moral and ethical justice, or lack thereof, in the vulnerable female Kenyan. Gender role definitions are yet another problem area and are a good pointer to trace the roots behind the low social and economic status of women, and gender-based violence. Within a society, gender roles determine policy-making in the social and public arena. In turn they reflect gendered social and economic high status of men and low status of the women respectively.

Unfortunately low economic statuses correspond to perception, regard, and treatment of women in the social, economic and family units. The system of education in the public schools in Kenya exemplifies the claim that there are significant gender-based status differentials between men and women. Given the tough economic situation in Kenya today, most families are constantly faced with the question of which child to educate and which child has to stay home for lack of finances. When such a decision has to be made, it is usually the girl child who must stop her education in favor of the boy child. The rationale is that the boy will grow to become a provider for his family and possibly the protective arm of his parents, while the girl will be provided for anyway in adulthood through marriage. Since its inception in 2002, the current government has been very responsive and sensitive to this gendered economic choice within families by providing free primary education. Consequently, there was a huge influx of children into the primary schools in the years following 2003. For instance between 2005 and 2009 number of children enrolled in the early childhood centers around the country grew from 1,643,175 to 1,914,222.[8] A similar increase was experienced in the primary schools enrollment between the period 2003 and 2009 (1,608,115 children)

8. "Table 3.5: Pupil Enrolment and Teacher Numbers in Early Childhood Development Centers, 2005–2009," Ministry of Education, www.education.go.ke.

compared to 1999 to 2003 (151, 565 children).[9] These figures reflect total number of boys and girls. However, that alone cannot curb the problem because when these children come to the age of high school, which is not free, the families have to tackle the same decision. The result is that many girls drop out of school after grade eight. Furthermore, the question of which children to send to school may have nothing to do with finances but rather with cultural traditions and beliefs along gender lines. Many parents reason that the girls will be of no use to their families of origin once they get married, so it would be a waste of resources to spend any money for education on them. Indeed, this has been a source of conflict: mothers trying to vie for their daughter's education get in heated disagreements with their husbands, who prefer for their sons to be educated. Even in communities where girls are enrolled for primary education, most of their educational endeavors are curtailed when they become of marriageable age (which in these societies is determined by the girl's onset of menstruation and therefore eligibility to give birth), at which time they are, in many cases, married off against their will. This practice, coupled with early pregnancies that require the girls to drop out of school so they can take care of the baby, and the punitive school rules of not accepting mothers in schools, contribute towards the very high dropout rate of girls as compared to boys.

For instance, consider these statistics: the transition of students from primary to secondary (high) school in the period between 1998 and 2002 averaging at about 45%, indicate a very small margin of only about 2.1% for boys over girls. Then in 2003 there was a sudden influx of girls transitioning at a higher rate of 6.2% over boys, followed by a slack between 2004–2008 averaging at 1.7%, and major influx again of girls over boys in 2009 and 2010 of about 6%.[10] One would expect similar numbers to be reflected by those of total students enrolled in high school. Yet, the number of boys in high school is consistently higher with the gap widening dramatically in year 2007–2009 (average of 7.2%) from 1999–2006 (average of 3.2%).[11] There could be varying explanations, but given the fact that there

9. Calculated from figures provided in "Primary School Net Enrollment Rate, 1999–2009," Ministry of Education tables, www.education.go.ke.

10. Calculated from tables published by Education Management Information System (EMIS), in "Primary to Secondary Transition Rate National, 1998–2009," Ministry of Education, www.education.go.ke.

11. Averages are calculated from table published by 2009 EMISS school census returns, titled "Secondary Schools Gross Enrollment Rate, 1999–2009," Ministry of Education: www.education.go.ke.

is not a significant difference between number of boys and the number of girls transitioning from primary to secondary, it is logical to assume that it gets more difficult for the girl child to maintain her high school status due to social cultural expectations in the society. What is most bothersome is the unrealistic popular myth that the main reason for higher dropout rate by girls in high school is that they are not smart or rigorous enough to attain high school diploma. Such hypothesis fails to acknowledge the demands and social pressures on the girl child by the society to marry and raise a family—especially when these two roles are tied to her identity in the community. It also does not take to consideration that many of the girls who drop out of high school do so because of familial economic decisions that favor the male child as discussed above.

The transition rate of students from high school to university is even more telling. Of the 169,357 candidates who obtained high school Diploma in 1998, only 30,243 candidates were qualified for entrance to universities. Of these only 8,150 (4%) were admitted to the 7 national universities, 64% of whom were male and 35% females. Very similar trends hold through 2003. After this year we observe a significant increase in the total number of those admitted to universities from an average of 5.1% (between 1999–2005) to 6.1% (2006), 6.5% (2007) and 7.2% (2008). This significant increase should however be viewed against the general staggering increase in student population registered for the national exam, KCSE, from 169,357 students (1998) to 276,192 students (2007) reflecting an increase of 106, 835 students over a 9 year period."[12]

Cultural expectations are that girls must be taught their maternal roles early in life: taking care of household chores and looking after all members of the family. These expectations can interrupt the girl's education and girls do not have a 'level playing field' when competing with male peers for entry into higher education. Yet at each educational level, both girls and boys sit for the same examinations which determine who goes on to the next year of schooling. The competition to go to the next level is always very stiff because the higher the level of education, the lower the number of institutions available to meet the large number of candidates. Hence, the 7.2 % (20,000) of candidates admitted to university in the year 2007 as reported above, should be viewed against the figure 276,192 students who sat the exam. A similar number may have been absorbed by private universities and technical colleges leaving about 236,000 young

12. Source: Commission of Higher Education, Ministry of Education: www.education.go.ke.

people with little or no purpose or means to better themselves. Given the statistics above, 66% (about 160,000) of these are young girls!

Despite the unfair gendered grounds on which the national exams are approached, final grades and their distribution in schools are largely taken to confirm the claim that girls are not as smart as boys in educational arenas. However, I believe that a closer look at the general school composition and curriculum is an even more accurate measure. Most schools in Kenya, especially the high schools, are segregated by gender. Boys' schools have strong science-oriented curriculums and are equipped with laboratories and other science facilities, while girls' schools concentrate on arts, humanities and home economics. This difference is a direct reflection of the gendered roles of the society.

Even at this higher level of education all students are required to sit for the same national exams to determine who will get entry into the national universities. The exams are also used to judge cognitive skills and educational strengths along gender lines; boys are perceived as mathematically and scientifically smart, while the girls are associated with interrelational strengths. The system therefore produces a greater number of male graduates from the state colleges. The disparity in the schools along gender lines also lays an educational foundation all the way from primary schools through secondary schools and colleges, thus producing young men as engineers, economists, architects, doctors, lawyers, statisticians, professors and other esteemed professions, while the greater number of women graduate in what the Kenyan society has termed "supportive staff." The issue here is that supportive service includes professions like teaching and nursing which are the cornerstones of economic development and stability of any country. The fact that by being referred to as supportive service, the pay is not commensurate to the work and its value and the concern is not the actual professions of teaching and nursing, but prestige and remuneration which translate to a fulfilled sense of self. The system makes sure that these, which are regarded as women's professions and therefore more populated by women, are relegated to second place, commanding very low salaries, while 'men's professions' are envied for esteem and pride, and better pay.

Of the six state universities established by 2004, Kenyatta University, which offers more of the education-based courses to prepare graduates for the teaching profession, has more correlate figures between males and females.[13]

---

13. All the other state universities indicate a ratio of about 1/2 or less female to

While many women do not get opportunities for higher education, even those who do, end up being economically poorer, because of the preponderance of women relegated to being in supportive professions. In turn, the economic and social status of women is very low. They find themselves heavily reliant on their husband's finances. Especially in the cities, the trend in the last few years has been one of women seeking higher levels of education by juggling their jobs, family, and school. This trend is a very significant indication of women's dissatisfaction with their low status in the society, and an undercurrent but a very powerful defiance against the system. It is noteworthy that with this recent trend, more and more of the traditionally male-gendered professions are being penetrated by greater numbers of women. While some people perceive this as an attempt by women to compete with men, I propose that these women confirm the argument that, when granted the opportunity for education, women are cognitively, emotionally and physically capable of excelling in positions of leadership and development while handling their family responsibilities. In my view, their efforts do not need to be perceived as "competition" with men because gender roles are not on an equal plane, and men are not a *yardstick* but a *partner* in development. The trend is also significant in pointing to a desired transformation of indicators for female identity in this society.

FEMALE IDENTITY AND INTIMATE VIOLENCE

Unfortunately, the low status of women in the economic and social structures of the country carries over to family relationships for many people in their homes, leading to mistreatment and violence against women in many families. The generally inferior economic status of women in Kenya, coupled with the cultural expectations of female identity as wife and mother, leaves them few choices when they are in an abusive relationship.

The foregoing contextual background is very important in the quest to understand the range of responses available to the female in intimate violence. Specifically, how is her high functionality (and other range of responses to intimate violence) to be understood within the contextual framework presented above? Is the apparent lack of easily identifiable trauma and PTSD effects to be linked to the Kenyan socio-cultural traditions that demand her to maintain her belongingness to the whole by

male enrollment. See *Enrollment by Gender in Universities 1999/2000–2003/2004.* Ministry of Education, Science and technology, www.education.go.ke.

maintaining her roles as a mother and a wife? What are some of the possible implications, both to the individuals and community, if indeed the
contextual framework makes a negative demand on the woman's formation of self? Might many of the females have psychological concerns whose
evidence may be clouded by a great need to fulfill primary roles? Is there a
possibility that such clouding, even though the woman appears to function well, may be curtailing an achievement drive and therefore loss of
potential to the community?

All of these considerations are specific and integral not only to the
socio-cultural and religious context, but also to its distinctive influence
along gender lines. While the man is held to the fulfillment of the marriage and childbearing role, he is free to actualize his identity in various
other ways, such as education, leadership and economic status. One might
argue that he too cannot self-actualize through these accomplishments in
the Western sense of the word because, as Sundermeier states, potentiality
in Africa "does not aim at defining life in the sense of our ideal personality." Rather it means the "internal potential of life to grow, the ideal being
the harmonious balance of all forces" (Sundermeier 1998, 19). In other
words, potentiality for the African in general is not achieved through personal achievement but must also balance with being connected with the
community through fulfillment of community expectations. I maintain,
however, that the harmonious maintenance "of all forces" presents for the
woman greater challenges than for the man because, even if she were to
strive to self-actualize in the African sense through both achievement and
maintenance of a sense of belonging, the society has already prescribed
her roles of motherhood and family as primary, if not exclusive. In this
regard I deviate from Bahemuka, who sees "in today's societies, social
class as achieved and not prescribed" (Bahemuku 1992, 129). While one
may reach a certain social class through financial status and educational
achievement, there still survives the traditional pull on women to find
fulfillment through prescribed reproductive and marital expectations,
if only from the societal perception. Might this shed some partial light
on why many women seek to be sequential wives despite the knowledge
that they will not gain the main status of first wife, or why they choose
to stay on in unfulfilling relationships? Although I cannot conclusively
prove that this is the main reason women participate as sequential wives,
it cannot be denied that motherhood and wifely female roles continue to
pervade the definitions of the status of women. These roles are so integral
that they cannot be ignored when considering identity formation. Most

other achievements become secondary. Unlike men, who can move on to self-actualize in other achievements that continue to uphold societal norms, and whose achievements are perceived with equal benevolence to the society as their family roles, for the woman, self-actualizing achievements are of secondary importance.

These differential communal demands on the identity formation of the female and male in Kenyan society lead to a perception of gender roles as the accepted mirror of societal expectations and definitions of a "good woman" and a "good man." A woman with a high level accomplishment in variables that could reflect achievement will first be evaluated by her success in her motherly and wifely role. As a result, even though she may have success in education and other social parameters, she may possess feelings of disillusionment and a fragmented sense of self if she is unmarried, divorced, or childless. The society may not give her a chance at leadership because she is not an integral part of the whole through maternal roles. A classic example of a real life situation in Kenya of such gendered evaluation of capability is the public utterance of our former president (1978-2002) regarding the incapability and ineffectiveness of insights from a woman who is divorced. The utterances were made at a public day rally in Nairobi stating that the public should not pay attention to this woman's plea to preserve the forest through her newly founded Green Belt movement since she was divorced and had therefore failed to hold her home together. As I write, this woman now deceased has since received the Nobel Peace Prize by forces outside of Kenya who do not evaluate a woman's worth only through her maternal roles of a wife and a mother! It is important to note that the demand on the man's identity for responsible roles as a father and husband are regarded only as rites of passage, and not necessarily lifelong roles. Hence as long as he has passed through these rites, any further failures, like that of not holding his family together or not providing for them, are secondary. In most cases such failures are regarded as the woman's fault unless it is tangibly evident that the man is to blame. Even then, he can still thrive on his other self-actualization achievements (including having more than one wife and male children in some communities), which can easily overshadow his general failure in his paternal role.

It is not surprising with this contextual background that wife beating has been normalized as a form of discipline for a non-submissive wife. Non-submission of the woman can be defined in various ways and is subject to the man's definition. Its definition may include: disrespect (talking back, asking for explanations); disobedience (not asking for permission, refusal of sexual demand); neglect of household duties (cooking, washing clothes, waiting up for him in the night); demand for fidelity (not accepting promiscuity, asking to use condoms); and financial stressors (lack of employment, limited availability of money and budgeting and/or allocation priorities). Indeed, for many couples, wife beating in the secular world is sometimes heroic. Discussing this sexist issue, Hinga states:

> In fact, many men think that wife beating is part of their husbandry rights and privileges if not obligation. Many women on their part seem generally to accept their destiny and will often cover up their husbands even when they have done them actual bodily harm. They too seem to assume that being battered is part of the marriage package. (Hinga 1994, 119)

A partial result of this perception of the asymmetric relationship between a man and a woman in the marriage is to indoctrinate the woman's mind that she is of less worth as a person in comparison to the man. In today's society, where both men and women are striving for similar jobs and education, her treatment by the society and persons significant in her life send contradicting messages. If the society around her were affirming her status and place in the society and telling her about her worth, and affirming that worth is not tied to her maternal roles, it would be the burden of the woman to live up to her potentiality. In reality, however, she is caught in the paradoxical situation of knowing her worth as an educated competitor in the economic life of the culture, but having experiences that counter that sense of worth by basing it primarily on marriage, procreation and motherhood.

Kenya as a society in general holds the cultural value of the need to keep family affairs secret, especially as they concern the relationship between the man and his wife. This is generally referred to as not "washing one's dirty linen in public." It is paradoxical that acts of violence against women, which are normally regarded as acceptable, should also be termed as "dirty." This belief ensures that intimate violence is kept as hidden as possible. Despite the secrecy surrounding the issue of intimate violence, it is openly talked of in general, implying that everyone knows that it happens but not with any specificity. For instance, women will jokingly talk of hurrying home before he gets there or making sure his food is ready or else, *Utatandikwa*, meaning, "you will be beaten." Beneath such joking masks, is there a real threat that one may actually be beaten?

Secrecy plays a big role in helping maintain the picture of the perfect family to the public. Secrecy is especially important when the family holds a position of prestige either in community leadership, has economic stability, or participates in church worship. At the same time it helps the man to rest assured that he never has to fear being "exposed" because if the woman ever admits to being beaten, she is revealing to the world that she is incapable of being a good wife. The dynamics within the culture and traditions demand that she collude in keeping the abuse as secret as possible.

When the abuse gets out of hand, the recourse is first and foremost family arbitration, usually of the man's side since this is the family that has the responsibility towards the couple. Unfortunately, this approach is not a very helpful recourse because, as already discussed, the family would most likely be aligned to support the man. Many women have resigned themselves to living silently with the violence after calculating the demand for their rights against loss—physical (including children, and property), financial, emotional and psychological (including family, attachments, identity and sense of self). If a woman has grown up in an abusive home herself, abuse in marriage as an adult can be easily incorporated as normative and therefore not responded to in an empowered, decisive manner. In many instances lack of what appears as an empowered response is misinterpreted as acceptance of the abuse. However, this is not to assume that the woman actually *thrives or enjoys* being abused. In many cases, even where they cannot challenge the violence, most women will maintain the hope that if they collude with their husbands and continue to be submissive, things will change. In this regard, Kibwana states:

> When men say that women have learnt to accept violence, they mean that women have learnt to rationalize that theirs is a violence-prone life and therefore must tolerate violence for their survival and that of their children. Nobody ever accepts violence. (Kibwana 1994, 174)

The consideration of "acceptance" of intimate violence raises a crucial question: How does one reconcile survivor's responses of denouncing violence and traditional perception of women's acceptance of violence? All these factors—the superior role of the man in the family, and society in general; traditions about what it takes to be a good woman; and therefore socio-cultural and religious beliefs about maternal roles attached to identity and place within the society, the nature of the marriage institution, and the lack of alternatives for most women due to low social and economic status—work together to ensure that women in abusive relationships collude with the perpetrators for their own survival.

EFFECTS OF INTIMATE VIOLENCE IN THE KENYAN CONTEXT

I submit that understanding the responses and functionality of survivors of intimate violence would best be achieved if studied with analytical interrogation between the socio-cultural and religious context and the latter's role in the psycho-social processes of the survivor's self-formation. It is from this perspective that I positioned myself as a researcher in the Kenyan context in an attempt to demystify the high level of functionality by analytically listening to my informants' narratives and being open to understanding this phenomenon from their own perspectives. In the next chapter I discuss in detail my orienting psychological and religious framework, the lens through which I investigated the subject.

However, my theory, is that the effects of violence, (which demand secrecy and collaboration, and thus prevent societal empathy), are adverse and have volatile outlets that could cause disorders both to the women and the children who witness the abusive violence. Dissociation is one of the most likely effects of continued violence. The toleration of abuse discussed above could actually be a form of dissociation where one trains oneself not to think of the beating at the time it is happening. Dissociation increases depression and dependency on the part of the survivor so that she increases her need to please the man in order to decrease the beatings. The battered women syndrome literature concludes that such dissociation would lead to the victim losing her ability to empathize, and can result in her killing the perpetrator; here, however, the cultural check to this effect would lead to introversion and associated post traumatic disorders. Along with these effects comes the risk for learned helplessness: the victim feels incompetent and unworthy, and has an undefined sense of self. These negative setbacks may be reflected in many areas of her life.

Children are also influenced by the abusive relationships of their parents. They may try to intervene indirectly because the culture once again does not allow them to have direct confrontation with their parents. They may also learn to consider aggression to be a way of solving problems, and may carry this strategy into adulthood, hence repeating the cycle of violence into their own newly-established homes. These effects can be very adverse, depending on the stage at which the child witnesses the violence and how constant the violence is. Some of these developmental effects may exhibit different symptoms at different stages, including trouble in learning and crankiness (0–3 years), stomach aches, headaches, and fear of being alone (3–6 years); blaming the mother for violence (6–11 years); and a great need to be very protective of the mother (12 years and over).

Adulthood effects include low self-esteem and poor interpersonal skills, and more severe effects include PTSD, which refers to an over-regulation of chemicals released in the brain motivating the body to certain reactions, so that one is always in a state of hyper-vigilance. Among other deleterious effects, PTSD may cause loss of memory or intrusive memories. Many women know that witnessing the abuse, or even knowing, (without actually being there) could affect their children. They therefore try to hide this violence as much as possible from their children. Children are, however, very observant and usually know what happens behind closed doors.

4

Theoretical Psycho-Social and Religious Frameworks for Understanding Intimate Violence in Kenya

The previous chapter explored the Kenyan socio-cultural and religious context as a case study in which the female is nurtured as she develops an identity and a sense of self. In this chapter I critically engage psycho-social and religious theories of identity formation with the contextual identity and sense of self-formation of women in Kenya, with the objective of formulating a theoretical framework with which to understand the survivor of intimate violence in Kenya.

I utilize Heinz Kohut's (1971, 1978) theory on formation of the self as an entry point of engagement. Kohut's theory provides a psychoanalytic lens into the inner workings and formation of a self through interpersonal relationships with the outer world with which I agree. Also, rather than approach narcissistic disorders from the traditional medical model of disease and pathology, Kohut proposes an understanding of individuals against the background of a meta-psychology of the person, the unique individual formation of the self (Kohut 1971, 3). However, I have made adjustment to some aspects of Kohut's theory that do not address a dominantly collective society like Kenya, and contextualized issues of gender that influence the formation of the self, while holding his fundamental structures in place.

Kohut's theory also omits consideration of the role that religion and perceptions of God play in the formation of the self. In this respect, I begin by acknowledging the discourse on the meaning of religion, drawing from John Mbiti's (1971, 1975, 1991) philosophical thoughts on African religiosity in conversation with other thinkers, and my own articulation of religion. To underscore the centrality of religion in the formation of the self, the work of Ana-Maria Rizzuto's (1979) formation of God's representations in human development is engaged. I argue that religion is central in the formation of core psychic structures and eventual integration into our sense of self. I conclude this chapter by postulating a context and gender-sensitive theoretical framework that would be most relevant to investigate understandings of intimate violence as held by survivors in the Kenyan context. I use this theoretical framework as an investigative lens in my field research to engage the experience of survivors of intimate violence in Kenya, noting that the framework may be used similarly with adaptations for other cultures.

KOHUT'S PERSONALITY DEVELOPMENT THEORY

An entry point to this discussion is Heinz Kohut's theory on the formation of a cohesive self, as discussed in selected writings in *Analysis of the Self* (1971) and *The Search for the Self* (1978). Kohut theorizes a second line of development parallel to, but independent from, the Freudian psychoanalytic line of development. Freud's view of development to mature adulthood is premised on a psychosexual framework, grounded in the Oedipal crises, from which all human behavioral explanations and neuroses are based and can be explained. In contrast, Kohut asserts that adult mature behavior emanates from the formation of a well-integrated self with a well-balanced ambition drive on one hand and a moral guide on the other. Agreeing with object relation theorists, Kohut believes that the infant, from birth to about the first year, does not experience him/herself as an independent self. He calls this period "primary narcissism" because of the nature of the self-absorption with which the child is in existence. He refers to it as the "I = You" (Kohut 1978, 430) stage, denoting that the child at this stage is in dyadic union with the mother. It is a perfect experience. As the child grows, differentiation due to what he calls "maturational pressures" or "shortcomings of maternal care" (Kohut 1971, 25; 1978, 430) begins to take place. Maturational pressures may range anywhere from very subtle (the breast not appearing immediately when the child is hungry, or the child is not picked up on the first cry) to traumatic experiences (infliction of pain, long periods of crying without response from the care taker).

The child begins to be aware of and experience "the other." At this stage however, the object of the other is still related to as though it were part of the self and will continue to undergo differentiation until it can be related to as "an-other-object." In the process of the ongoing differentiation, the child replaces the primary perfection by "(a) establishing a Grandiose and exhibitionistic image of the self: *the Grandiose Self,* and (b) giving over the previous perfection to an admired omnipotent (transitional) self-object: *idealized parent imago*" (Kohut 1971, 25). The term Grandiose Self refers to a spectrum of experience including, at the child's stage, the "undisguised pleasured in being admired" and the feeling that everything good is inside of self. The idealized parent imago on the other hand refers to the psychic structure representing an admired omnipotent self-object (usually the parent), and related to in an idealized manner that functions to preserve primary narcissism. According to Kohut, the mechanisms ("I am perfect, you are perfect, but I am part of you"), which these two psychic configurations use to preserve a part of the original experience of self-perfection, are antithetical. Yet they co-exist and in Kohut's words, have "largely independent lines of development" (Kohut 1971, 27).

Under optimal development conditions the child gradually learns that she/he is not perfect in every way and that she/he is not the center of the universe. This process may be referred to as "the gradual recognition of the realistic imperfections and limitations of the self" (Kohut 1971, 108). Progressively, the primary Grandiosity and exhibitionistic nature is tamed, "and the whole structure ultimately becomes integrated into adulthood personality." The structure thus "supplies the instinctual fuel" of human drive for achievement and sense of worth, which Kohut refers to as "ego-syntonic ambitions and purposes, for the enjoyment of our activities and important aspects of our self-esteem" (Kohut 1971, 27-28).

Under optimal circumstances, the child gradually faces the realistic limitations of the counter self-object, *the idealized parent imago*:

> While the child idealizes the parent, the idealized constellation is open to correction and modification through actual experience (the child's recognition of the actual qualities of the parents), and the empathic parent's gradual revelation of their shortcomings enables the child during the pre-oedipal phases to withdraw a part of their idealizing libido [energy] from the parental imagoes and to employ them in the building up of drive controlling structures. (Kohut 1971, 40-41)

Kohut states, "normally it is, of course, the parent of the same sex as the child who plays the most important role in this context" (Kohut 1971, 41). The child gives up the idealization, recognizing the parents' short-comings as well as appreciating their valuable characteristics. This leads to withdrawal of part of the energy that was invested in this parental image idealization and its gradual redirection to "internalization, i.e., to the acquisition of permanent psychological structures..." which continue "the functions that the idealized self-object had served" (Kohut 1971, 45). In other words, the child transmutes the internalization of realistic ideals into the developing psychic structure of the super-ego. In the adult personality the super-ego is the important component of our psychic organization that holds up to us the guiding leadership of its ideals. In Kohut's words, the super-ego "leads to the building up of those aspects of the super-ego which direct toward the ego, the commands and prohibitions, the praise, scolding and punishment that formerly the parents directed towards the child" (Kohut 1971, 41). Along with these developments, it is the "internalization of the narcissistic aspects of the child's relationship to the oedipal parents [which] however, leads to narcissistic dimension of the super-ego, i.e., to its idealization" (Kohut 1971, 41). So while the idealized "object-cathected aspects" transmute to the "content and functions of the super-ego . . . the narcissistic aspects account for the exalted position which these contents and functions have. . . ." (1971:41). Standards found in the super-ego define the "ideal self" (that ideal of what the child should be as held up to the child by the parents and accepted by the child) (Kohut 1971, 41). Thus, the content of the super-ego is decisively influenced by the specific values and ideals held by the parents, The resulting integration into the personality of a well-tamed Grandiose Self and a well-transmuted, value-laden idealized parent imago is termed a *cohesive self* (Kohut 1971, 32). In Diagram 1, I have attempted to map Kohut's theory in a most simplified form:

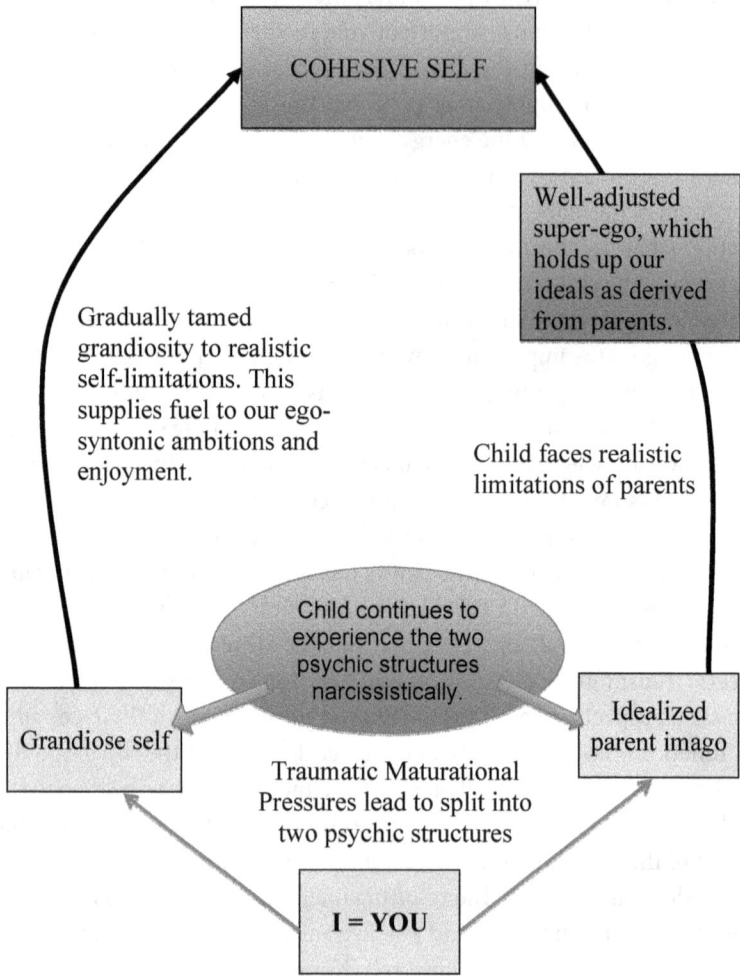

COHESIVE SELF

Well-adjusted super-ego, which holds up our ideals as derived from parents.

Gradually tamed grandiosity to realistic self-limitations. This supplies fuel to our ego-syntonic ambitions and enjoyment.

Child faces realistic limitations of parents

Child continues to experience the two psychic structures narcissistically.

Grandiose self

Idealized parent imago

Traumatic Maturational Pressures lead to split into two psychic structures

I = YOU

DIAGRAM 1: Mapping Kohut's Optimal Development of Self

Under unfavorable circumstances, where the child experiences severe traumas that do not allow a gradual letting go of the primary narcissism and Grandiosity, the "Grandiose Self does not merge into the relevant ego content" (Kohut 1971, 28). It is not tamed and is retained in its "archaic" (unaltered form), striving to fulfill its primary narcissistic aims. Similarly, "if the child experiences traumatic disappointments in the admired adult, then the idealized parent imago, too, is retained in its unaltered form" (1971:28). The child, in other words, "does not acquire the needed internal structure, his psyche remains fixated" on the primary objects. Realistic parental ideals are not transmuted into an accessible, internalized tension-regulating structure (of the super-ego). According to Kohut, the grown child's life throughout is dependent on what seems to be "an intense form of object hunger for an [idealized] object" almost as a replacement for the missing psychic structure (Kohut 1971, 45). The intensity of the dependency on such object is because "they are striven for as a substitute for the missing segments of the psychic structure" (Kohut 1971, 45). The unrealistic perfectionism is not given up, and the object continues to serve the purpose of primary self-fulfillment. Hence "within the sequence of development from (1) the archaic self object, via (2) psychic structure, to (3) the true object, the idealized parent imago falls clearly within the category of the archaic self object" (Kohut 1971, 33). The psyche now tries to save some part of the lost experience of primary narcissism by assigning it to a "transitional" self-object, the idealized parent imago. According to Kohut, "severe disappointment with the idealized oedipal object even at the beginning of latency. . . may lead to a renewed insistence on, and search for, an external object of perfection." (Kohut 1971, 44). "Since all bliss and power now reside in the idealized parent imago, the child feels empty and powerless when he is separated from this transitional object and will therefore attempt to maintain continuous union with it" (Kohut 1971, 37). Both the Grandiose Self and the idealized parent imago become cathected with intense narcissistic libido (internal energy). Such intensity with the primary narcissistic objects interferes with a sufficient integration of a tamed Grandiosity and development of a super-ego from a successfully transmuted idealized parent imago. Kohut calls the resulting psychic self-structure a *delimited cohesive self*. See Diagram 2 in which I have attempted to map Kohut's development of a delimited cohesive self.

Although Kohut states that the gradual recognition of self-limitation and realistic imperfections are associated with normal human development and are pre-conditions for mental health in the narcissistic sector of personality, he acknowledges the exceptions that may be associated with gifted persons. He cites people like Churchill and Goethe as good examples of gifted persons whose egos have been pushed to the utmost capacities, resulting in outstanding performances (Kohut 1971, 108-109).

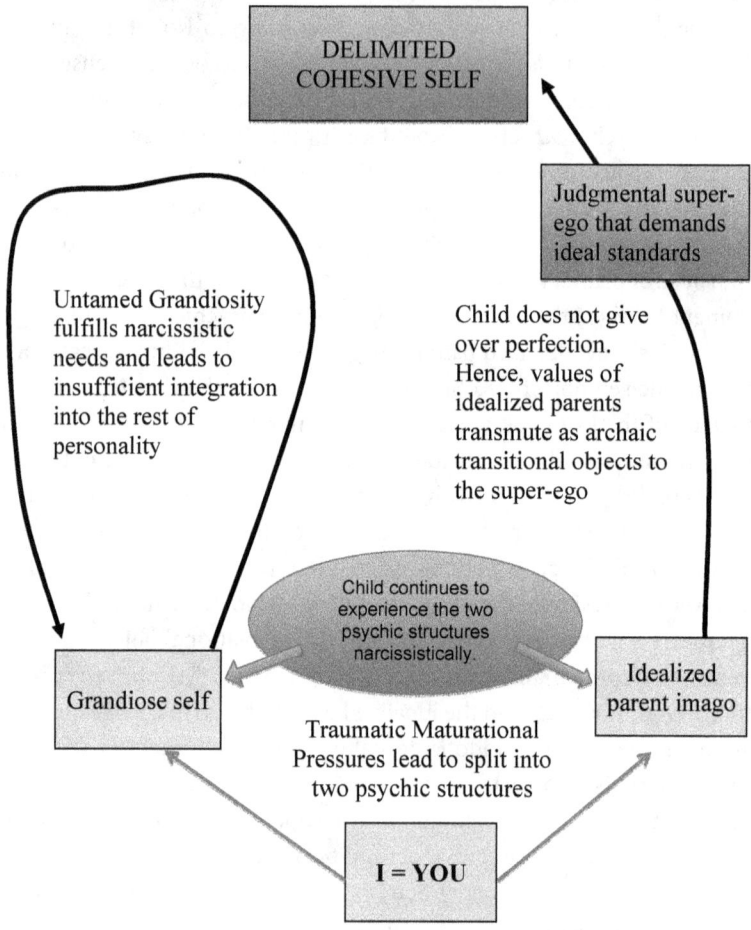

DIAGRAM 2: Mapping Kohut's Non-Optimal Development of the Self

In narcissistic personality disturbances, according to Kohut, psychopathology concerns primarily the self and archaic narcissistic objects. Psychopathology can occur in two main ways:

- The objects may be "insufficiently cathected," making the sense of self, liable to fragmentation (Kohut 1971, 19).

- The objects may be sufficiently or even "hyper-cathected" but not integrated into the rest of the personality. Hence mature personality is deprived of a sufficient supply of narcissistic or self-investment, necessary for the enjoyment of achievement and self-worth (Kohut 1971, 19).

Symptoms may be observed both in a therapeutic setting as well as outside of analysis. For instance, a patient may have an upsurge of self-confidence and sudden liveliness in the world possibly coming from attentive praise from outside of one self. It is however, not long-lived and is soon replaced by a chronic sense of dullness and passivity either displayed openly or disguised by long hours of mechanically performed duties. The main source of discomfort is "the psyche's inability to regulate self-esteem and maintain it at normal levels" (Kohut 1971, 20). Such discomfort can manifest itself in anxious Grandiosity and excitement or in mild embarrassment to severe shame and depression, or both. According to Kohut, then, the emergence of a self is a function of the content of the mental apparatus.

LIMITING ASPECTS OF KOHUT'S THEORY FOR APPLICATION IN THE KENYAN CONTEXT

Extensive Multi-parental Image Influences

An analytical engagement with Kohut's theory for its applicability in a collective society reveals a number of the theory's limiting aspects. Most fundamental is the fact that the theory is based on ontological assumptions of a self that emanates, develops, and gets constructs as an individual entity. Although Kohut's theory is developed mainly from a variety of intense social interactions between the developing child and the caregivers, I believe that from his theory the range of sociality is limited as compared to the African collective settings. Kohut's notion of self is predominantly Euro-centric, which is largely not relevant for interpreting the dominant collective African cultures and especially Kenya. Feshbach et al. (1996) speak to this notion of individual self:

> our western view of the self tends to treat it as a ghostly entity inside which has, or should have, absolute power to regulate the individual. The self is thus "separate, encapsulated and godlike, in that it is presumed to be the originator, creator and controller of behavior" (p. 402). Such a self puts an enormous emphasis on mastery and control, and healthy individuals are seen as exercising self-control as well as control of the situations they are in. This self is also seen as having its own stable identity that it

> maintains independent of the contexts it is in . . . . Such a self can
> be described without reference to other people. (Feshbach et al.
> 1996, 54 citing Landrine 1992)

Kohut's theory is replete with aspects that suggest an individualized self, modeled in the Western sense, even though he recognizes parental influence in the formation of such a self. Its applicability is limited in the Kenyan society, where the sense of self fundamentally emanates from broad relationality, including the members of the family (both nuclear and extended), members of the community, inanimate nature including the land and its offerings, as well as the person's relationship with the ancestral world and those yet to be born. Mbiti's assertions are clear indications of such formation of a sense of self:

> Even where there is no biological life in an object, African
> peoples attribute (mystical) life to it in order to establish a more
> direct relationship with the world around them. In this way, the
> visible and invisible parts of the universe are at man's disposal
> through physical, mystical and religious means. Man is not the
> master of the universe; he is only the center, the friend, the ben-
> eficiary, the user. For that reason he has to live in harmony with
> the universe, obeying the laws of natural, moral and mystical
> order. . . . He is an integral part of nature and the priest of nature.
> (Mbiti 1991, 44)

In dominant Kenyan cultures, the child would be exposed to a greater number of other things that can be assigned the idealization of self-objects, in the Kohutian sense of the word.

Furthermore, the idealized parent imago in Kohut's theory assumes the nuclear Western notion of the parental system. In Kenya, as in many other African cultures, female relatives and neighbors (*aturi*) are significantly involved in all aspects of child-rearing beginning from infancy. Speaking with regard to the birth of a child, Mbiti states,

> There are many parts of Africa where following the birth of a
> baby, both mother and baby (or just the baby alone) are kept
> in seclusion inside the house for several days . . . .Then in great
> jubilation, the baby and mother are brought out of seclusion to
> be introduced to their family, relatives and friends. This is like
> a social birth for them. In some places it is believed that even
> the living dead are present for the occasion. In other areas the
> baby is introduced to the moon, to the sun or to God, in a short
> ceremony . . . It also shows that the baby is now separated from

mother's womb, so that from that moment onwards it belongs
to the whole family and the whole community. (Mbiti 1991, 92)

Among the Meru people in traditional Kenya, for instance, the new mother was held in seclusion while she recovered from the birth of a child.
Her duties were reduced to the necessary nursing of the child while other
females came into the home and took over the household duties. With
the beginning of industrialization, and the ensuing onset of paid jobs and
smaller families, seclusions especially in the cities are not always observed.
However, many families continue to ensure that a number of helpers are
in the vicinity to assist with taking care of the newborn and the other children in the home. In many cases, the caretakers include but are not limited
to older siblings, aunts, grandparents, hired house-help and friends. More
often than not they are female caretakers. The reference to a parental image, therefore, cannot be limited to the mother and the father alone, but
must add the whole cadre of caretakers as suggested above, in the early
months of the child, and added male caretakers as the child grows beyond
the first year of life. I therefore posit that Kohut's self-object of idealized
parent imago be referred to, for the purpose of this discussion and for
the sake of its applicability in Kenya, as *"multi-parent idealized imagos"*
connoting the Kenyan context of multiple caretakers and relationality to
other objects that are not necessarily parents or animate. This is not only
a fundamental adjustment to Kohut's theory for relevance in investigating the Kenyan context, but also a salient statement of the differences in
social-cultural locations, and how these affect theories that have been historically taken as universal.

The theory of the nature of maturational pressures changes when
taking into account forms of the child's engagement with the extended
animate and inanimate systems in her differentiation process. The process
is no longer a simple and direct one of the child attempting to figure where
"the breast" that feeds him appears from, or who gives her the comfort
when she cries. The process is now seen as a more complex individuation that calls for interpretation of many aspects of the care taking. Some
children may have to contend with interpreting mother's (or any other
caretaker's) sad or happy face at seeing the child, the songs sung during
household chores, or messages of praise for beauty or of curses depending
on the circumstances which the caretaker is in.

Gender-specific Social Cultural Influences

Kohut's theory points to a sense of self-reflecting Euro-centric *male* development. It does not take into consideration socio-cultural gender nuances that influence parenting styles, state of being, and personal and communal worldview, nor does it consider gender roles and the worth attached to them. These are all very real female experiences of the Kenyan girl child as she develops a sense of self in the context she is in. . This aspect of socio-cultural gendered influence—which is ignored in Kohut's theory, but which I demonstrate here as part of the orienting system in which a child develops, and therefore a component of the maturational pressures—I will call *gendered messages*. They influence the girl's relation to the idealized images and determine the nature of maturational pressure and some specific contents of both the idealized image and the Grandiose self-structure. These, as claimed later in the chapter, are necessary for understanding her self-identity formation.

Religion and the Formation of a Self

The third important adjustment to Kohut's theory for applicability in Kenya is the addition of the role of religion, a fundamental aspect in the quest to understand the formation of the self. I treat religion in this theoretical formulation as separate from the socio-cultural and traditional images discussed above, because consideration of the religious influence in the formation of a self in Kenya implies the development of God images and, thus, an engagement with what is regarded as the superhuman, or the Divine. Religion as discussed in here further implies the presence of a personified image that could be related to with some special significance. Indeed, in *The Birth of the Living God*, Ana-Maria Rizzuto put forward a credible theory that human beings begin forming a God representation or image right from infancy and continue throughout adulthood. I use Rizzuto's postulations to demonstrate the role that religion plays in the formation of a self.

Religious Role in Human Life

To understand the role of religion in female identity in Africa, one must understand the pervasiveness of religion in the African context, of which Kenya provides one specific example. Mbiti, as already stated in chapter 2, tells us that religion has to do with every aspect of life and cannot be distinguished from culture. It is inescapable, and provides a way of being in the world and understanding the world, and it produces social and personal identities of kinds specific to religious communities.

The social and personal identities generated by religion in the Kenyan context can be interpreted using Clifford Geertz's (1973, 90) perspective of the power of symbolism associated with religion: religion has the power to color our external worldviews and experiences. Much as religion finds expression through external cultural patterns and symbolism, Geertz points out that it elicits powerful and pervasive moods and motivations within the person. Religion in its cultural expression generates powerful psychological realities for individual persons. Hence, the African way of being is an interaction with religion whereby meaning is given to both social and psychological reality, and correspondingly religious practices and symbolism give meaning to human experience within the culture. Geertz's perspective provides a lens through which these social and personal identities can be interpreted as a process of developing symbol systems and cultural practices that elicit kinds of moods and motivations, whose power can shape the human formation of the self, human behavior, and the response to situations.

The psychological and spiritual dimensions of this mood or way of being are akin to, but not identical with, Western psychologies that interpret religion in more personal or interior terms. For the purposes of my discussion, I look at how identity and the sense of self of Kenyan women are structured by communal religion that gives rise to a certain sense of self and a social-psychological identity that puts more emphasis upon interior religiosity than most interpreters of African religions emphasize.

It is important for me to make this move because, as much as African religion is predominantly expressed communally and in relation, it also has individual and interior psycho-spiritual dimensions. Westernized religious doctrines that demand personal investment in the faith are just as powerful and influential in the life of the African convert as the communal and relational aspects derived from cultural traditions. The role of communal religion in structuring the more personal and interior psychological sense of self and social identities provides a most insightful lens for examining how individuals within the community may appropriate cultural practices and gender roles religiously. The appropriation of cultural practices through interior religiosity, even though emanating from socially structured identities, has great bearing on the possible response by females who experience intimate violence.

In summary, to be religious is to experience a highly personalized state of being that emanates from a deep-seated and developmentally engendered representation of a power that is acknowledged and experienced as being beyond ourselves, and that finds expression in cultural and social symbolism of our context. Believing in the existence of a Deity, and engaging in communal religious rituals and ceremonies, is an expression of this acknowledgment.

Object relations theorists provide a positive framework from which an individual and his/her behavior can be understood in relation to religion. Winnicott, for instance, perceives religion as a transitory area that helps human beings to make sense of the inner and outer realities (Winnicott 1953, 14), and "transitional phenomena are healthy and universal" (Winnicott 1953, 96). Discussing Winnicott's theory, Wulff notes that just as the infant ventures out and assimilates outer reality through the help of transitional objects, so does the adult continue to make sense of the outer reality through diverse forms of orienting systems available to him/her, including religion and cultural traditions (Wulff 2001, 23).

Winnicott asserts that religion plays a positive role in human life and mental health. His perception of religion's role in human life and especially in stressful situations, offers a viable approach to attempt to explain how survivors of violence in Kenya have used religion in their coping mechanisms, a subject of focus in the next chapter.

Advancing on Winnicott's theory, Rizzuto perceives religion as one of the most powerful regulatory agencies in organized life (Rizzuto 1979, 89). Human beings, according to Rizzuto, go to great lengths to organize their world in a coherent manner. In the course of the life cycle, she observes, an individual produces a "highly personalized representation of God" begun in infancy as object relations (Rizzuto 1979, 90). It evolves through years of life experiences beginning with the parents, and draws from environmental systems of beliefs. Rizzuto states that the God representation is one among the many transitional objects that children populate their "transitional space" with (Rizzuto 1979, 190). Soon, however, the God representation acquires special and superior characteristics on account of the multiple cultural, social, religious and ritualistic practices within the family, and encountered in the larger world. At each developmental stage, the old God representation is "tweaked" according to the new experiences leading to repression, refinement, transformation or utilization of the representation (Rizzuto 1979, 90). She states:

> I conclude therefore that formation of the image of God does
> not depend upon the oedipal conflict. It is an object related rep-
> resentational process marked by the emotional configuration of
> the individual prevailing at the moment he forms the represen-
> tation, at any developmental stage. The clinical cases show God
> belonging to each level of development from oral to Oedipal.
> (Rizzuto 1979, 44)

With every adjustment of the God representation, there is an alteration
of the self-representation. If, for instance, a God representation has been
transformed over the years to remain more or less a satisfactory transitional object, a sudden change in self-representation may strain the
reshaping of God representation and cause internal conflict within the
person (Rizzuto 1979, 52).

My own derivation from Rizzuto's assertions is that all humans have
the potential to be religious through their developing God representation.
The level of, and claim to be religious however, is varied by each person's
personal, social, and cultural experience and ensuing engagement with
his/her representation of the Divine. Rizzuto's statement is most explicit
and fills the gap in Freud's position regarding non-believers and its correlation with maturity. She states that

> in this context the nonbeliever is a person who has decided con-
> sciously or unconsciously for reasons based on his own histori-
> cal evolution, not to believe in a God whose representation he
> has. … Some people cannot believe because they are terrified of
> their God. Some do not dare to believe because they are afraid
> of their own regressive wishes. Others do not need to believe
> because they have created other types of gods that sustain them
> equally well. Maturity and belief are not related issues. Only
> detailed study of each individual can reveal the reason for that
> person's belief in God. (Rizzuto 1979, 47)

Rizzuto's arguments illustrate that a person acquires God representations early in life and makes a conscious or unconscious decision
to be or not to be religious. Her arguments also illustrate that religion
through God representation shapes our own self-perception, and therefore, our behavior. Her theory is an explicit example of the importance
of understanding religion, at least God representations, as a significant
component of human behavior, and therefore an indispensable contribution in understanding the survivors of intimate violence. It is this religious
role and perspective of religious origins through the formation of God

representations that I bring to the discourse a religious role in female self-formation. Hence, women are highly personalized but also very culturally oriented, and encountered with transformations at every stage of their human development, as exposited by Rizzuto.

Role of Religion in the Formation of a Sense of Self

Having discussed the role of religion in human life, I now proceed to discuss the role that religion plays in the formation of a sense of self. This role comes as a third substantial adjustment to Kohut's theoretical aspects, an adjustment that would make his theory appropriate and viable for investigations made in Kenya. The other two already discussed are 1) the complexity of a highly collective society which affects the concept of early mother-child relationships and the nature of maturational pressures and 2) his insensitivity to gender issues regarding development and self-formation.

To grasp religion's role in formation of a self, I will attempt to illustrate that religion is a phenomenon acquired through human development. Rizzuto once again puts forth a remarkably good case in making this argument. Her work on the formation of God representation interestingly stems from Freudian psychoanalytic works that discredit religion as an article of faith in the mature human beings. Freud's general outlook on origins of religion and the image of a God may be found in his popular and humorous descriptions that reverse the Genesis text, from "God created man in his own image" to "Man created God in his own image" (Freud 1910, 19). For Freud, the development of the idea of man's creation of superhuman beings, (both good (God) and evil (the devil),) was originating from the human mind at the individual and anthropological level. Rizzuto states that for Freud, man's creation of God pivoted on the Oedipus complex where the image of God was provided by the image of the father, thus accounting for the male's God image from a father-son relationship, and the origins of the need for religion in males (Rizzuto 1979, 15). She cites Freud's notion that God is psychologically nothing but an "exalted father" figure (Freud 1910, 123). Freud further states:

> Thus we recognize the roots of the need for religion are in the parental complex; the almighty and just God, and kindly Nature, appear to us as grand sublimations of father and mother, or rather as revivals and restorations of the young child's ideas of them. (Freud 1910, 123)

Although Freud later adds an explanation of how women become religious as a *cultural* inheritance through men, Rizzuto notes that he was not concerned with either the origins of religion in women or the possibility of religion forming through other object relations. She states:

> In the placing of the formation of the inner God image in the context of the father-son relationship alone, Freud excludes other possible early objects relations: son-mother, daughter-father, daughter-mother. This exclusion obliged him to find further explanation for the *cultural* transmission of religion. Inheritance is for Freud, the explanation: 'The male sex seems to have taken the lead in all these moral acquisitions; and they seem to have been transmitted to women by cross inheritance. (Rizzuto 1979, 15 citing Freud 1923b)

This is a very important aspect in my discussion because, as I later demonstrate in my data analysis section regarding female development within the socio-cultural and religious systems in Kenya, the male, in the psychological hierarchy of psychic structures, appears to emerge as exalted, and closer to God. Rizzuto offers an avenue that allows the exploration of the possibilities of other influences in the formation of God representations that are more inclusive of women's experiences. Rizzuto also observes that Freud does not concern himself with the question about how some people come to believe in the existence of a God (Rizzuto 1979, 15). In talking about the formation of God representation, Freud uses several terms in his different works that indicate the process of transformation of the paternal image into a God. These are: an "exalted father," "a transfiguration of," "a likeness of," a "sublimation of," "a surrogate of," "a copy of," to the ultimate conclusion that "God is really the father" (Rizzuto 1979, 31). Rizzuto's claims bring women on board as direct participants in the origination of a God image and therefore religion. Her assertions also provide for the possibility of a very mature relationship between humans and their God representation. She states:

> But if my analysis is correct, the God representation is more than the cornerstone upon which it was built. It is a *new* original representation which, because it is new, may have the varied components to soothe and comfort, provide inspiration and courage—or terror and dread—far beyond that inspired by the actual parents. This reasoning also provides an explanation for belief in God by people who are neither infantile nor so regressed as to make us suspect that they constantly reactivate

their childhood drama or cling to a parental divinity. (Rizzuto 1979, 46)

She further states, "Those who are capable of mature religious belief renew their God representation to make it compatible with their emotional conscious and unconscious situation, as well as with their cognitive and object-related development" (Rizzuto 1979, 46). The resulting God representation is not just a private creation but also one in constant interaction with our experiences of the outer world and social-cultural systems.

Indeed, for one who may not have matured in religious belief, the God representation may be simply one that has been offered by the social-cultural system. This is an important point, as demonstrated in Chapter 5, in understanding how the experience of a personal traumatic event like intimate violence can push one's imagination, emotional exertion and mental process to take to task their God representation, thereby affecting the sense of self in relation to the transformed God representation. On a similar note Rizzuto states "perhaps we have forgotten the powerful reality of nonexistent objects, objects of our creation" (Rizzuto 1979, 47). Included in such objects of our creation are angels, the devil, God, and heroes. I concur with her assertion that it is "an integral part of being human, truly human in our capacity to create non-visible but meaningful realities capable of containing our potential for imaginative expansion beyond the boundaries of the senses" (Rizzuto 1979, 47). From Rizzuto's and my perspective, therefore, religion originates and gains status as an agency in human life. This is a focal point from which I begin to address the role of religion in the experiences of women in intimate violence.

In considering Rizzuto's views of God representation and my thoughts of how such representations present the potential for people to become religious in the Kenyan context, it is important to keep in mind that multiple factors beyond the mother-child relationship influence the origination of God representation. Personalized religious sentiments about who God is, what God is capable of, and what role God plays in one's life are deeply rooted in the social-cultural system that nurtures the person, and through which the person develops a sense of self. Hence my argument is that these ongoing interactions between the social-cultural systems and development of a God representation within the psyche, are important aspects that are not considered in Kohut's theory of the development of a cohesive self, but which find expression through religious participation and symbolism. The three adjustments made to Kohut's theory are: (1) Extensive multi-parental image influences, (2) Gender-specific messages absorbed as part of the maturational pressures, and (3) Religious influence in the formation of a sense of self.

If the above proposed adjustments are incorporated into the Kohut's theory, fundamental changes must occur to make the theory relevant for investigation of women's self-formation on the Kenyan context. In the ensuing discussion I propose what I have analytically postulated as a viable psycho-social and religious theoretical framework that takes into account the collective aspects of the society, female experience and religious reality. This framework will best be understood against the backdrop of the social, cultural, and religious Kenyan context as discussed in Chapter 3. It will be proven as the narratives of women survivors of intimate violence are investigated.

PSYCHO-SOCIAL AND RELIGIOUS FEMALE SELF-FORMATION IN KENYA

Postulated Theoretical Framework

Having made an important adjustment to Kohut's theory for relevance in investigating the survivor's understanding of, and response to, intimate violence, I now present my hypothesized gender- and context-sensitive theoretical framework of understanding development of a female sense of self (identity) in Kenya. To facilitate an effective tracking of the arguments, I have divided the discussion into maturational pressures, the idealized parent imago, and the Grandiose Self.

Maturational Pressures

According to Kohut's theory, maturational pressures are a big determinant of the psychic split and eventual formation of the two major psychic structures: *the idealized parent imago* and the *Grandiose Self.* I make the case that in the Kenyan context these take the added dimension of *availed gendered messages* like social cultural beliefs and practices, and rites of passage, including naming, birth ceremony and circumcision. For instance, in various traditional cultures of Kenya, the girl child and the boy child are welcomed into the community in certain ways. Mbiti states in this regard that the "sex of the baby is announced through various methods, such as shouts or screams by the mother or other women attending her" (Mbiti 1991, 90). Among the Meru, when a girl is born, the announcement is made by three ululations. The boy's announcement is made by five ululations. Whatever the rationale used in the allocation of the number of ululations, the fact is that there is likely to be a very young child in that family or community that is observing these differences and making interpretations for herself. Furthermore, a casual comment may be made to the child in a very loving way about how "we welcomed you with three ululations and your brother with five ululations." While these are not meant in any way to discredit the girl child and although she is in the pre-latency period where she may not be able to voice her curiosity as to the mystery behind the differential number of ululations, she will nevertheless make gendered attributions that become part of the dialogue in her ongoing psychic differentiation. It is possible to quickly dismiss such traditional examples in the modern context of Kenya, until one hears a supposedly congratulatory comment such as I received from a friend when, on the birth of our child, I announced it was a boy. He added to his already given congratulations, "Wow! That is a child and a half," which when analytically engaged illustrates the continuity, only in a different form, of our traditional ululations.

While the care-taking of and therefore influence on, the infant are primarily done by the female figures for both boys and girls up to pre-school age (about 6 to 8 years), the content of the messages will have gender-specific aspects. A popular link in this regard is the subtle but powerful comments that join beauty or education with the yielding of many cows (or whatever the bride price the community uses). I have frequently heard endearing comments from fathers like "What a beauty you are my girl, you will yield me [_____ number] of cows," [to the family through her marriage]. The girl may also be praised for her beauty, execution of household duties or loving attitude she shows towards the play doll, while the boy may be praised for being protective of the sister or be encouraged to affirm his position and ideas on the playground. Of ultimate importance is the fact that such praise and comments are from very early in infancy connected with the observation that the girls will become either good mothers or great wives. Indeed, what is happening is the beginning of the formation of a gendered sense of self, through which significant gender roles for the girl are disseminated. They influence the contents of the two developing psychic structures as discussed in the next two sections.

Multi-idealized Parent Imagos

"Multi-idealized imagos," as I choose to call the psychic structure that would be equivalent to Kohut's *idealized parent imago*, refers to the multiple objects, which in a collective society are bound to influence with idealization, the self-formation of a person in a typical Kenyan society. They include, but are not limited to, multiple caretakers, inanimate objects like mountains and natural life, as well as religion.

I have made the claim that the main caretakers of the child at infancy are multiple females, at least in the Kenyan context. Object relation theorists talk of mothers mirroring their own self-reflection to the babies and state that this has implications for the child's self-image. If my analysis of the cultural and social status of women is correct, the mirroring that happens for the girl child is of an inferior image. It is not as idealized as the child had conjured and assigned to the self-object because the caretaker's behavior as a female, when relating to a male mirrors different values to the child. It is likely that the caretaker is herself suffering some inferiority complex or dissatisfaction, which in turn is mirrored to the girl child. This may be compounded by other *gendered messages* including, but not limited to, the value of the girl child in relation to a boy child. Evelyn Keller (1978), although writing from a different context, captures the different cultural and ensuing psychological forces that influence gendered development right from infancy:

> Whatever intellectual or personality characteristics may be affected by sexual hormones, it has become abundantly clear that our ideas about the differences between the sexes far exceed what can be traced to mere biology; that once formed, these ideas take on a life of their own—a life sustained by powerful cultural and psychological forces. (Keller 1978, 199)

She argues that although boys and girls have a similar need for autonomy in differentiation development, boys determine their identity through an opposition to "what is both experienced and defined as feminine" and that this is likely to "accentuate their process of separation." The girl's development of separateness, on the other hand, according to Keller may be hindered by her continued identification with the female. She states:

> It has been suggested that the girl's development of a sense of separateness may to some degree be hampered by her ongoing identification with her mother. Although she too must disentangle herself from the early experience of oneness, she continues to look towards her mother as a model for her gender identity. Whatever vicissitudes her relation to her mother may suffer during subsequent development, a strong identification based

on common gender is likely to persist—her need for "dis-identification" is not so radical. Cultural forces may further compli-
cate her development of autonomy by stressing dependency and
subjectivity as feminine characteristics. (Keller 1978, 199)

While I agree with Keller on the issue of continued identification of
the girl with the mother, and the boy's need for "dis-identification" from
the mother, the collective patriarchal culture poses some challenges for
the girl child in Kenya. Rather than an easygoing continued identification,
I am arguing for a conflicted continued identification of the girl child to
the females (more than one parent) in her life because of lower female status. The conflict created by difficulties in continuing to idealize the female
multi-parents, and the persisting need for identification with the same, is
bound to drive the girl child to greater idealization of the male with the
effect of lower self-esteem. It may elicit internal conflicts since that inferiority reflects a physical self-image, which she normally should identify
with, but cannot now idealize. This internal conflict may be expressed by
"I am you, but you are not perfect, and I do not want to be you."

I would like to briefly digress at this point to make a link between
the influences of idealized parent imago, availed gender messages, and the
possibility of the inception of a formation of a God representation. It is
important to note that this is the same period that Rizzuto claims to be the
onset of the first impressions of God representation. She states:

Around the age of three, the child matures cognitively to the
point of becoming concerned with animistic notions of causal-
ity. He wants to know the why of everything. Through questioning he tries to arrive at the final answer and is not satisfied with
scientific explanation. The child wants to know who moves the
clouds and why. If told "The wind," he wants to know who moves
the wind, and so on. Finally he is told by parents or adults that
God does these things. . . . This ceaseless chaining of causes in-
evitably ends up in a "superior being." That notion suits the child
well because in his mind his parents and adults as "superior beings" of great power and size gifted with a remarkable ability to
know the child's intentions. In psychoanalytic terms the child is
dealing with idealized representations of his parents to whom
he attributes great perfection and power. He is also struggling
with his own grandiose wishes for extra-ordinary powers of his
own. The knowledge that his parents themselves submit to a
greater being and that God can do things they cannot do im-
presses the child immensely. But his capacity for admiration of
such a great being does not diminish the child's animistic-that is

anthropomorphic –understanding of God as being like his parents, only greater. (Rizzuto 1979, 45)

I have argued that various aspects of the socio-cultural and religious context are likely to influence the psychic differentiation and self-formation of the girl child. Simultaneously these aspects influence her developing God image. A number of psychic configurations are bound to take place given these added facets of social cultural, maturational pressures, multi-idealized images and onset of religious sentiments and God representations.

Effects on Multi-parent Idealized Imago Psychic Structure

It is at this stage, according to Kohut, that the child should be giving over perfection to an idealized object. I submit that, given multi-parents and the social cultural gender-availed messages involved in the self-formation process, the girl child gives over that perfection with specific value attached along gender lines and the omnipotence of her images. Before the end of the Oedipal period, at which point Kohut theorizes that the child has incorporated aspects of the idealized parent imago into the super-ego structure that is now forming, I postulate that the child's psychic structure splits further to appropriate the three major influencing entities in her life: God representation, male figures, and female figures.

God Representation: This is the most likely first image a child will have in the Kenyan context of God, as omnipotent in nature. I make this assertion in light of the context's worldview and orienting system. Mbiti suggests that African peoples' origin of the belief in God may have arisen from their reflections of the universe, from the realization of their own limitations, and from observation of forces of nature, leading to acknowledging the creator to be God. God is associated with powers like storms, lightning, warmth, and calamities, and is perceived as one more powerful than people and the observable. The general religious orienting system in the Kenyan context presents God as superhuman, omnipotent and omniscient, through songs and other ways that people, right from childhood, are taught to relate to God as an object of worship. Rizzuto stated,

> The type of God each individual produces as a first representation
> is the compounded image resulting from all these contributing
> factors—the pre-oedipal psychic situation, the beginning stage
> of the oedipal complex, the characteristics of the parents, the
> predicament of the child with each of his parents and siblings,

the general religious, social and intellectual background of the
household. (Rizzuto 1979, 45)

One can inductively conclude that a child's earliest representations of God
in the Kenyan context are omnipotent in nature. The fact that children are
participators and witnesses of the worship of God, even by their idealized
parents, can account for the position that God would be assigned in the
psychic hierarchies.

Male Figures: Male figures are highly idealized because of the very high
status they are accorded in the society and the special acknowledgement
and accomplishment that is bestowed on them. The child may observe
how the women in the household (community) relate to the men. The
male is reified to a position of being similar in physical likeness and character to the superhuman being and apparently must be greater than even
the females. The child may attribute to the male power, ability, intelligence,
leadership and high status. In cases where the male does not live up to the
child's idealization, then, in "depriving the psyche a source of instinctual
gratification," the object imago (in this case the male figure) is changed
into an "introject," or as Kohut describes, "a structure of the psychic apparatus that takes over functions previously performed by the object" (Kohut
1978, 432). In this way, male idealization may continue to be perpetuated
by the cultural context, despite disappointments of individual males in the
life of the particular female.

Female Figures: For the girl child, female caretakers would most likely be
a conflicted image of the child's self and therefore the lowest in the psychic
hierarchy of idealized figures. Disappointments with the status of female
figures as idealized images would be considered by Kohut as a loss of an
idealized object. Kohut further states, "Every shortcoming detected in
the idealized parent leads to a corresponding internal preservation of the
externally lost quality of the object" (Kohut 1978, 433). The corresponding qualities would therefore be part of the internalization of the female
child into the super-ego. However, it must be noted that the female figures
have some very positive traits admired by the child. The woman represents
goodness, obedience, sacrifice and maternal attributes of caring and loving. This side of her does represent some Godliness (attributes that are
most likely used in the household to ascribe value to God and therefore,
super-humanness for the child), which too would undoubtedly find its
way into the eventual integration of the super-ego.

Kohut states that the "form and content of the psychic representation of the idealized parent" varies with "the maturational stage of the child's cognitive apparatus" (Kohut 1978, 480). Since her cognitive ability (at about six to eight years of age) is developed to an adequate state to comprehend reality, there is every likelihood that the girl child in Kenya can very well figure her lower status in the society and the value of holding on to the societal prescribed expectation. She knows (though may be not cognitively) that society expectations formulate her place in the society as well as needed self Grandiosity. She has the cognitive realization of differential treatment and status of the male and the female, whether in simple conditions like division of labor in the home, or in educational opportunities. The girl may become preoccupied by the need to secure a place in the society by conforming to the prescribed expectations and gender roles. These aspects of gender roles,(a high regard of the male figure and the omnipotence of God), are what get transmuted to become the substance of the super-ego. The "good" attributes of the female may offer a reflection of God's image as discussed in the household (community) and may thus be appropriated to the ongoing formation of a God representation. Most of the other attributes of God, however, are likely approximated to the male figure because of his fantasized and actual high status in the society. This most likely includes the use of masculine language for God, which not only influences the individual God-representation being formed, but also the image and status of the males. The self is forming with pedestal-led image of God representation, the idealized male and a tag-along mirrored female self-image. The female image therefore needs to be in some form of relation with the other mightier idealized images, whether in service to, relationship to, or fantasized attempts to be like them. Roles that fuel the fulfillment of her Grandiosity become part of her idealized moral standards (the super-ego) internalized through the multi-layered idealized parent imago that has now appropriated God, male and female respectively. As Rizzuto observes, the God representation, which is highest on the hierarchy, has characteristics of both parents and a "general social and intellectual religious background of the household" (Rizzuto 1979, 45). The culminating self in adulthood is a self anchored on societally prescribed expectations as an integral part of her self-cohesiveness. While the early childhood experience of Kenyan girls enables them to internalize a positive identity as female that correlates with some positive cultural views of God, on the whole the culture sees this identity as inferior and subordinate to the characteristics of male children whose internalized

God representations are of higher value socially and religiously, thereby marking the girl child with a sense of inferiority.

Grandiose Self Psychic Structure

The dynamics of gender-specific messages, female praise for gender role attributes (obedience, goodness, care-taking, sacrificial-ness), and the psychic structure hierarchies of God, male, female respectively, all coalesce to structure a female's thinking and behavior in conformity to societal expectations. The more she fulfills these roles, the more she gains praise and the more it fuels her Grandiose Self.

A major departure from Kohut's theorization is that the two lines of development along the two major psychic structures are not independent of each other. It is deductively apparent that the two psychological structures—the idealized parent imago (now developed to a multi-layered psychic structure, and characterized by idealized socio-cultural and religious expectations) and the Grandiose self (either inferior self-image or a Grandiose Self-image when conforming to gender roles)—fuel each other. This in turn determines the content of the Grandiose self for the girl. Her relation to the mother figures at this stage, however, is likely to be conflicted because though her execution of the mirrored positive but humble gender roles (also godly attributes) puff up her Grandiosity, the low and powerless status she holds (also mirrored by the females in general and compounded by *gendered messages*), counters her feelings of Grandiosity.Unlike Kohut's theory, which asserts the child's relation with the self-object as "You are perfect and I am part of you," the more *likely* relation with the idealized object begins taking the shape of "You are not perfect and I do not want to be you." Or, it could as well be, "You are not perfect, and because I am female like you, neither am I." I use the word "likely" because I am taking Kohut's concept and mapping it onto the girl child's context and reality in Kenya.

Grandiosity for the girl child therefore is more often fueled by execution of idealized mirrored characteristics that are gender specific, as reflected in my qualifying the name of the Grandiose Self structure to reflect the female experience of Grandiosity in Kenya (see Diagram 3). Along the Grandiose Self line of development, there is the likelihood of insufficient integration into the rest of personality because female Grandiosity, if my social cultural assessment is correct, curtails the drive for the women to fuel ambitions and potential areas of achievement. Drive for achievement takes secondary status, second to the primary psychic need of fulfillment through gender roles. It is a self that is characterized by a super-ego that functions as a tension-generating structure holding up the do's and don'ts as informed by highly-revered gender roles and a world view character- ized by gendered hierarchies of the psychic structures. The very location of these values and gender roles in the super-ego, warrants them great importance and emotional value. Kohut states:

> the original narcissism has passed through a cherished object before its re-internalization and that the narcissistic investment itself has been raised to the new developmental level of idealiza- tion account for the unique emotional importance of our stan- dards, values and ideals in so far as they are part of our super-ego. . . . Similarly the unique position held by those of our values and ideals which belong to the realm of the super-ego is determined neither by their (variable) content . . . nor by their (variable) form . . . but by their genesis and psychic location. (Kohut 1978, 434)

While for some females the latency period may be a smooth transitional period, for many girls it is a very traumatic realization of their place in the society that may cause high vulnerability. Kohut perceives this latency pe- riod to constitute the "last of the several periods of danger in early child- hood during which the psyche is especially susceptible to traumatization" (Kohut 1978, 480). There is a greater likelihood of her experience leading to a strong cathexis of both the gender roles in their archaic form (as mir- rored by the multi-parents and centered on the self-identity), and a Gran- diosity that is centered on that for which she is praised, gender roles. (See Diagram 3 on p. 88 for the figurative illustration of my postulated theo- retical framework with the various adjustments made to Kohut's theory.)

In a sense, then, even in Kohut's most optimal scenario, there may be a sufficiently internalized idealized parent imago but it is not inde- pendent of the multi-layered status offered by the context. On the other hand, it may be said that the self-Grandiose structure is over-tamed so that ego ambitions are insufficiently integrated into the rest of personality, requiring the societal gender roles to be fulfilled first. My postulation is, therefore, that cohesiveness for a female in the Kenyan society is rather an integration centered around the idealized, internalized identity roles that help her hold together what is ordained by the culture as forming her sense of self, or her belonging in the community.

Based on these considerations, I will advance a general view of func- tionality among victims of violence in Kenya as a form of resilience that can be primarily explained by adaptive striving for identity based on the content of their structural psychic formation. I will propose that religion is a fundamental, integral part of their psychic structural organization of the self, and therefore religion plays a significant role in their self-organization. Qualitative research, focusing on survivors' accounts of their violent and general developmental experiences, gives insight into their actual self-formations and hence their psychological and adaptive response to intimate violence. It became a true testing ground of the theoretical formulations developed in this chapter. The ensuing chapters present such conceptualized data and offers analytical discussions.

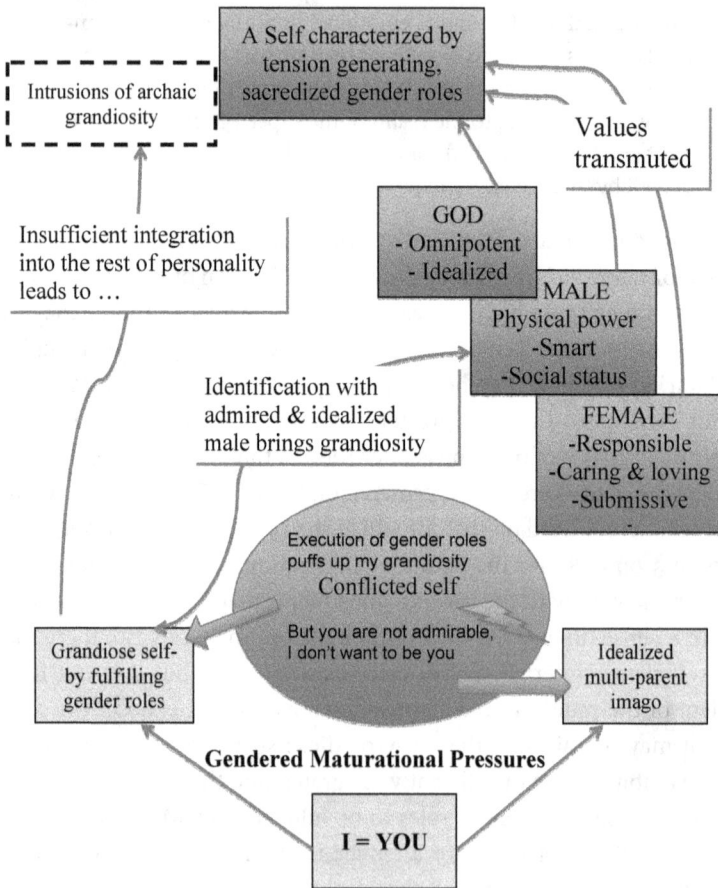

DIAGRAM 3: Gender and Context Sensitive Theoretical Framework for Females in Kenya

Section II

The Violence Phenomenon:
Conceptualization of Female
Response to Intimate Violence

5

The Violence Phenomenon

Psycho-Social Concepts in Survivor Response

INTRODUCTION

Many notions that emerged from my field study are typical of general intimate violence research, including low self-esteem and symptoms suggesting implications for minor post-traumatic stress disorders, such as slight
memory spacing, repression, and "learned helplessness."[1] This chapter
focuses on analyzing those concepts that emerged from the study that are
specific to collective characteristics of a context like Kenya (and in many
ways African) context, or that may differ from the Western[2] context from
which most of the intimate violence literature has evolved. I demonstrate
through the emerging psycho-social concepts from the study that social

---

1. "Learned helplessness," associated with psychologist Martin Seligman, is defined
by Feshbach et al. as the "acquired expectation that one's actions will exert little control
over outcomes" (1996, 580). It is understood in Walker's argument to be responsible
for "emotional cognitive and behavioral deficits in battered women" which adversely
keep her from leaving an abusive relationship (1984, 2).

2. Clearly neither the "Kenyan context" nor the "Western context" exists as a homogeneous reality. However, there are marked differences that are specific to each
context even though there are variations within the variable. I am simply using these
general terms to denote generally shared perceptions and identities and to make salient statements of the differences in context for academic studies.

cultural demands on psychic formation of selves for females lead to an unhealthy configuration that is primarily and unconsciously narcissistic in agenda, even though, on the surface, the female is executing noble "giving" and relation-building roles. This unhealthy configuration curtails her drive for enjoyment of creativity and achievement on one hand, and results in a tension-generating, judgmental and reprimanding super-ego on the other. In turn these profoundly curtail her capacity for creativity beyond her gender roles and limit her range of decisions when faced by circumstances such as intimate violence that threaten a fragmentation of the self.

Specifically, four psycho-social concepts emerged from my study: psychological female socialization to perceive the male as a socially idealized figure; notions of a sense of self which is organized around a strong investment in gender roles; profound empowerment and purpose in life found in bearing and rearing children; and high functionality that has some characteristics of self-righting tendencies. For most of my informants, this last concept, I argue, emanates from a psychic need to maintain their roles in the family and society as an integral part of the sense of self. Such a need can energize the person to keep doing what is necessary despite the obstacles created by violence. I call this concept "mechanical self-righting functionalism." After presenting all four concepts and their supporting data, I have provided a data analysis section for each of the concepts. In Chapter 6, I discuss an overarching finding across all the women interviewed: the role of religion in coping, making meaning, and its transformative power in these survivors responses to violence.

I begin this chapter by giving a brief overview of the participants of the study.[3] As clearly stated in my introductory chapter and guided by my research questions, the study had three objectives: to explore how females in Kenya form a sense of self given their social-cultural and religious context; to find out the understanding held by survivors regarding the phenomenon of intimate violence; and to explore possible effects that such a sense of self and understandings of violence have on their response, as a quest to gain insight into their operating mechanism. The second objective is informed by the survivors' self-disclosures in the interviews, largely taken at face value. The first and third objectives are, however, achieved through inferences I draw from interpretation of the data, in conjunction with prevalent social-cultural and religious theories already discussed.

---

3. See Table 5, Appendix 3, for a more detailed demographic presentation of the participants. See also Appendix 5 for more detailed narratives of key participants in the study.

THE PARTICIPANTS

In observance of confidentiality, all the participants in the study are identified by pseudonyms. Other demographic information that could lead to identification, like specific age or reference to specific names of towns or friends and family members, has also been altered. Further, names that identify the specific language group of the participant have been avoided in order to screen out any negative stereotype of any particular group. Larger ethnic identifications have been used where necessary.

I interviewed a total of twenty-three participants, nineteen of whom had experienced or were currently in abusive relationships. Four of the participants had not experienced gender violence and served the purpose of a deviant sample in the study. My main focus is on survivors of intimate violence. Of the nineteen survivors, five were interviewed both privately and in a small group setting, to allow for observation of group dynamics as opposed to the narratives that I obtained very privately. Some general informational analysis regarding the participants is summarized in Table 3 below. More detailed narratives of the five most-referenced survivors, namely Rose, Nancy, Millicent, Nelly and Angela, are presented in Appendix 4. Also included are brief details of all the other informants.

Table 1: Demographic Summaries of participants and Key Tables

Total number of participants	23
Survivors sample	19
Deviant sample	4
Age groups	
Young adults (18–30) years	11
Young middle aged adults (31–40):	7
Older adults (41–50)	5
Education	
Grade 8 and below	9
Up to form four (high school)	4
College training (commercial/ Skill colleges)	6
University and beyond	4

Religious Affiliation

Islam faith tradition	2
Christian faith—adherent	7
Christian faith—nominal	12
Belief—no specified affiliation	2

Employment:

No income	3
Low income employment	2
Roadside / small day-to-day business	9
Community-based development org.	1
Full-time professional jobs	4
High income business & retail / employment	4

Ethnic general grouping

Agricultural Bantus	9
Coastal Bantus	1
Plain Nilotes	3
Lake Nilotes	7
Cushites	1
Swahili	2

Ethnic group figures may appear on the surface biased towards large representation of certain groups. However, the numbers are generally reflective of the ratios of the various group populations in Nairobi, Kenya.

PSYCHO-SOCIAL CONCEPTS EMERGING FROM THE STUDY

Psychological Idealization of the Male Image

The term "idealization" as used in this particular concept refers to the unrealistic romanticism with which females are socialized to perceive the male. Such idealization is instilled over a long period of time through observation of the differential gender treatment and through direct inferences that suggest superior mental, spiritual, and physical worth of the male over the female. Indicators of such idealization in women experiencing violence from their spouses include, but are not limited to: a genuine belief and idealist praise for their spouse despite an apparent cognitive acknowledgement of their failures; persistent conviction that the spouse's irresponsibilities are beyond his control; and unrealistically holding on to a belief that the man will change his violent and irresponsible behaviors.

Eighteen out of the twenty-three women I interviewed voiced sentiments that implied their belief that the male is superior to the female and he is positioned higher in the socio-cultural hierarchy. I directly asked if it was acceptable in some cases for a man to beat a woman. Eight of the women answered positively that yes, a man can beat a woman. Even though the verbal response by fifteen of the women was somewhat negative, the body message did not match the emotion attached to the response. Indeed, fourteen of the women found some instances, naming infidelity, neglecting children and disrespect, to justify some form of this discipline from the male abuser, adding, however, statements like " a little" or "*si-kuua*" (not to kill) to qualify the apparently subtle disciplining violence which they had deemed justifiable. Rose, responding to the question of whether a beating by a male is justified, stated, "Yes if you are found with another man, it is wrong and you can be beaten." Nelly, responding to the advice she would give a battered woman, stated:

> I would tell her there are people who are beaten because they have some weaknesses. I would want to know why you are beaten. Some bad things can make a woman be beaten. But if a woman has for instance men friends, she can be beaten. In fact there was a woman like that. When I asked her why she was doing that she told me I was foolish, I should use the men to buy me beer. The husband was so good and social, but she would always come home drunk.

From the above responses two main derivations may be made. First, it is socially acceptable for a woman to be beaten by a man if she is found guilty of committing a crime that is socially unacceptable for a woman in Kenya. Apparently the same does not apply for the man. He can cheat on his wife and do other unacceptable things but they are acceptable in this social context. It is also notable that the male is the judge in the above instance of the female behavior, and he can decide what is unacceptable and therefore punishable by violence.

Second, the woman referred to by Nelly in the narrative does, on a symbolic level (using men for beer,) what many women in the Kenyan context will do in relationships with men. Even though Nelly despises this other woman who uses men to buy beer, she herself, elsewhere, implies a similar relationship to men. She states, "I was however, really looking forward to have a husband . . . he would take me out to eat and to the movies . . . ." There is a very common perception of men being valued for their financial, economic, educational, and social successes and achievement. Hence it can be argued that men are perceived as the gender that is successful, economically stable, socially powerful, and capable of achievement. These are all derivations that support my argument that even women themselves are socialized to support the idealized position of males in the society. When reactions to the question of whether it was acceptable for a woman to beat a man were compared, the difference in responses was distinctive. I observed that thirteen of the women almost recoiled when I asked the question about retaliating with violence to their abusers. The reactions included rolling of eyes, sudden jerking of the head and looking me straight in the eye (not very acceptable culturally–except in cases of ridicule), or a remark like "eeh?" suggesting that I had no idea what I was talking about. I would not characterize the recoil as emanating from fear but rather from the notion that what I had asked was unthinkable, unacceptable, and simply disrespectful of the position that the male holds in society. An intense internal conflict was evident when participants responded as to why the woman could not retaliate. Respondents made such statements as follows:

"How? You just can't do that."

"It is simply not right."

"I cannot think of a woman beating the man."

"You would have to be out of your mind."

These statements may simply be reflecting the greater physical and social power of men over women. However, the way that the male superiority is lodged in the psychological organization of the inferior positioned female is what I refer to as male idealization. Within the framework of this concept is the sense that I heard of a "need" to hold the abusive male figure in his reified position in society and the family despite the fact that the women disagreed with what he was doing. All the respondents talked of many years of making excuses and covering up the abuse they experienced from their partners. Even those that had eventually managed to break from the relationships and move on, expressed a deep predicament of "wanting to understand" why the man had been abusive. Many talked of how the man had been brought up witnessing abuse, how the alcohol he consumed took hold of his senses, how she knew that he had a bad temper, how he was frustrated at his work and the bad economy, and how she was sure he had been bewitched, among others. The conviction with which these explanations were voiced were such that one cannot dismiss them just as excuses that are normally associated with survivors of intimate violence in their attempts to make rational sense of the behavior, or repression associated with PTSD. It is almost as if the survivors were saying, "He is a good man. You cannot blame him, instead blame the happenings outside of him that make him become abusive." Clearly there appears to be a picture of the idealized male image in what I hypothesize to be part of the psychic contents of the woman. Annastasia's statement describing her marriage and locating her husband's behavior outside of him clearly illustrates how women protect their idealized image of their husband:

> Marriage was my decision. Six and a half years ago. To begin with life in marriage was very good. Taking care of kids was okay. He sent my children to the private school. His problem is staying with bad people with bad characters. He is otherwise okay about the children. The problem is when they go to the bars, they drink beer up to the morning.

Clearly Annastasia considered her husband to be a "good" man whose problem must be the people around him and the alcohol.

Rose, another of the survivors, found the cause of her husband's abusive behavior toward her to be the other woman in his life. She calls it "bewitching" by this woman. She states:

> This woman was a loose woman. She had another man in the house. She would get them and then spoil them; bewitched they become "*ovio, ovio*" (useless). They could urinate anywhere, they wash for her the clothes and dishes, I don't know what she would do to the men. The men would be so tamed they just follow her directions without questions.

Rose's pronouncement above that the men were *bewitched* is of particular interest in the analysis of idealization of men in the society. She cannot understand how a man can wash clothes and dishes for the woman—roles that are relegated to female servitude in the society. The ridiculousness of this whole situation warrants her to pronounce the men bewitched.

Nelly, is yet another who seemed to hold on to the husband's "good-ness" as a provider, even if these provisions were done irresponsibly, and despite his heavy drinking and violence, saying,

> soon enough I realized he drunk a lot and no one had told me that he was a drunkard. He was so good because he would come from work, buy food and bring it home. When he has no money he would go to the shops and get loan for food and pay later . . . The day I went to deliver the baby, the father was so drunk he did not even know where he was. He could not even take me to the hospital when I was ready. So I just took myself to the nearby hospital and gave birth. I paid the bill but had no money to buy anything for the baby. . . . We got home; he has no money even for food. . . . I had hidden some money so I gave him and told him to go buy some food instead of loaning. Instead of going to buy food he went and drunk alcohol. It was Kshs. 500. What he had left he bought some *maini* (intestines) and some cornmeal. When he came he was so drunk so I was forced to cook. I had just given birth but I was strong enough to cook. . . . When he got his salary, he would not even buy the child baby soap. He would say the child can use the normal soaps and *Omo* (Regular detergent).

Note that Nelly first states that "he was so good" before proceeding to talk about his failures. Even when she discusses the failures, she finds an ex-planation of his being drunk and overlooks his conscious decision (before he gets drunk) to use money that she had given him for food. In her nar-ratives, she similarly locates responsibility for bad behavior outside her husband with respect to physical abuse, his infidelity, and his general irre-sponsibility as a husband. She cognitively knows that it is irresponsible for him to have her cook while he goes out drinking on the very day they have received their baby, but diverts her attention from this atrocity by trans-forming this to a situation where she thrives on her womanly strength to walk to the hospital just before she gives birth, and come home by herself to cook. The inference here is that in spite of suffering such hardships, she maintained her roles as a mother and a wife effectively.

Like Nelly, Jane is convinced that all their marital problems lie with the husband's family, especially the husband's sister. Despite her acknowl-edgement that he has been unfaithful, abusive, and secretive, she explains away her husband's behavior by citing the sister's influence. She states:

> Their people interfere with my relationship. In fact, (a long si-lence) they have been trying to get my husband to go away out

of Kenya to mess our marriage, especially his sister. Even before
I got married the sister used to tell him she is not the right person. At first he said he had chosen me but now he listened to her.
. . . The sister has been very bad for us. She tells him he made a
mistake all these years and now he has decided to listen to her.

Jane, despite her intelligence, and her ability to use computer technology
to find out secrets about her husband and despite her willingness to seek
legal police help in securing her children, does not show similar acumen
in perceiving her husband for who he is. Elsewhere she states that he has
been seeing many other women behind her back for many years, and has
been trying to get out of the country without her knowledge. Yet she would
rather blame the disintegration of her relationship with her husband on
the sister-in-law and all the other systems outside of the husband. This
incongruence, I argue, has much to do with the psychological organization in the female mind of who a male is. Consistently, survivors explain
their husband's unacceptable behavior by locating it outside of his control.
I theorize that this has something to do with female socialization in Kenya
which creates a psychic need to be in relationship with a significant male.
By placing her male partner's irresponsibility and unacceptable behavior
outside of his control, the female still has an idealized image she can hang
on to. This psychic need defines female sense of self in that it has the power
to cause the female to overlook and justify the bad while holding on to the
good for a sense of self. While this may be mistaken for her love for her
male partner, I posit that it is more accurate to explain it as a desperate
move to hold her sense of self together, which would be threatened by
disintegration in the face of having no idealized male to define her self.

This concept of an idealized male image and therefore a psychic need
to define a sense of self through him expressed by most of the women I
interviewed, (which I will more fully discuss in my data analysis section,)
may be contrasted with the two women in the sample who, because of
their upbringing, did not have a similar idealization of the man. One of
them, Nancy, states:

That is what was annoying me, because he could have gone to the
public with the lies that I was *dogging* (colloquial for cheating)
or stealing his money and they could have justified it. Knowing
that that could have happened, it really upset me. It is my body!
Nobody should leave marks on me. If I had dogged, he should
have moved on, after all he was not short of women.

She goes on to say:

> If he had learnt his lesson and changed I would not even have
> pressed the charges. But he went around talking saying I stole
> from him and was moving around. That hurt and I decided I
> was going to court . . . People were saying why don't you just
> agree at home, in the tribal council. But the guy was not even
> agreeing to that because he was saying it is even cheaper to just
> bribe the magistrate than pay a traditional fine. My dad actually
> called his family and they came but with so much arrogance.
> They said, if Nancy wants Kshs. 1 million and we finish this case
> she can get it. But anything more, she will not get. They think it
> is money that buys anything. I said never call me to this kind of
> a kangaroo court. . . .
>
> But after he started messing me up, I decided I was not in
> the wrong. I did nothing. I had not even provoked him. In Ke-
> nya you can get away for beating a woman if she provoked. You
> only get a day or a fine. So I wanted it straight in the record that
> I did not even provoke. Let him say what money I stole. Did he
> put it in the safe or write me a check? . . . if he says that I stole the
> money, he should go to court and have me refund it.

Although they had been living together and their families were aware of
this arrangement, which was the case with many of the other women,
Nancy was the only one in my sample who would not describe the man
as her husband. She immediately corrected me, "Not my husband really,
my fiancé." In the analysis section I will discuss further the contrast in the
formation of a sense of self between Nancy and the other informants.

Viewed from this angle, the situations of eight respondents—who
demonstrated high intellectual capacity and made very tough decisions
in workplaces and other areas of their lives, but not in their abusive relationships—made more sense. It might also provide insight into the decisions of those respondents who voiced their financial dependence on their
husbands as a reason for choosing to stay in the abusive relationship even
though it was very clear from their own narratives that they were the main
or the sole providers for the family. Five of these women actually suffered
the abuse of having to surrender everything they were making, sometimes
hoarding the little they could save so that the husband did not spend it on
other women or a drinking spree. One woman talked of her frustration
at her husband's irresponsibility in spending, so much so that even if he
had much money it always got wasted and he had to borrow from her to
survive until he made more money. Yet she, like most other women in my
study, voiced her main reason for staying on in the relationship as being
financially based.

Clearly, from an outsider's view, these were not women who were financially dependent on their men. The men were not only financially dependent on the women, but in most cases were a financial liability. Again this is an example of a person who knows that the relationship she is in is slowly depleting her livelihood and emotional resources, but who is overpowered by the need to be in union with the idealized figure that has taken a significant position in her own sense of self. Whereas literature on intimate violence emphasizes financial dependence and notions of learned helplessness in explaining why women stay on in abusive relationships, I submit that in the Kenyan and other collective contexts, the concept of psychic need to be in union with a significant male should be considered a primary influence alongside those influences elucidated by Western research.

Conceptual Data Analysis: Idealized Male Image

One way to comprehend the concept of the idealized male image is to visualize a psychic schema that represents masculinity as superior, insightful, and powerful in comparison to femininity. The reality experienced by women is obviously not necessarily congruent with this psychic image. Following my theoretical postulations in Chapter 4, light may be shed on how such idealization of the male image may come about in the Kenyan context. As already discussed, Kohut theorizes a child development in which the primary sense of self (the I) is not separate from the object (the other), and he names this psychic structure "I=You." As the child develops and realizes that there is life outside of the self, the I=You structure differentiates culminating in the formation of two psychic structures: the Grandiose Self and the Idealized Parent Imago. With regard to the development of self-Grandiosity, if my cultural analysis shows that most Kenyan women's self view is of a lower status by virtue of their gender and the corresponding cultural status, it would be expected that this low esteemed self-image is what is reflected for the girl child trying to identify with the female parental multi-figures. Females, especially those intricately involved in the care of young children like aunts and *yayas* (househelp) generally exhibit characteristics far from Grandiosity. The girl child's experiences of disappointment absorbed from the caretaker's sense of self-esteem cannot be removed far from her own self-image. The ultimate result is a greater developmental tendency toward idealizing the male figure more than the female figure.

The male idealization comes into being from early infancy in the development of the girl in Kenya by a number of likely avenues. I suggest two possibilities as follows:

The first possibility is a narcissistic hold onto the Grandiose Self that finds expression when in union with the male figures (the better mirror). The attempt here is to move as far away as possible from the disappointing image of the female estimation of the self by viewing a self in narcissistic relation with the idealized male image. In adulthood, such development may manifest itself in the forms of a great need to be in psychological union with significant males in life, an assertive unconscious competition to be similar to or more than the male figures, and a love-hate relationship with significant males in one's life. Being a psychic function, this configuration may be a source of inner conflict in that the real-life males in one's life are not living up to the idealization held within the psychic realms.

The second possibility is that, although the child continues to experience the multi-parent idealized images narcissistically as she develops into latency period (about age 5 to 9), the male and the female are experienced differently. There is bound to be a conflicted relationship with the image of her mirror (the woman—who holds an inferior and not very admirable place but who simultaneously reflects roles of intrinsic worth in the society). The girl gains praise by playing the maternal roles of caregiving, obedience, and sacrifice. Being praised in these respects of service to her family (in adulthood to children and husband) expands her Grandiosity and the good feelings of self. Upholding the roles that have been learned through mirroring of her self in the female idealized objects[4] serves to fuel her self-Grandiosity. One may argue that the idealized objects are not only women but include men. While this may be true, the girl's relation to either of these idealized objects is different. From the female mother figures, the mirror is of roles that make her be termed "good" and "valuable." The male father figures, on the other hand, if they have been very good images (strong, protective, and good providers), are admired and exalted. If they have been abusive, the real-life male figure is repressed and replaced with the archaic idealized male figure, thus filling a psychic need for the girl to maintain her Grandiosity.

---

4. This refers to my postulation that more than one person is involved in the rearing of the child. More often than not these are females caretakers. In-depth discussion regarding adjustments to Kohut's theory regarding collective societies where more than the biological mother is involved in the rearing of the child has been discussed in Chapter 4.

Either way, the socio-cultural elevation accorded males works to strengthen this dual process of idealization of the male figure so that he emerges in the psychic organization as almost being second to a Deity. Analytically, the narrative's statements,(that the male is like a deity), may be emanating from a deeper conviction which the women may not even be aware of, . Rose's explanation of her husband's behavior is a good illustration of this argument. Even as she blames this other woman for her husband's infidelity and abusive behavior, her narrative also exemplifies her general idealization of men such that men who will clean dishes and wash clothes among other "small" household duties and men who will even follow a woman's directions are regarded as not being masculine. It may be inferred that what would be manly is the opposite of what she observes in these men, whom she states must be "bewitched" and "tamed." The opposite, which would be more congruent with her masculinity image, is a man who does not do household duties (generally designated as a female chore,) and who does not follow a woman's instructions. Flowing from this is the image of a man as superior and in a more idealized position than the woman.

Clearly, whether the woman is adapted to appraise the man with very high ideals emanating from both the Grandiose Self and the idealized self object, or from her own very low self-image, the ultimate end is one of relating to the man as superior to herself. The resulting psychic organization is of an idealized male image on the one hand and the maintenance of a Grandiose self that finds fulfillment when "in union with"[5] a male image on the other. My initial supposition in the theoretical framework was that the female idealizes the male as one of the idealized objects, while females are related to as conflicted images. The notion of Grandiosity through "union with a male" is a new revelation from the field research. This notion of "union with a male" is anchored both by the general female idealization of the male already argued for, and by the female gendered messages. Gendered messages may for instance take the form of: a good girl knows how to cook, care for children, humble herself before men, is beautiful enough to yield a good dowry in marriage, will make a good

5. This is a notion derived from the hypothesized postulations that from infancy women, through the subtle but strong medium of gendered messages (e.g., of beauty or smartness that will yield greater bride price, or patriarchal naming, etc., observation of gender relations between significant males and females in their lives and other social cultural and religious symbolism), are likely to figure the gender hierarchies and their lower status. Consciously or unconsciously there is bound to be a configuration of grandiosity that finds great fulfilment if attached to a male figure.

wife, etc. They not only fuel Grandiosity but also demand female identity through relationship with a male. The notion has the power to shift
all thinking towards rationalizing and excusing the actions of the male
batterer.

In a situation where the girl child has been reared to believe in herself
and anchor her self-formation on achievements outside of gender roles
and marriage, the woman in adulthood does not develop a Grandiosity
pegged to union with a male. Nancy is a good example to illustrate this
claim. Nancy's need to clarify that her former partner was not her husband, and her clarity regarding alternatives she has and how the partner, if
he was good, should have handled their situation, emanates from a sense
of self that is self-replenishing. Unlike most of the other women in my
sample, Nancy's sense of self is not anchored in male idealization. Nancy
had been brought up to believe in herself and her capabilities. Education,
achievement, hard work, discipline and pride in herself are characteristics
that speak of her parental influence. The following segments of the interview were illuminating:

> My chances in life were good; I was in a stable family. We were
> a stable family, middle class I think. Actually we were a wealthy
> family. My parents were happy, we were all happy. They were just
> this loving couple. . . . Their love was so obvious, so guaranteed.
>
> We went to good schools, had nice homes, and went on
> holidays. I was brought up to work hard and to believe in my-
> self. Dad would take us to Mombasa (form of a tourist holiday
> resort) and he would say, "I don't want a man to come and con-
> fuse you saying they are taking you to Mombasa and get you so
> excited. I want you to have everything so you do not have to rely
> on other people." We were two girls and two boys.
>
> But now when I look back, I realize that my mother's strict-
> ness really helped us grow with values. I remember sometimes
> when we were a bit grown up, she would give the house girl off
> so we can be in charge. She wanted us to know how to take care
> of the house and all.
>
> If I was not brought up the way I did to believe in myself, I
> would have most likely said let me persevere, even if I am beaten
> a little here and there, I am living in a beautiful house in [high
> class part of town], I am driving a great BMW, what else do I
> want? You know the financial gain!

These are just a few of the statements drawn from a narrative that demonstrates a girl who has grown thinking very highly of her parents and

herself. The greatest influence came from a parental system that believed in her and worked to instill the drive for achievement in areas that would normally be male-oriented. Any later societal influences and messages of being inferior as a woman in a patriarchal society get averted by strong values of a worthy self already instilled in her. Her self-mirroring reflections from the mother are positive. Idealization of the father is positive, too, and the messages she receives from both parents regarding her self are full of promise for a great future. She has no need to idealize the male figure above the female or feel the psychological narcissistic need to be in union with the male.

It is important to grasp this concept by perceiving its power as resting in the narcissistic agenda. By justifying the man's actions, the survivor still has an idealized figure in place that she can feel good about. Intimate violence, because it is inflicted by one from whom the woman expects love, attacks the deepest core of the self, threatening fragmentation of that self organized around the male image. It is as if a part of the self (the male image) is injuring figuratively the other part of the self.

For a girl child, the trauma of witnessing violence at an early age may affect psychic configuration in various ways. Her early socialization may result in low self-esteem, especially if she grows up in a situation where she witnesses continuing occurrences of violence against her mother, (who is both the idealized 'passer of societal expectations' and the image from which she is trying to distance herself) inflicted by her father (who is the ideal image to be in union with) or another male figure. In this case, greater cathexis to the narcissistic father image may be likely. The traumatizing reality of the father figure requires the girl child to hold even more tightly to the primary narcissistic image of a father (idealized male) who is beyond any fault. The real father figure is therefore repressed and an ideal modified one is held onto. One cannot but wonder whether, in marital relations, the husband figure replaces the male image as an object to narcissistically cathect[6] to in the face of the threat of self-fragmentation posed by traumatic situations like intimate violence. Might this be a plausible explanation for the need to continue to hold onto a violent relationship and continue to be identified with the male figure? Might it further be an explanation for why some women will justify in all possible ways the acts of their male partners? If this analytical speculation holds true, it might

---

6. The notion of cathexis has also been discussed in detail in Chapter 4. It refers to a powerful hold, or underlying energy (libido), which a person invests towards an object given the possible threat of that object being taken away.

help in clarifing why some women have found ways to explain away the violent nature of their husbands with explanations that then collectively develop into normalization of the practice within culturally accepted mores. Walker alludes to this argument when she states:

> Institutionalized acceptance of violence against women would further reinforce this learned response of acceptance of a certain level of battering, provided it was defined as occurring for socially acceptable reasons, like punishment. (Walker 1984, 9)

Walker's statement also explains the survivors' thinking that there are instances when violence against a woman can be justified, such as infidelity, as already stated in the case of Rose and Nelly.

Formation of a Self, Organized Along Gendered Roles

A second concept that clearly emerged is a sense of self attached to family, children, and husband/partner. As discussed in Chapter 3, being a mother and wife are two major roles for females in Kenya. However, the idea that these roles define her psychological selfhood and sense of well-being is an aspect that clearly runs through the women's narratives, giving invaluable insight to my research question: how does a woman form a sense of self and respond subsequently to intimate violence?

Without exception, the main goal and aspiration of all the women was first to bring up and provide for their children. Even when I directly asked for specific aspirations in terms of personal achievement, the responses always found their way back to children especially. In all instances I had to directly state that I was also looking to hear of aspirations like work, careers, and education to get any answers in this direction. One woman took me by surprise when she stated that she had refused to grant a divorce to her abusive and openly unfaithful husband in court because she was willing to give up everything else, including her freedom from violence and unfaithfulness, as long as he provided for the children. Responding to why she would not take the presented court alternative of holding him to legal provision for the children after a divorce, she responded that she needed to be in her rightful place in the family as she reared her children. Clearly the question of physical provision is not the gist of her perseverance – it is rather the social preservation of the marriage unit in which children are reared by their own mother with the presence of the father figure. This greatly challenged my own thinking of what family and marriage was all about in the Kenyan context. It helped me listen with more openness to the women survivors as I continued the research.

Rose's and Nelly's responses to violence are good examples that illustrate this concept of forming a self around maternal and wifely female roles as prescribed by society. Rose, narrating her violent experience, says:

> I got beaten every day. Especially when he lived with this woman. Before then, it was once in a while since I was mainly in the rural area. Anytime I came here (Nairobi) it was violence and suffering for lack of food. But when I came and stayed here and he had the other woman he would beat me to the pulp every single day, until my eyes would begin oozing pus. Yet I could not stay home in peace because this is my husband even though any time I met him it was violence. Whenever I am home in the village, I would ask myself, why couldn't I live with my husband like other women. So I would come again, then he would beat me, and I would go back. But I just could not get peace being there in the village alone. (Silence) I would feel empty, and alone. That is when I eventually decided to just move here. . . . And you know, when you are frustrated and in heartache, there cannot be any love. Most of the time we never slept together. . . . He used to beat me every day, no reason at all. It might be even just the way I was sitting that he would pick on. Those times there was even no food in that house. No one ever came. My children use to call him Lion. They would say "the Lion is here" and they all knew what would happen.

One would have expected that she would prefer to stay on in the village and get a break from daily beatings and suffering, but she chose to be where he was in Nairobi and she states it was for image, as she was ashamed not to be like other women who could live with their husbands.

Rose's eventual decision to take back a man now old and dying from sickness, after he had left her for over 15 years with ten children to bring up by herself and had not even come to the burial of his own child, is a good illustration of the power with which wifely and maternal roles shape identity in the society. She states:

> I said I am saved, and that is why I took back my husband. . . . You see he had gone back home, and even though I have a house here, if he dies since he has children, they are going to look for him as traditionally I am still his wife. Also having children, I realized I would be leaving a curse on them if I did not take back their father.

> You see if he died, I would go with all the children. Each tribe has it its own traditions and I cannot tell the children, who are now almost adults not to go to their father's funeral. Also, all the time there would be someone coming here from home telling me words that pierced my heart. His people always came and they would look for me. Some would say "Oh that husband of yours cannot make it one more day" and then I would be worried wondering what was happening. So I decided to just bring him here and then I can work in peace. Even if I were not saved I would still do it I think.

It is apparent that Rose's decision to take her husband back has nothing to do with love or an affectionate relationship with her husband. It is so that she can "work in peace" by fulfilling societal expectations and thereby retain her respectful place in the society. It also has something to do with her concern for what is proper and least shameful for her children.

Nelly's response is similar:

> Since I gave birth the drinking got worse. He would come home very late. He does not eat cold *ugali* (cornmeal) so at 2:00 am I would wake up to make *ugali* for him. He would bring a quarter kilo of meat just for himself to eat with the *ugali*. I would just cook for him and that time if I asked why he was coming late, he would tell me I knew I was getting married to a drunkard so I should learn to live with it. When I asked about his living with other women he would say if I want to live with him, I should stop listening to other people. So I stopped listening to these things, because I wanted to make a home and for my kids to have a father for them . . . My biggest frustration was to see I cannot provide for my kids, and my husband is useless in doing so. I would ask why this has to be. They will never know it was the father, because they will always think it was their mother who did not care. So I had to go look for some work and get them food. They were so happy when I did so.

Nelly's decision to turn a blind eye to her husband's behavior and to take on providing for the family is a powerful illustration of the importance of maintaining her maternal and wifely roles.

While these roles may not form the ultimate sense of self for all women in Kenya, it needs to be recognized that it is sufficient for the majority of women to have their sense of self first and foremost anchored in their children and in marital roles. This concept is indeed closely related to the sense of satisfaction that children brought into the lives of survivors.

Conceptual Data Analysis: Self Organized Around Gender Roles

The theoretical hypothesis of self-development of the girl child in Kenya, according to my postulated theoretical framework, supports an understanding of some of the survivors' responses to violence and the construction of the self around gender roles. As the girl child develops, the messages that in infancy brought about good feelings of esteem (Grandiosity), only do so in latency and beyond when attached to the execution of gender roles of duties and/or marriage. Her experience as a girl in the community is definitely different from that of a boy. Two excellent selections from the survivors' narratives illustrate the challenges the girl child faces in the early years of her life. Here is Rose, describing who she is:

> Me, I am a parent. A parent [*note the emphasis*] and I have children. In my home, I am the mother and the father. In my youth as a girl, I used to think. I use to talk well and looked forward to a good life. But things did not turn out that way. I started in form one. Okay before form one I was in primary, but my father had three wives so my mother had lots of problems. . . . So when I went to secondary, my father married yet another wife. I waited two years out of school hoping father will pay for my school fees. He worked but also wanted so many women so he could not afford our school fees.
>
> My mother was my friend because we have undergone a lot of poverty with her. My father left her and she had to struggle with us for so long. My mother is now long dead. But I learnt a lot from her especially her perseverance in hardship.

Rose can identify with her mother's plight and in this way become good friends with her. It may be inferred that learning from her mother how to suffer hardships and persevere in the face of mistreatment are skills that have been reflected by a female as ideal to the girl child. Although not as clearly expressed, there is a hint of disappointment in her mother as an ideal figure because she gives the impression of really thinking and wanting something greater (looked forward to a good life). However, what stands out most from her mother is her perseverance in hardship and her execution of gender roles of being a nurturer and a good parent.

Nelly's narrative describes similar aspects of gendered values and disappointments passed on by the idealized parents:

> My mother never told us that our father had died. We just used to wonder why whenever we needed anything it would have to be mom to get it. From knickers to school fees. The man we

knew as our father always said he had no money. . . . I use to be
such a nice kid everyone wanted me around. I mean in terms
of helping at home, by the time mom came home from work,
I had cooked, fetched water, tidied the house. We had trouble
with water in [town] so the distance to fetch water was far. I
would take the wheelbarrow and get water without being asked.
I would go to school in the morning, and then in the evening, I
would fetch water. I would work at home. I woke in the morning
at 5:00 AM and then read and after that then I would get ready
for school. Even if a neighbor sends me, I would just go. I was a
very clean kid. I also loved kids. If you left me with your child, I
would really take care of the child. You would find I have bathed
the child, he has eaten he is just happy. People would even bring
me candies and even clothes because of how I took care of their
children. I would even wash their clothes.

Nelly's case is also an excellent illustration of my argument that constant
praise of the girl child in her execution of female roles will have the "oper-
ant conditioning" effect of making her engage even more in these roles to
fulfill her Grandiosity. Hence, she becomes the favorite in the community
for execution of gender roles.

Around latency, according to Kohut (1971, 43), the psychic structures take on some degree of permanency. Their transmutation and integration into the super-ego structure entails values that are passed on
through the multi-parent idealized images. For the girl child, such values
are mirrored by females as being caring, obedient, submissive, and sacri-
ficial, and embrace the whole realm of cultural maternal-ness; and from
the man, as being an ideal, achieving, intellectual, organizer, requiring to
be served, sometimes brutal, and rightfully judgmental, depending on the
influencing male figures in the household and community. In many ways
she cannot identify with these male characteristics except as argued above
in relationship with him. She therefore holds onto, in a narcissistic manner, the idealization of gender roles mirrored through the females- the
only aspect of being female that commands recognition. In adulthood this
may manifest in women as genuine difficulties to love and view oneself
as worthy of praise, except in her execution of gender-roles. Grandiosity
may be experienced when one achieves in other ways but if such achievement is not coupled with maternal and wifely endowments, Grandiosity
is very temporary and short lived, quickly being replaced by feelings of
helplessness and unworthiness, because of the primary intrusions that demand Grandiosity through gender roles as she has been socialized. Such

organization translates into a sense of self that is anchored on maternal roles that fuel Grandiosity, and that have been integrated into the super-ego as life mandates. Unfortunately, such a self can be very vulnerable because it is secured by roles which must be performed outside of the self. While there may be great cost in performing them, there is even greater cost in not doing so.

When faced with the trauma of intimate violence later on in marriage, the woman survivor will most likely tend to function on an internal mechanism centered on maintaining her identity (place in the society). Her sense of self is characterized by psychic tensions, with the greater weight toward conformity to internalized ideations of what it means to be a woman and to belong in the society. These have, over time been internalized as an integral part of her super-ego. She figures, either consciously or unconsciously, that she would be more mentally stable if she were to tow the line of fulfilling her maternal and marital roles, because this way she retains her special place as a person, a part of the whole. The absence of these roles poses a threat of vulnerability and fragmentation to the self. Viewed from Mbiti's "African perspective," as discussed in Chapter 3, as a woman who is not married and/or who is childless she would become a nonentity.

Yet she cannot also be viewed as a healthy and fully functional being even in the Kenyan context, because there is a part of her that must be repressed or dissociated if she is to cope. If she were to choose divorce from her abusive partner, she would have to deal with being loathed as a nonentity within the society, unless she is an exceptional case (as demonstrated by Nelly's narrative above,) and can redeem that identity in other acceptable and justifiable means. She may even have to deal with being regarded as an outcast if we are to follow Mbiti's philosophical thoughts of distancing oneself from the main society (Mbiti 1991, 104). This notion is compounded by the fact that a divorce also means giving up the role of rearing her children and, therefore, becoming the one who severs the connection between life and death and therefore invites a curse upon herself and family. Her reasons for divorce in this case become secondary. Her economic and social contributions are also secondary to her identity value, which is pegged to her reproductive and wifely roles.

Children: Empowerment for Self-esteem and/or Purpose in Life

Not even one of the respondents expressed any regrets for having children with their abusive partners. Indeed, children emerged as influential in the roles of either being catalysts to decision making of their mothers regarding abusive relationships; giving a purpose in life; bringing fulfillment; and/or empowering the survivors to take on challenging responsibilities and ventures in life, resonated through all the narratives. By purpose in life and empowerment, I mean the capacity of the survivor to take more self-direction for herself and her children through courage and entrepreneurship. Three areas in which children played an important role are discussed here to demonstrate empowerment and/or purposefulness of life which they brought to the survivors.

Children's Role in Women's Response to Intimate Violence

The notion of children in the survivors' lives was empowering and fulfilling. Many of their decisions and responses to violence revolved around the welfare of their children. The responses of the women to intimate violence, which in many ways were influenced by the presence of children in the relationship, were as varied as the unique circumstances of each woman. Nelly, already discussed above, decided to stay on in her abusive relationship to provide a family for her children.

Rose, when asked why she took back the man after he had abandoned her for other women for over 15 years, states:

> If he dies and since he has children they will go looking for him.
> Also having children, I realized that I would be leaving a curse
> on them if I did not take back the father.

Millicent, now out of the abusive relationship, is very worried about her children and expresses a sense of being lost without them and a longing for the assurance that they will be okay. Her job does not really substitute for her loss of children.

> Even now I am out of home, I am not happy because sometimes
> when my children tell me that sometimes there is no food and
> when they ask him for money he says there is nothing. Some-
> times they will look for money themselves, buy some food cook
> and eat and wash the dishes . . . I wanted to have four children:
> two boys, and two girls, I wanted to get away from poverty so
> much. Now all I have after all the effort is this job. If I lose it, it is
> all gone. I have told the children that the house at the base and

the other house is not theirs. Their real home is only the rural one I built. It is why I don't live with two of my children. I told them if dad was to pay their fees, they should just live with him so they can get education because I could not manage to pay . . . But I worry about my girls living there. At times, you can see the frustration of the children. The last-born came and threw his bags on the floor and told me he would not go back even if it meant leaving school.

These facts, as she cites later, are motivators as she considers going back to her abusive relationship, even though she assumes she would be walking to a death sentence. In this regard, children played the role of giving purpose of life to the survivor. The survivor was willing to receive the abuse rather than miss the chance to physically raise her children if it gave them the opportunity to a future through education.

Children Brought about Self-fulfillment

The feeling of pride through their children was clearly apparent on the faces of the survivors as they talked about their children. Rose, describing who she is, states, "Me, I am a mother. I am a parent and I have children." This is a good example of a clear identity which gives Rose a sense of worth. Her centering on the notion of parenthood in describing who she is indicates the importance of that role in defining her sense of self. The image of one of the younger women, Irene, is illustrative of the central role of parenthood in identity, a view that was mirrored by all the women I interviewed. I would have thought that, being so young, she would regret that her life was curtailed through giving birth very early, placing her in a non-progressive situation with no financial means and with a husband who had vanished leaving her with no real plans for the immediate future. However, a strong sense of self emanated from her as she latched on dearly and lovingly to her six-month old baby. The baby was tangible proof that she was still somebody, the "mother of so and so." No one, not even the man who had lied to her, beaten her, mistreated her by leaving her to bleed to death and refused to take her to the hospital, could take this status away from her. Her sadness as she told her experiences was heart rending, up to the point when she began to talk about giving birth, about the joy of naming the baby after her own father in response to the husband warning her not to give it any name from his family. At this point her sadness broke into a deep smile.

Nancy, though taught to believe in herself and accomplished in many ways, states that she may not have a husband and is not interested in one because she already has her family, her children. She then goes on to state that she is "guilty" of asking her own unmarried friends what they are thinking as they have no children at this age and they do not seem to be taking any initiative even though "it looks like there is no boyfriend in the horizon" to give them a child.

Children Gave Survivors Empowerment and Status

We have already met Nelly, who had resigned herself to an abusive relationship to provide for her children. Eventually, it is the same perception of her children's welfare that gave Nelly the impetus to get out of the house and work to provide for them when the husband had failed. She expressed feelings of great frustration when she could not provide for her children. The realization that her husband was useless in providing for the children drove her to begin a small entrepreneurial business of "walking retail merchandise" to provide for her children. Angela is another great example of a woman who felt empowered by her children. She exuded pride as she informed me in a matter of fact way:

> My kids are going to some of the best schools in Nairobi, and he is paying for every penny of it. . . . He can keep as many women as he wants but he is losing it all. I get to stay on the farm, make money from the farm, and live a life of my own, and take care of my kids. My-father-in law keeps telling the other women married in the family and who are beaten every day to learn from my example. He says, (imitating father-in-law's voice) "You see Angela? She knows what matters. My son can keep moving around because he could not put up with a tough woman, but she will stay here and develop herself and her children."

Notice that the father-in-law's perception of toughness in a woman requires that she hold onto her role as the main wife and the mother in the home, apparently an attitude that works to puff up Angela's Grandiosity. This is followed by a hearty laugh about how she has won the game in which her husband thought he was punishing her. Although Angela may not be relating to the husband in the marital sense of sharing the same bed, house, and resources, she still holds her very highly regarded place as his wife and the mother of his children and is doing very well in providing for her children through that status. In fact, her father-in-law seems very proud of her for maintaining these roles, and criticizes his son for not fulfilling his duties as husband. I cannot help wondering if her fulfillment in her status is not fueled and sustained by the father-in-law's (an idealized male) high regard of her maintenance of maternal roles.

Jane is yet another good example. After resigning herself to a cycle that blinded her to her husband's schemes of secretive travels, business, and women behind her back, and blaming everyone else but him for their soured relationship, she suddenly finds voice and agency when he tricks her and takes the children away. She states, "I went to look for him in [city], he beat me there and I went to the police in [place]. We discussed the situation. Then I came back to Nairobi. That is why I am here at FIDA, so that he can pay school fees for my children." Her confidence as she narrates her life is indicative of the empowerment that the very thought of losing her children has brought about.

Nancy's amazing story of survival also implies a power energized through her child. She stated, "So I just said my last prayers and decided to die quietly. But any time I kept quiet my daughter would call me and I would regain energy to try again." As Nancy lay expecting to die, and everything else seemed bleak in terms of chances of survival, Nancy's one hope came through hearing the voice of her child calling her. One can almost envision her child's hand reaching out to the dying mother, and the mother feeling that she needed to try harder, to meet her child's figurative outstretched hand, to keep alive for the sake of her child.[7]

Conceptual Data Analysis: Children's Role in Self-definition and Response to Intimate Violence

Throughout the narratives, indisputably the children are important and therefore pivotal in the decision-making, empowerment, and defining of a sense of self for the survivors. The importance of this centrality of children is the ultimate place that children held in the sense of self in the women's lives. The thought that they might not be able to continue to raise their children, or that they were not being good mothers to their children, not only gave the women new-found energy to look for alternatives when there seemed to be none, but also gave them a purpose for striving to make their lives better. The fact that they had children gave them a status that no one could take away, as in the case of Irene who glowed with pride about her baby, and of Angela (who had refused the court offer for a divorce and seemed very happy to have her rightful place as mother of her children in

---

7. A longer excerpt of Nancy's ordeal is related later in this chapter and in Appendix 4.

the home). If one wanted to push this idea further, one could ask whether, if Angela had had no biological children, she would have felt empowered and confident to let her husband move around while she kept her status as his wife or whether her life would have taken a different dimension. Would the father-in-law have been as proud of her as he was? Would she be deriving the same feeling of Grandiosity from her place as wife and her role as mother that she now expresses? We may never know the answers, but I would hypothesize that her situation would be very different, most likely one of being shunned as infertile and therefore justifying her husband's infidelity. The role that children play cannot be underestimated in the formation of a sense of self and subsequently the woman's response to intimate violence. I argue that a deeper need (psychologically) is being fulfilled through this maternal role than the mere call of motherly responsibility, involving the mother's coping responses to intimate violence.

Mechanical Self-righting Functionalism

Intimate violence is a very traumatic experience especially since the perpetrator should, in normal circumstances, be envisioned as a loving, kind and protective figure. Extensive literature may be found regarding the traumatizing experience of intimate violence and its related effects of psychological symptoms, notably PTSD and the battered woman syndrome.[8] Generally, when people think of a survivor of violence, they picture a helpless, traumatized individual. Yet as I listened to each of the narratives of my respondents, I kept expecting to hear and observe signs of traumatization, but these were not forthcoming. I did not see or hear strong indicators of depression, stress, total helplessness, rock bottom low esteem or many of the other factors associated with violence trauma and PTSD. What I saw were individuals who presented themselves in almost all aspects as normal human beings. This notion of functionality among survivors of violence, whichis discussed in the analysis section, is neither new to intimate violence literature, nor unique to the Kenyan context only.

However, a number of the women in my survivor sample expressed sadness and showed it on their faces. Interestingly, such sadness was only detected among the young women, and those women in shorter relationships. Yet even these women did not sit in their homes helpless or depressed. Eight of them were engaged in small scale businesses selling

---

8. These psychological effects have been discussed in the general literature review of domestic violence in Chapter 1.

produce by the roadside, or having "walking, retail merchandise," or, as in the case of Rose, doing community work. Only one of these eight women had gone beyond eighth grade. They had very few options (if any) open to them in terms of employment. Yet among these eight, seven not only supported their families, but also educated the children with their meager earnings in the face of their husbands either having left to live with another woman or being outright irresponsible.

Five other women worked in full time office career jobs and seemed very settled in what they did. For example, Jackie worked as an assistant in a shop in town and really seemed to enjoy her job, and her employer, (who referred her to me,) described Jackie as her best worker. There was no way of discerning, just by looking at these women or relating with them, the heavy burden of violence and abuse that weighed on their shoulders. Julie, one of these career women, especially took me by surprise. I remember walking into her office on our first appointment and thinking I had come to the wrong office. I asked if I could speak to Julie and could not hide my surprise when she introduced herself as Julie. Later, I reflected in my journal on having expected to find the downtrodden face of a woman burdened with a heavy heart. I had instead been greeted by one of the most vivacious women I have ever known. She exuded life! I remember trying to rationalize this bountiful energy as coming from the fact that Julie had been able to break from the cycle of violence and was already out of the abusive relationship. While this explanation may be plausible, it is watered down by the fact that she had only been out of that hole for just over two weeks. That was not long enough to normalize a life after horrible experiences for years. She even expressed confusion and some regret at walking out of the relationship, aspects reflecting a psychological conflict that would be expected to show through her face. Even though I am aware that people can compartmentalize, deny, repress, and otherwise cut off from painful psychological realities, I saw that, in Julie's case, she was more than willing to talk about it and expressed the pain it was causing her. What is more important is that her tough experiences did not deter her from performing her regular duties in any way.

Nancy is yet another woman whose experience is worthy of note. She ran her own business, dressed to rival any other middle class professional woman, and spoke with an aura of confidence that just did not reflect the trauma she had gone through. As she narrated her experience of psychological violence for years, which had culminated in a near-death physically violent event, it was hard to match the experience with the narrator.

Nancy told of how she had been warned by several people about the furi-
ous temper of her husband-to-be, with whom she was already living. She
had been told that he had been in another relationship, which had broken
up, because of his violence. He had dismissed these allegations, but she
occasionally had to live with considerable verbal and psychological abuse.
She always hoped he would change, especially since he was very loving
and caring when he was not in his bad moods. As she narrated her ordeal,
which sounds unbelievable, she showed no sign of trauma, or even tears:

> He had not been going to the office. He would leave his place
> and come to my house and sometimes I would go to his house.
> His messages would be brought to him at home from women.
> He would put them on the bedside. So I asked him, you get all
> these messages from women in the office and then you come
> and put them here so I can read them. I am moving. I said that
> then I put on my nightgown and was getting out to go sleep in
> another room. He grabbed me and the next thing I saw was a
> knife tearing into my stomach and my leg. I don't know what
> he was thinking. He locked me in the room. My intestines were
> spread on the floor. You know I had tried to shield myself with
> the hand and it got injured too in the process. Then he locked
> the door, and locked the grill door, and locked the other door,
> four doors in total before going. My tendons had been cut, I
> could not stand I tried to stand and I collapsed. As far as he
> knew he had killed me. You see my [relative] and my [relative],
> were trying to break the door and they could not. They were
> upstairs in another room and they came when they heard me
> screaming, but he pushed her away and told the *shamba* boys
> (gardener) and the cook not to go to the house or open it un-
> der any circumstance. Nobody knew what had happened to me
> whether I had just been slapped or what. I pushed the EARS
> (Security) button and they spoke with us but they said they are
> trained for thieves and not to break into people's houses. I told
> them they have to break. When they called the police, the police
> decided they did not have a car. So I just said my last prayers and
> decided to die quietly. But any time I kept quiet my daughter
> would call me. At about 5 A.M. I called his [relative] and told
> her what had happened to me was so bad and if she does not
> come and break the house, she should not bother to come. She
> was actually good, she got some people who came and broke
> the house and I was taken to the hospital. I was in theatre for
> 8 hours from 8:00 in the morning to 5:00 in the evening. Every
> time I had tried to stand up or move, I would feel all this gush

of blood so I had stopped moving and I did not know what else was on the floor. So I pulled the duvet cover and stayed on the floor. I tell you it is by God's grace I am here alive today. Even when I went to the hospital, the man's [relative] called the matron and said Nancy is so hurt, please prepare for her as she is on her way in the ambulance. I found doctors waiting for me. They had actually to remove the intestines completely and then put them back. There were many doctors working on me. They checked everything to see if there was anything ripped. They said we have done our best now let us wait and see if they settle. I woke up at 8:00 AM. I was given good medical attention.

These horrific narrations and this analysis of the missing symptoms of trauma (that would normally be expected from an extreme experience like this) clearly show the high level of functionality these women displayed in the face of trauma. It just was incomprehensible that someone should go through such a terrible traumatic experience and yet function at a similar level of any other person without having attended any "formal counseling session" or therapy! There was nothing about their style, or presentation of their job performances, or *anything* out of the normal that would reveal their lives of hidden violence. One could not distinguish, just by looking at her or visiting with her, a woman who was traumatized, sometimes daily, in her intimate relationships, from one who was not. On the surface, this may not seem a novel issue because, as literature on intimate violence PTSD shows, it is common for victims to repress any signs of trauma in their survivorship. However, as is discussed in the analysis section, common is not necessarily normal. For me, the high functionality of the women in the first place is what led me to this study because, although commonplace, it is not normal.

Conceptual Data Analysis: Self-righting Functionalism of Survivors

Walker's discussion of the battered woman syndrome gives some insight into what seems like an absence of effects of trauma on the survivors in Kenya and helps address my initial perplexity at the high functionality of female survivors of violence. She states that although women experience the effects of trauma from abusive relationships,

> this did not affect areas of the battered women's lives other than her family life. Most of the women interviewed were intelligent, well-educated, competent people who held responsible jobs . . .

> In fact they were quite successful in appearing to be just like
> other people . . . (1984, 150)

Apparently, from Walker's statement above, high functionality that makes
the survivor appear like any other person is not necessarily unique to the
Kenyan situation. It is an adaptation which she points out to be typical to
PTSD patients, and which she has brought to the fore in the West, successfully helping the legal systems understand the volatile eruptions of
repressed anger and the sometimes lethal nature of survivors of intimate
violence. Although acknowledging that the concept is not unique to Kenya, it is important to note how survivors' high functionality has been used
to normalize violence to the women in Kenya and claim it as harmless.

In considering the functionality of survivors, I realized I had been
influenced by the commonplace generalization that women in violence
cycles are helpless victims. I realized I was applying to these women some
psychological assumptions of how a traumatized person should behave
and present herself in terms of being helpless, depressed, dependent, and
generally non-functional. It is this common knowledge (that survivors of
violence do not always display these indicators of trauma,) that has been
used to construct powerful myths of the acceptance of violence which allows violence to continue in our homes.

Writing about how science has been engendered through mythical
beliefs, Keller illustrates the extent of power that myths have in our lives:

> The survival of myth-like beliefs in our thinking about science,
> the very archetype of anti-myth, ought, it would seem, to invite
> our curiosity and demand investigation. Unexamined myths,
> wherever they survive, have a subterranean potency; they affect
> our thinking in ways we are not aware of, and to the extent that
> we lack awareness, our capacity to resist their influence is un-
> dermined. (Keller 1978, 187)

Keller's statements summarize what I perceive to be the situation regarding intimate violence survivors. I had failed to recognize the relationship
between response to plurality and therefore specificity of the contexts,
conditions, and needs of the women in violence, and therefore expected
them to behave in certain generic ways. Fortunately, this led me to become
curious as to why they did not conform to these standard ways and instead
functioned so efficiently in their responsibilities and social roles. Although
Walker discusses the observation that survivors present themselves like
everyone else, (which is common with PTSD in survivors of violence,)
the fact that women in Kenya have generally not had an opportunity for

diagnosis and treatment led me to look further, unraveling deeper revelations of female psychic organizations that are very much a function of the social-cultural and religious context. By failing to acknowledge the commonplace knowledge, my curiosity had demanded investigation and led me to this study!

Indeed, the incomprehensibility of the range of the survivor's response to violence has been used by those who would like to deny the presence of intimate violence and its adverse effects on survivors in the Kenyan communities. The survivor's "normal" functionalism has been a great source of misinterpretation in the Kenyan context. Since the survivor's life is not regarded as a clinical concern, many view it as normal to be beaten as a wife, whether for discipline or as a form of expressing love (Nasimiyu-Wasike 1994, 103). Theresa Hinga, speaking to the similar response by women in Kenya about intimate violence, states,

> Many women on their part seem generally to accept their destiny and will often cover up their husbands even when they have done them actual bodily harm. They too seem to assume that being battered is a part of their marriage package as evident in the recent survey conducted by some female researchers on women's awareness of their rights. In the survey women were asked whether men have a right to discipline and beat their wives. Of this, about 45% answered that men had a right to discipline their wives, while 8% did not know whether he had such a right or not. (Hinga 1994, 119)

The societal view of the violence as normal has been a reason for a stance of noninvolvement by most people, including those in helping professions who are in a position to address the situation. Their rationale is that the survivor of violence, although facing a hard fate in the relationship, still stands in a better position than if she were robbed of her societal identity role. After all, marriage and the children are her securities and the basis for positive identity. Designating intimate violence as a non-clinical, domestic concern allows it to escape society's limelight. Organizations like FIDA (Federation of Women lawyers), COVAW (Coalition of Violence Against Women Kenya), WRAP (Women's Rights Awareness Programme) and GVRC (Gender Violence Recovery Center—Nairobi women's Hospital), which have defied the commonplace acceptance and are initiating women's rights education and advocacy, are in many ways spoken of negatively, and perceived with suspicion. Many theories of the cycle of violence view the survivor's "normal" circumstances as emanating from the fact that most survivors of violence who stay in abusive relationships have also grown up witnessing similar abuse to their mothers. Survivors are used to the violence because of their exposure to it in homes of origin. Such popular theories in Kenya have also led to false perception that women in intimate violence situations accept their fate. I disagree with such sentiments of "acceptance" of violence by any normal human being. Instead, the constant negative feedback works on the survivor's self-concept. The effect on the functions of the Grandiose Self in union with the male, and the survivor's archaic and narcissistic need to maintain identity through fulfillment of role obligations (guided by the idealized parent imago[s],) have more to do with these survivors remaining as highly functional beings in abusive relationships than with the survivor's acceptance of violence as normal. This concept of "acceptance" is nothing but a myth, one that helps perpetuate resistance to changing the socio-cultural set up of the communities in Kenya. Any change would threaten the male psychological position in the society and risk fragmentation of the female's psychological identity and social role within that same society.

The question then that many opposed to activist work against Violence ask is, "If survivors of violence function well enough, at least on the surface, even though adaptively, why is there a need for change?" This question takes me back to my root argument that these survivors of violence very rarely have the opportunity for a self-cohesiveness that balances maternal and wifely roles with the human drive for endeavors and achievement beyond parenting. This argument offers some insight into the dynamics of why and what in the context makes one continue to be highly functional in the face of intimate violence trauma. I have suggested in this work, that a major clue to understanding the survivor's functionality, is embedded in the social, cultural, and religious context and its influence in the formations of the sense of self. In the Kenyan context, even as I acknowledge that contextualizing trauma will affect the presenting symptoms, I do not totally ignore the presence of some dysfunctionality, which may be embedded in the very way in which survivors appear to be very functional. The respondents' presentation of themselves was not unlike other women in the same community at their respective economic and social levels. Yet for those continuing to be caught up in the violence cycle, all their energies were focused on survival for themselves as wives and as supporters and protectors of their children. This is a claim that is consistent with Kohut's theory that narcissistic personalities are not entirely dysfunctional. The self may still cohere around something, but it loses creativity, empathy, wisdom and zest. Similarly, though the women survivors of intimate violence cohere, they do so around the very limited focus of fulfilling the gender roles of marriage and motherhood, hence re-directing all their energies towards the fulfillment of these roles. They relate to these roles as though fulfilling legal mandates. In this way they lose the passion for self-development and achievement that would open up avenues for greater creativity.

Rose's statement alludes to this concept of redirected energy: "You know when you are having problems, your whole heart is in those problems, and so I never thought of anything else." Similarly, Annastasia's association of the word "anger" with captivity reflects a negative energy. She stated, "Anger can make people to be frustrated. When I am not happy I cannot be comfortable. I cannot do anything. Even I cannot pray because I am not free."

For most women who had managed to move on, there seemed to be a psychological entrapment by their abusers still, as was the case with Rose (who goes to the village to get her husband so she can be like other women), and with Millicent (who wishes she could go back to her estranged husband and worries herself about his welfare without her).

A clear line of how I conceptualize this idea of functionalism through the self-righting tendency is built upon my argument about the development of the self for a woman in a collective context. By the latency period, her cognitive ability is developed adequately to comprehend that her societal role is an important part of her identity within the community. I have made the case that the greatest of these societal roles is her dual role as a mother and a wife. Given this theoretical framework, the woman's cohesiveness is strongly centered around these two roles and developed through the values of the idealized imagos and the Grandiose self. These values are transmuted to the super-ego. The fact that these roles are part of the super-ego content aligned along with other do's and don'ts, and integrated as cultural and religious beliefs, accord them a sacred status. The survivor's experience of violence causes her to even more strongly engage her idealized roles to maintain her now-threatened cohesiveness. She must not only hold onto these roles but also execute them in the most acceptable ways in the society. For many of the women, the provision of food and other family necessities falls under their responsibility as mother and wife. So does a positive presentation of oneself and the family in the larger society. From this responsibility comes the saying that "we [women] should not wash our dirty linen in public." There is no bigger shame than that which is attached to exposing the ills and dysfunctionality of one's family by a woman. The drive is very strong not only to maintain her place as a part of the whole through maintaining her roles in the family, but also to continue to execute these roles with utmost efficiency.

Furthermore, if one is to take the example of a woman whose line of development culminated in an already low self-esteem with regard to achievement outside of these roles, the presence of intimate violence is a devastating blow to the already injured esteem. The physical attack on the person goes beyond criticizing her for actions she has done, whether true or not.

I am convinced, from this theoretical base, that survivors of intimate violence continually suffer the blow of negative self-concept, and that this may indeed be a factor in their staying on in abusive relationships. A negative self-concept, combined with the fact that one gains some identity and respect through maintaining her roles in the family and a sense of self through union with a significant male figure, are powerful enough to keep many women in an abusive relationship. This negative self-concept is enlarged by the absence of social support, and by the few life-options available to women who would choose to reject or modify expected social roles. All this is enough to keep one in disorientation of one's true capability and endeavors. The probable stir of a desire and passion for creativity while balancing societal obligations, as Kohut would theorize, is lost.

I am arguing that given the socio-cultural and religious context that condones and justifies intimate violence against women, survivors' adaptation through repression, dissociation and tapping into archaic forms of primary narcissistic existence, contribute to their successful functioning, especially with regard to reproductive and marriage roles.

In conclusion then, while Kenyan female survivors of intimate abuse may appear to be adaptive, highly functioning, and in some ways even thriving, this functionalism is an outward depiction of her desperate hold on her self-identity as a wife and mother, and expresses her desire to maintain her sense of self. When examined in the light of Kohut's cohesiveness theory, there are considerable hidden costs to the psychological integrity of these women. Their potential for healthy cohesion is severely curtailed, if not rendered impossible.

There are more chances for this potential to be lost for the survivors of intimate violence, as they endeavor to adapt. The effects of such a loss, given the considerable number of women in violent situations, should not only be a source of clinical concern, but also of economic and social concern because it entails deprivation for society as a whole. A myriad of developmentally-related activities that fuel the ego-driven creativity and contribution to the development of any society is being lost as long as we condone gender violence and ignore the impact of its roots in the subsuming socio-cultural and religious setting.

A publication focusing on Zambia and the need to investigate that judicial system's response to gender violence recognizes this lost potential by survivors of violence. It states:

> Gender violence whether in public or private sphere creates permanent constraints in the ability of survivors especially women and girls. Thus violence in this way retards development at the individual and national levels. Considering that Zambia's population is currently estimated as 10 million people, 51% of whom are women, this is why gender violence and how the justice system responds to it becomes important. (Women and Law in South African Trust 2001, 9)

The need for appropriate intervention that begins by addressing the social, and cultural demands cannot be ignored if we are to have a society with a fully creative and functional population. My recommendation is to begin with a psycho-social and cultural analysis of the context that nurtures the formation of women's sense of self. Such analysis will lead to more effective intervention in intimate violence. A clear understanding, however, of how that sense of self has developed and been nurtured in the gendered context over the years would present a realistic and empowering approach to intervention that begins by a quest to understand women's responses to abusive relationships. It is a clear lens for addressing the root issues embedded in the society's socio-cultural and religious patterns that gives rise to a limited sense of self. The full picture of the formation of the self and the response to traumatic situations, (which reveal an amazing creativity on the part of the female survivor) cannot, however, be complete without consideration of the role of religion. Chapter 6 is an attempt at the analysis of this role from my data.

6

The Violence Phenomenon

Religious Concepts

THE ROLE OF RELIGION IN SURVIVORS' LIVES

Engagement with religion emerged as a strong practice that ran among all my respondents. I conceptualize religion as a dynamic encounter between the women in violence and their views of the Divine, as the women constantly sought to make sense of a reality that was incomprehensible. Such an encounter encompasses religious symbolism and doctrines in their respective faiths and belief systems. This chapter is devoted to a critical examination of how the ordinary female survivor of violence in Kenya engaged religion, even as she experienced the violence perpetrated on her. Specifically, how does she use religion first to cope, then to make sense of her reality, and ultimately to respond decisively to that reality?

By exploring these questions I will be attempting to address my research objectives as well: How does religion influence the female's formation of sense of self in Kenya? How does religion colors women's understanding of the violence they experience? And how does such sense of self affect the survivor's response to intimate violence?. Although Christianity mixed with African traditional religions is primarily the focus of this chapter, where necessary other religious traditions have been mentioned since they play a significant role in the lives of the survivors in my sample.

In attempting to understand how the survivors engaged religion, it is important to ask why they engaged religion in the first place. In other words, what makes religion in the circumstance so important that it ran pervasively among all my respondents? I begin by presenting some excerpts from my interviews, demonstrating that religion did indeed emerge as a significant moral and psychic regulating agency. I then argue for religion as an orienting system, readily available and appealing to the survivors of violence, by outlining its presenting characteristics, its agency, and its embedded-ness in the social cultural context. From these perspectives, I engaged the survivors to determine how they used religion to ascribe meaning to their experiences.

A biographical data analysis of each respondent would enable a determination of several aspects of her engagement with religion in her violent experiences. These would include, but are not limited to: the individual's position in relation to her belief in God; prevailing characteristics of her God; elaborations and transformations of her God images,[1] and the metamorphosis of these, from parental figures; use of the God image in the maintenance of one's psychic balance; possible discrepancies or alignment between the social God and the private God image; and the particular needs of the individual for her God. These are all aspects derived from a guiding analysis set forth by Rizzuto in interpreting the individual formation of the God image and its prevailing use in life through religious encounters (1979, 91). This task, however appealing it may seem, is beyond the scope of this discussion. These aspects have nevertheless been highlighted whenever necessary to illustrate the theoretical framework I propose for understanding survivors of intimate violence. It may also be noted that the conceptual analysis presented in this chapter after the data presentation, does not concern the origins of the God image of the respondents, but rather the way they have used God images and religion to maintain their psychic equilibrium. For now it is important to know the

1. See Rizzuto (1979). A discussion engaging Rizzuto's theory on human development of God images from childhood into adulthood is presented in Chapter 4. The most important notion to note in this chapter is that such God image, as Rizzuto conceives it, does not remain static once formed (44). Through one's life experiences, one continues to engage and construct images or representations of the Divine and therefore reshape, reconstruct, and/or repress the image at every stage of development. The social image presented by the society and the private image may or may not be congruent, calling for further reshaping and renegotiating into what she calls a "highly personalized God representation."

categories I utilize in analyzing the religious roles in their lives. Rizzuto outlines four categories when she states:

> The positions encountered are four: (1) those who have a God whose existence they do not doubt; (2) those wondering whether or not to believe in a God they are not sure exists; (3) those amazed, angered, or quietly surprised to see others invested in a God who does not interest them; (4) those who struggle with a demanding God they would like to get rid of if they were not convinced of His existence and power. (Rizzuto 1979, 91)

The importance of outlining these positions at the beginning is to assert that the interviewee was asking questions about God and therefore engaging religion whether any survivor reacted to God and religious sentiments with anger, or with gladness or somewhere in between. It also points to the fact that even if some of the survivors may be said to have a similar religious base in terms of traditions and beliefs, their engagement with the Divine is not homogenous. It is at different levels.

THE SURVIVORS' ENGAGEMENT OF RELIGION

Without exception, all my respondents engaged religion in various ways and at various levels. Religious engagement ran so strongly in my sample that I had to go back to my data and determine if the finding was influenced by the way I had identified the informants. However, my sources were as varied as the survivors themselves, with most being referred by organizations working with women in violence, which have nothing to do with religion per se. In a profound way it illustrates Mbiti's statement that, in the African sense, "to be human is to be religious." It is for this reason I have included a detailed discussion of religion as an orienting system within the Kenyan society.

In this part of the chapter, I point out instances where religious sentiments came up in the narrative, sometimes as a direct response but most often in the ordinary narrative. As I do so, I mention, as necessary, levels and categories that I think the survivor is engaging religion at. This way I keep the analysis section strictly concerning how the survivors were engaging religion to cope, make sense of, and respond to violence.

Dorcas is a good example of a 'category one' person—someone who does not doubt the existence of her God. She says:

I decided to go to the chief's. Neighbors told me that the people who had helped him move were his friends and brother whose house I had gone to look for him earlier. When I reached the chief's place, I met a representative of WRAP (Women's Rights Awareness Program) who told me about WRAP and we came here together. God had without question brought this person to me!

Her statement reveals her belief in the existence of a God who intervenes at her lowest point—a God with power to control the actions of other people whether they know it or not. Kindness, goodness and caring could be associated with Dorcas's God. Elsewhere, in her reply to where God was in her experiences, Dorcas expresses an *undefined* personal relationship with her God, yet an acceptance that God definitely exists and *must* help those who are in need. She states:

I don't really know. But I know God helped me because when I got beaten, I could not even hear or talk and the head was hurting so much I did not know if I would recover.

In contrast, Annastasia's statements reflect a knowledge and possible acceptance of the existence of God but ambivalence about whether such a belief is relevant to her circumstances. Her perception of God is reflected through third person relationships. She replies when asked about her relationship with God:

I guess one is just supposed to persevere with marriage because of children. The fellowship group gives one encouragement.
Well, they can pray, Pastor can help by talking to the couple. [This came after a further probe of how God has helped.]

She almost avoids directly reflecting on God and therefore she settles for a less threatening engagement with religion. Or it could be that religion does not feature prominently in her life, so she cannot talk of personal investment in religion, and instead circumvents the subject and responds in relation to the religious community. Elsewhere Annastasia states, "When I am not happy I cannot be comfortable. I cannot do anything. Even I cannot pray because I am not free."

This statement does point to the possibility of an inner struggle regarding religious beliefs and her experience, which is causing discomfort. Her first recounting of a childhood memory was one where she witnessed violence meted out against her mother by the father. She says:

> We loved mother more than father because dad remarried a second time, which brought lots of chaos in the family: quarrelling between the two women. Stepmother left the family to another farm. Then father left and joined the second wife. Mother was very hard working. She was a businesswoman. She had business in [town] up to-date, though little. I felt very bad when dad remarried. One day, which I never forget, we went to church all of us. We left our dad at home. When we came back we found mom beaten by dad and the other lady.

Annastasia may be struggling with the issue of the existence of God, and maybe belief in religious doctrine, but would be inclined to go with the conventional faith of not doubting the existence of God and God's power through prayer. It is interesting that her most vivid memory is of a violent incident against her mother, one that happened on a Sunday right after church. It is also notable that in her narrative, at her lowest point, a woman came by and helped her by taking her to the hospital and to WRAP. On the way, however, they did stop at a church and they went inside and prayed. However, that was the only help she received from church as opposed to the woman who takes her in and gives physical help. I cannot help but wonder if both these have contributed to her apparent ambivalence around religion.

Irene's position is not only a belief in the existence of God but also of Satan (evil spirit[2]). She states:

> I thought we were a man and wife, but I do not know how he perceived me. He did not beat me before. I just wonder where Satan came to him because he was not bad. He had even taken me to the hospital and paid the bill. We have now looked for him all over and cannot find him, even the police have been looking for him through WRAP. . . . I guess all I can now do is to pray to God.

A similar view is held by Nelly's mother-in-law who, when told of the behavior of her son, states that he must have *shetani* (Satan) in him. She

---

2. The word *Shetani* (Satan) is inter-changeable and loosely used to mean an evil spirit. In the African context, it does not necessarily point to the common place knowledge of the "devil," the opponent of God. It points to the existence of evil forces that can direct the actions and thinking of human beings. I therefore hesitate to call it Satan in my analysis and attribute a more general and encompassing meaning of a third dimension, an evil spirit world, which however is believed to be under the influence of the devil.

stated that the evil spirit must have closed his eyes so he cannot see, and he therefore needed prayers.

I also encountered this third dimension of the spirit world from Millicent, who states:

> One day we were going to the market, I told him, when you wanted to marry me, I was told that there are evil spirits that close your eyes and you could kill me. I realized that the violence was not only just directed at me, but also to the kids, whoever was at hand.

As she concluded her narrative she stated:

> I know God is there and I believe in God. But I also know that there is strong witchcraft. I even know why I am out of my home now. Jealousy!

These are just a few of the examples I use to illustrate the strength of the role of religion in piloting the lives of the survivors of violence. They also demonstrate the varying positions of belief from which people engage religion, showing how context and experience can shape such positions of belief. These positions do not always remain constant throughout one's life. What may remain in place is the fact that one has already acquired, and over the years developed, an image representation of God, the piloting aspect of Rizzuto's theory, and religious influence. A number of respondents, including Millicent and Rose, also alluded to the presence of, and belief in, ancestral spirits, evil spirits and the supernatural world. These all point to the fusion between aspects of African traditional religious beliefs and other mainline religions. The role of religion, as discussed in this chapter, takes into account these broader dimensions when encountered in the narratives.

RELIGION AS AN ORIENTING SYSTEM

Religion is an influencing reality in the lives of its adherents. I hold a basic assumption that religion plays an important role in the lives of women in intimate violence because in times of stress or trauma, people draw on orienting systems to find ways of coping. For religious people, religion or religious belief is one of these resources. While Pargament and Park (1997) refer to this resource as a search process emanating from belief systems, McIntosh (1997) refers to it as a cognitive schema already in place that can keep being reconstructed with life experiences.

Religion presents itself in various forms including symbols, social norms, ethics and mores, and traditions and values of a given culture. It finds expression through texts, formal and informal conversations, liturgy and lyrics within and without communities of faith. It is an integral part of the Kenyan contexts, beginning from infancy, where the family of origin is the greatest influence, continuing to larger and more complex contexts. Although religious rites and practices are born in social and cultural contexts, the development of representations of God in the child prepares him to incorporate social symbolism and religious appropriation. Rizzuto's statement presents a clear argument:

> From the point of view of integration to society and family (the adaptive point of view of Rapaport and Gill), religion remains one of the most regulatory structures of organized social life. If one religion disappears, new systems of belief spring up to organize the meaning of the universe at large. No man can avoid the task because as an intelligent human being, he cannot deal with a world he cannot approach with understanding. In this respect, archaeology and cultural and social anthropology have shown beyond doubt that "in his search to understand the world around him, man has gone to extra-ordinary lengths to organize his surroundings in a coherent manner, one which he could relate to his own existence" [Silverman, 1976]. From this point of view, the maturational ability of the child to form a representation of God prepares a child to link himself with cultural traditions and adapt to the type of culture in which he was born. (Rizzuto 1979, 90)

In the Kenyan context I note three main characteristics that present religion in particular traditions as available orienting systems. For the purpose of illustration in this work, the Kenyan Christian religion (which is heavily characterized by aspects of African traditional religion) will hold the main focus, although other mainline religions in Kenya, like Islam and African traditional religious beliefs, are not altogether ignored. Christianity's main presentation with reference to being a framework for gender relations is found in three specific characteristics: a) interpretations of the Bible through communities of faith; b) beliefs surrounding marital relations negotiated through mores and values that are held almost canonically; and c) an omnipotent and omniscient nature of God mediated through lyrics, informal conversations and testimonies.

Scriptural Interpretations

Communities of faith hold a very high standing in their interpretation of the scriptures through the medium of worship services. In the Kenyan context biblical interpretations reflect a highly patriarchal bias. They are historically laden with inherited and generational nuances from their Jewish origin and packaged with colonial forces that coincided with the patriarchal African culture. Saint Paul's letters to the churches in Corinth and Philippi are examples of texts that are extensively used to subdue the woman's position in society.[3] An additional text that demonstrates gender hierarchical views of the marital relationship and that are constantly utilized in marriage and counseling occasions is as follows:

> Wives be subject to your own husband as to the Lord. For the husband is the head of the wife, as Christ also is the head of the church, He Himself being the savior of the body. But as the Church is subject to Christ, so also the wives ought to be to their husbands in everything. (Eph 5:21–24)

This is one of the texts taken literally as a directive for marital relations. Both individuals and communities of faith have historically interpreted unconditional obedience on the part of the woman as a requirement of marriage. It is one of the texts I encountered from the women's narratives. Consider the following response from Annastasia:

> INT: Is there any circumstance that would make it okay for a woman to beat her husband?
>
> ANNASTASIA: I cannot say so, even in defense. Even the Bible says we have to respect the men. Because the man is the head of the house. So you cannot beat him and *mama hana nguvu kama mwanaume* (the woman is not as strong as the man).

In the pulpit, a popular interpretation of the Ephesians text is the visual aid of recognizing the physical head's position in relation to the other parts of the body to depict the configuration of a Christian family as God intended it to be: with the husband as the head, the wife as the neck (helper) and the children as the rest of the body parts. In this way the man possesses those intellectual and cognitive functions of the family, including handling of finances, disciplinary actions (which includes violence) and executive

---

3. I have in a different work discussed the use of these texts by communities of faith as authoritative definers of the role and status of women in Kenya. See Chapter 3 (Gatobu, 2003)

decisions. It is a position that also comes with the bonus "privilege" of not being accountable to any other human power with respect to family relations. The woman is depicted as the helper, indispensable especially in her role as the connection between the husband and children. She is the two-way lifeline through which the wisdom of her husband is passed on to the children and simultaneously through whom the children become a source of satisfaction and esteem for the husband in terms of his place in the society. Clearly such an analogy of a scriptural text is embedded in the cultural worldview of marital relationships with gender-specific roles of the male and the female. The text has been said not only to exemplify the perfect Christian family but also to be a guide for successfully maintaining family unity. In many societies in Kenya, this model has been used to define a "good Christian family." Indeed this interpretive model is used as the homily at the matrimonial celebration of many Christian marriages. Imagine the kind of psychological power such a model would have on the decisions a female survivor of violence has to make!

Consider two additional texts that describe marriage in religious terms:

> Then God said, Let us make man in our image, according to our likeness; and let them rule over the fish of the sea and over the birds of the sky and over the cattle and over all the earth, and over every creeping thing that creeps on the earth.

> God created man in His own image and in the image of God He created him; male and female He created them. (Gen 1:26, 27)

> Then the Lord God said, "It is not good for man to be alone; I will make him a helper suitable for him." . . . So the Lord God caused a deep sleep to fall upon the man, and he slept; then He took one of his ribs and closed up the flesh at that place. The Lord God fashioned into a woman the rib which He had taken from the man, and brought her to the man. (Gen 2:18, 21–22)

These texts are used extensively in matrimonial rites to depict the Christian origin of marriage between a man and a woman. While from a Christian perspective they may demonstrate that origin as ordained by God, their interpretations are problematic for gender relations. In the first text the man is presented as a creation of the direct image of God with overwhelming authority that subjects all the rest of God's creation including the woman under his rule. Proponents of this exegesis ignore the latter part of verse 22, which mentions the woman as part of that creation in God's image. Their arguments assert that the first part of the verse is a clear indication of the man as a creation in God's image, while the second part of the verse simply refers to God having created both male and female, not necessarily in His image on the part of the woman. This argument is made authoritative once perceived through the lens of the next text, which goes into the details of how God created the woman from the body of man, and only after realizing that the man needed a helper! These two texts literally translated from a patriarchal perspective not only strengthen the role of the woman as a helper who has to be "suitable for the man"; they also build the sacred space and define the role of the man as the one closest to God in terms of authority, wisdom, and power. While individual informal interpretations around these texts may elicit healthy diverse discussions, the same directive given from the pulpit carries Divine authority. When it is especially used for matrimonial religious rites, it becomes a frame of reference from which gender relations in marital status are defined. These texts, among others, are the basis for an immediate orienting system used by the woman who is faced with the pain and suffering of intimate violence. However, as discussed later in this chapter, similar scriptural texts have been transformational agencies just as powerful in empowering women to find comfort, guidance and strength in making decisions regarding violent relationships.

Canonically Held Beliefs

"Canonically held beliefs" (as I choose to call them) within the community are the second characteristic that points to religion as a readily available orienting system in the Kenyan context. Like scriptural interpretations, these emerge from textual interpretations and seemingly authoritative subjective opinions handed down through communities of faith and text-study fellowships, circles of family and friends, lyrics and liturgical mores, mythical norms, values and traditional virtues. Consider the following excerpts from Annastasia's narrative, which reveal examples of what I refer to here as "canonical beliefs" because of their function as authoritative guiding principles in gender relations.

> Sometime he would come so late. He would be so drunk. He couldn't even see well . . . I would advise him to buy a piece of land and build but . . . One day he told me he would be coming home early. He drunk and drunk and came back at 8:00 in the morning. Luckily his aunt had come and when I asked where he was, he just started beating me in front of the aunt. Another day a friend of mine came to visit me and found me cooking. When

I was done, I saw her off to the house and we met her husband who demanded to know where she was coming from. She explained, but he went on to beat her right in front of people. I told the man she was coming from my house. They went to verify from my husband, who said yes she was, but he started beating her in our house and my husband told him to go beat her outside his home. On the last day . . . I waited for him till midnight then I slept. I was worried and started praying. He came in the morning. As soon as I opened he started making noise that he had come and banged on the gate and no one opened. He found me breastfeeding the baby but had not fully gotten up. I reminded him he had a key. He said why did you not come looking for me. As I was trying to get out of bed, he hit me and I fell on the baby. I reminded him that the last Sunday he slept out of home and had pleaded the car had broken down, and now this. He said I had abused him and he hit me again. I started crying then he said sorry and that he doesn't know why he hit me. I said I would not be asking why he is coming late I will just be giving him his food and go to sleep.

From Annastasia's narrative, we can draw some gender relations guiding principles that are simply accepted at their face value, but which, when applied to women's experiences, elicit personal inner conflict. It seems okay for the man to come home whenever he wants and the woman has no right to ask, and if she does she is inviting trouble. In the narrative, the man's aunt does not intervene to stop him from beating his wife when she asks his whereabouts the whole night. After all, she "should have looked for him" when he did not come home, even though it seems like a pattern as she reminds him of doing the same last Sunday. When the second woman (in the second excerpt) is not home when she is supposed to be, she must explain her whereabouts and the husband alone can decide whether the explanation is plausible. Hence, no one objects when the husband of Annastasia's friend starts beating his wife in public. The above expectation of what it means to be a woman and a man in relationship might appear like individual negotiations between couples. However, I present them as general expectations in the society that are taken so seriously that they direct the response of a considerable portion of the society when society becomes a witness to violence. Millicent has a similar experience of being beaten in public. She states:

One sergeant came and tried to tell him that I only went to church and they were there with me. The neighbors tried to tell him that

I was not harlot-ing. He started daring anyone who wanted to shed some blood to come any closer and they took off. . . .

I took only Kshs. 450 from his pay to buy the child school shoes. For that I was beaten during the day outside till I almost died. It was a cinema for everyone.

What would make such expectations of gender relations so ingrained as to supersede what seems outright injustice? I believe it is their integration in the minds of the people as cultural-religious expectations with the dimensions of sacredness.

These general expectations also influence the individual female's response when she faces violence. They dictate the definition of violence by providing guidelines for what is acceptable and what is not. For instance, in response to the question of whether there were instances when the woman could be justifiably beaten, consider the following responses. Nancy, who earlier stated that no one has a right to put a mark on her, and also recognizes her husband's attack on her as totally unjustified, states

if you are dogging (colloquial for cheating on your spouse) for real and you know in your heart that you are dogging . . . if you continue dogging you know that you are going to get beaten . . . you stop dogging so that you do not get the beating . . . decide that you want to be with the person you are dogging with or stop dogging so that you don't get the beating. . . .

Further prompting on the same question draws the answer: "No . . . I do not think anything justifies beating . . . But you know people react differently . . . maybe it would have to be case by case."

Rose, on the same question of whether there is such a thing as justified violence, answers,

Yes, if for example you are found with another man, it is wrong and you can be beaten. . . . It would be okay if you are beaten in that case. Also let us say the husband has asked you to get his clothes ready when he is going on a trip. He comes and finds they are still not ready. A second day they are still there, he can take a whip and beat you. You see in that case you are looking for trouble yourself. If you did what he wanted he will look for trouble and not find it.

These two women come from very different backgrounds with regard to traditions, education, social and economic status. Yet they state the one main justifying reason that appears to be affirmed by most of the women in my study. It seems that a woman who is "dogging" is committing a socially and culturally "canonical" sin that can justify her husband beating her, even in the view of a woman like Nancy, who would normally not find it justifiable for any woman to be beaten. This view is not specifically stated in the laws, either social or religious, but is simply "known." In this way it is an integral part of the available orienting system that can be found in both cultural and religious spheres.

Such "canonical beliefs" direct the thinking of people in the context showing what it means to be a "good mother" and a "good wife" and a "good father." The beliefs are rarely questioned concerning either their value or their origin. They even spell out, in some cases, the consequences for not living up to one's part of the role, which may vary according to the social-cultural context. Millicent, in her narrative, talks of why the husband had psychotic violent episodes:

> I realized that there was something. Any time he beats me he would go to the witch. But God was on my side because somebody would always tell me they met my husband there. So I asked him why he keeps on going to the witches, and he said he wanted to know why we kept on fighting. I said it would be best if we had talked instead. I have tried to ask him what the problem was because there must be something. Only those in his family who were brought up in the town away from home had this problem. Their first born and last born who were brought up at home by uncle had no problems. The father stayed in town and beat the wife so much so that the last-born decided to go back home and stay with uncle too, as he could not take his mom's beating any more. The mother also decided eventually to leave the husband and go back to the rural home. I came to realize it all comes from home, from the mother and the brother's wives. . . . They are all jealous. They are the ones who close his eyes so he can beat me.
>
> I am almost convinced there is something they have done that they cannot stay with their wives. In our culture as [ethnic tribe removed] a person cannot fail to live well with the wife unless he has done something really bad. Their fighting is not normal. If he gets hold of a woman he is going to kill her if she does not take off.

This passage may be difficult for someone outside the culture to understand. That very fact demonstrates that the canonically held beliefs I am referring to are very contextual. Clearly the influence of the spirit world in this relationship is not just fiction but a reality that causes anxiety. Note that Millicent relates this belief, which someone from a different context may dismiss as cultural superstition of the past, to her Christian religious faith. Note also that she has definitions of what would be "normal" beatings of the wife, which the husband apparently has surpassed, leading to her decision to look into the spirit world. Her perspective of looking at her cultural religious reasoning, in conjunction with her Christian religion, is strengthened by the fact that her priest says exactly the same thing. She thus reports:

> Father [name] of Catholic Church I used to attend, called for a meeting with his [the husband's] seniors. When my husband appeared his eyes were red like flame. The Father immediately postponed the meeting and the next day traveled to our rural homeland. There he asked for our home and asked what kind of a family it was. You know, people know. He was told that the woman (meaning Millicent) is just waiting for her death, no woman survives in that family. But she has no choice, she married in it.

Satisfied with his research, the priest returned and advised Millicent to persevere as a good wife. Since the villagers had told him that the family is known for beating their women to death, I would have expected the priest to tell Millicent that she was in danger if she continued to be in her marriage. It may be noteworthy to see that the priest comes from generally the same cultural context as Millicent. My supposition is that he might have concluded from what the neighbors said that advising her to leave would be even more dangerous, especially since the man had warned her never to leave. This may also explain why, after looking at the man's red eyes, he moved to a different location, and decided that this was not a matter of deliberation with the man's employers. It required further consultation about family and the socio-cultural setting. This decision in itself speaks of some canonically held beliefs of behaviors that require, for explanation, a different framework of reference other than the purely Christian one. Both the priest and the senior officers seem to be in agreement in seeking answers beyond the conventional ones, and hence the priest travels upcountry to inquire about the family. That he takes seriously what the villagers said about the family reflects his integrative awareness of the spirit world and Christian doctrine. However, when he—a priest—communicates his advice to her, to persevere as a good wife, she is bound to see it as the rightful Christian thing to do. Her cultural beliefs have a sacred dimension and subsequently, have canonical status.

By living her role as a good Christian wife who is obedient and tries to pray for the husband and talk him out of his violence, while at the same time fulfilling her cultural role of holding onto the marriage and taking the best care of his children, Millicent believes that she stands in a better position with God than her husband does. The biblical connotation, added to these cultural values, gives being a "good wife" and a "good mother" an intrinsic value of religious worth. The roles now occupy a sacred space, which can be observed in the anxiety any differing suggestion raises in many women who express that belief. One can easily overlook the simultaneous inner conflict that emerges as the belief is stated. I followed up one of these statements:

> Millicent: You know as a woman you just can't walk out of your home. No one will understand, especially not as a Christian. In my [tribe] tradition, if you do that it will haunt you. God will even overlook the sins of your husband and have you pay for it.

> INT: So you are afraid God would punish you if you left, even after everything you have persevered through?

> Millicent: Yes! So I persevered till he himself threw me out. He told me to go out in [month]. He wrote to the air force commander with my picture at the gate that I should never go back there. On that day he brought a woman friend home he was seeing. It is okay if he wants to get another woman but not bring her to my home. Our culture does not allow that. He should leave me alone especially now with all the diseases. He should have left me with my children in my house . . . Even the Bible says if the man sends you out it is not good. If that happens though, you are not to look for other men. Jesus says that if it were he, he would stay single and that is what I am doing.

An excerpt from the interview with Lillian, another subject who is from a very different cultural background, shows that she shares Millicent's perspective:

> It is important to watch what you do with your problems because they are your burdens and you will carry them yourself. We are told in our beliefs to straighten our way so that our children are not followed by bad omen. You see in our culture, when a woman is ready for marriage, the aunt researches to see if that is a good family first. If the women or the men leave their marriages, then it is not a good home to go to.

Both of these excerpts are indeed strong examples of how the Christian religion is intertwined with cultural traditions in what many African theologians present as the contextualization of Christianity. That synthesis in itself gives the contextualization a powerful agency to become a strongly placed orienting system, even to those people who would normally not describe themselves as religious.

Nelly presents another example illustrating this contextualization of Christianity. Although she had resolved to stay with her abusive husband for the sake of her children and marital relations, this decision was affected by her traditional beliefs, which may be viewed as cultural religious beliefs. As it turned out, it was not her husband's drinking, beating, lack of provision, or any of the other many sources of dissatisfaction that caused Nelly to take a stand and leave. It was his sleeping with a woman whose husband had died and his refusal to submit to a cleansing ritual, thereby breaking what she termed a traditional taboo that led her to deny him, with dignity, his "conjugal rights." Nelly said:

> The lady that sells the *changaa* is the one who made them go because my husband would always take his whole salary there to pay for the beer. Then one time, the *changaa* woman's husband died. That day my husband slept outside. . . .I went to his mother's brother and told them what he was doing. That he was staying with a woman whose husband had died and we had a child in the home. You know in our traditions, if a man has sex with a woman whose husband has died, he cannot come and have sex with his wife. He must first be purified with herbs and take some herbal baths so that it does not affect the children. You know the children can begin to diarrhea and then die including the wife. So I was very afraid. His people came and spoke to him, but he said I was making it up. I was so afraid because I did not know why he was even breaking such a taboo.

Clearly, traditional rites and their strength in ancestral relations, which can also be argued to be part of the contents of the idealized images, gave Nelly empowerment to stand up against her husband. She could in her own way, justify leaving him, but retain a sense of self through observations of her traditional relations, giving her a psychic balance and hence a new perspective of sense of self. When, as in the above two excerpts, noncompliance with cultural expectations carries an implication of consequences for children, such a belief is doubly strengthened.

Much has been said about Kenya becoming modern and having effaced cultural traditions in favor of Christianity and other Western influences. Nelly's response to her experience, despite the fact that she regarded herself as a strong Christian, is a good example that demonstrates the very-present power of cultural traditions on people's psychic organization. Modernity has not negated the powerful cultural values and traditions passed on to us through the generations. Aspects of traditional gendered beliefs and values are powerful, and they become a very present psychic influence in the lives of many Kenyan women.

The influence of religion is a common and powerful theme in the interviewees' responses to violence, even though the interviewees could not all be categorized as knowing, without doubt, of the existence of God. The excerpts above are also very good examples of instances in which religion is seen to be an influence in the survivors' decisions to remain in abusive relationships. It is important to acknowledge that the power of most of these "canonically held beliefs" is their synthesis into "religious" beliefs.[4]

The Omnipotent and Omniscient Nature of God Presented by Orienting Systems

The last characteristic I consider is the omnipotent and omniscient nature of God as understood in the Kenyan context. It demonstrates that religion is a very present and available orienting system for the survivor of intimate violence. These characteristics of God are overwhelmingly pervasive and very powerful. They are found in the music, lyrics, and myths that play very strong roles elucidating the moods and feelings which may sway human thinking. Consider the following lyrics of a song popular within Christian circles:

> Hakuna Mungu Kama wewe (There is no God like You)
> Hakuna Upendo Kama wako (There is no love like yours)
> Hakuna Uwezo kama wako (There is no ability like yours).

There are more verses speaking of the attributes of God throughout the song.

This is the kind of chorus many people will draw strength and hope from when faced by adversity. Other songs with lyrics of this kind include:

---

4. Canonically held beliefs are, in many cases, perceived by the persons concerned and the society at large as religious beliefs, even when they cannot be traced back to any particular religious doctrine.

Ni wewe tu Bwana, ni wewe tu. (It is only You Oh Lord, when I am
in pain, in my family, for my children, for my husband etc.)

Wastahili ewe Bwana kupokea utukufu
(You alone are worthy to receive praise).

God's mightiness may also be heard in the following lyric:

He is a mighty God
Jesus is a mighty God
Everybody bows before Him, He is a mighty God

Indiscriminately, everyone bows before Him, according to this song. The lyric goes on to mention all the different groups in terms of gender, age, financial and economic status, who, when the day comes, will have to bow before God. The all-powerfulness and trustworthiness of God expressed in these lyrics reflects people's belief in God's omnipotence, whatever their circumstances. The omnipotence of God is found everyday in the kitchen, the street and in everyday conversation. People will give testimonies of what God has been doing in their lives, and in this way preserve the ripple effect of testifying about God's greatness everywhere.

The omnipotence of God is a perception I noticed in my interviews even before the topics of God and religion were brought into the interview, as when Nancy, speaking of her court victory, said,

> I was prepared for a tough court battle. You can imagine you are going to court with a lawyer of 20 years who knows his way well in the courts. But God has a way to close people's eyes and hears. When he came to court, he was blundering all over. This is a man whose life is to build good cases and he couldn't even defend himself. God just knows how to do this and fight for the rights of people.

Elsewhere Nancy stated, "You know it is only God who saved my life and I was so thankful for that."

CONCEPTUAL ANALYSIS OF THE ROLE OF RELIGION

The role that religion plays in the lives of survivors of violence is especially important because it brings insights from a psycho-religious perspective, to my three-fold research questions. Specifically, how does religion influence female formation of a sense of self? How does it influence women's appropriation and therefore understanding of violence, and how do the appropriations and understandings manifest themselves in the women's responses to violence? The discussion of the role of religion has asserted that survivors draw on religion, and that it is a powerful orienting system for women in violent relationships. In this section, I analyze, from their narratives, how they seem to have been utilizing religion in (i) coping with their experiences; (ii) making sense of the experiences; and (iii) responding/making decisions regarding the experiences. I will end with a general analysis of how this role of religion fits within my postulated psycho-social framework.

RELIGIOUS COPING IN INTIMATE VIOLENCE

My assessment is that religion is readily available and very compelling, and is a very strong presence in the coping mechanism for the survivors of violence. It also gains efficacy through ready witness by those who have experienced its power. However, my focus here is not the coping mechanisms, but the internal, transformative dynamics that take place in the psychic realms during the process of coping. However, I will first briefly discuss how survivors used religion to cope when faced with violence.

According to Kenneth Pargament and Crystal Park, "people cope with crises to maximize whatever is of significance to them," whether that be material, psychological or spiritual (1997, 44). They do so by drawing on prevalent systems available to them to generate specific ways of coping with negative events. I have made a strong case that many Kenyan women care deeply for their identity and their place society. I have also argued for a psycho-social perspective of the formation of a self among Kenyan women. That self is centered around a societally prescribed identity, and I have asserted that while she may have an integrated cohesive self, the content of the woman's psychic structure is populated with a self that is anchored in union with a significant male figure and societally prescribed gender roles and expectations. In this section, I am arguing that this content is overlaid with religious symbolism that is therefore an integral part of the psychic structures. Then, when a woman is faced with crises originating in intimate violence, religion (in all its symbolic and psychic presentation) is one of the orienting systems immediately available to her, and she can draw on it to cope and to appraise and give meaning to her experience.

Coping, schema, and attribution theories demonstrate how religion functions as a cognitive system that enables the adherent to reduce anxiety, appraise, and psychically accommodate traumatic events that would normally stretch one's sanity. In times of crisis, a person who cannot construe and make satisfactory interpretations of the world around threatens to fall apart. Geertz names three events that threaten a person's stable world, as "the limit of human analytic capacity;" "limits of powers of endurance" and "limits of moral insights" (1973, 101–8). Geertz recognizes the importance of comprehending situations in his assertion that a person's highest characteristic function and asset is conception (1973, 99). Geertz states that what becomes important at this point, whether consciously or not, is that the elusiveness of the event be accounted for in a rational and logical manner (1973, 99). Once accounted for, the threat no longer seems insurmountable and the person is able to clearly assimilate the facts of the situation and respond accordingly. This aspect of human psychology is increasingly associated with better adjustment to difficult and challenging situations. Many people turn to religion when faced by problems that challenge their worldview. Religion in many ways provides a framework from which to make sense of, or account for, such life situations, and it therefore facilitates adjustment and healing.

Like other traumatic situations, intimate violence challenges the survivor's human capacity to cope. Religion plays the important role of providing people with ways and means of coping in times of crisis—in traumatic and stressful situations in which other human resources of reasoning, power, and control are not sufficient. It can be assumed that in times of severe stress, such as intimate violence, many Kenyan women will turn to religion because of its availability as an orienting system.

Religion as an orienting system provides a special coping strategy for these women because of its association with a supernatural Deity. Religion, like coping, is concerned with seeking meaning to life (Pargament and Park 1997, 45). Geertz views the meaning-making function of religion as a fulfillment of a basic human need to find something comprehensive and interpretable about the deepest problems of human existence (Geertz 1973, 99). Earlier psychological schools of thought viewed religion negatively as a resource for coping, interpreting it as a defense mechanism to avoid confronting real life issues from the secular standpoint. I acknowledge that even in appraising a painful situation, religion can lead to negative results. A good example of a negative outcome arises when stressful events are viewed as punishment from God, or when stress is met by passively responding, in the belief that solutions are entirely from the outside of self and come from God (Pargament and Park, 1997, 47). The type of religious schema and the development level of God's image are relevant in determining the attributions one makes, and thereby the efficacy of coping which ensues (1997, 48).

Looking at religion academically as a useful source of coping does not exclude the possibility of denial and the repressive tendencies that may be associated with it. On the other hand, one cannot ignore the tremendous benefits of human psychological adjustment through the help of religion in situations that threaten the very core of a sense of self. Coping is not simply a reactive reflex to tragedy, but "is a *goal-directed process*" (1997, 44) that gives meaning to life's situations. Religious coping is definitely different from the stereotypical definitions of coping as avoidance of reality and anxiety. Through religion, people are able to comprehend the reality of the situation and thereby determine the probable challenges, losses, and other painful experiences, rather than deny their existence.

Religious resources become especially healthy when coping is collaborative. In this way, religious coping becomes a form of partnership with a Deity to "walk through" the traumatic event. This surely cannot be viewed as a form of escape from reality because it calls for the person to be co-author with the Deity in strategizing the path to be followed in comprehending the situation. Pargament and Park make this clear stating that religious coping "does not simply entail avoidance of difficult or undesirable situations" (1997, 46). It is a process that calls for the person to face the reality of the situation, but see it from a different perspective that enables a non-threatening environment of partnership with a support system.

Julie's narrative is of specific interest in determining the positive role of religion. She talks of how she used to feel guilty even for having thought of separating from her husband. Her church and the Bible preach that marriages are forever. She had walked into her marriage and had not been forced. Her mother always reminded her of that, telling her a little beating was normal for all women. After eleven years of marriage, Julie concluded that although God had ordained marriage as a lifelong institution, her husband had broken all the vows by beating her, sleeping with women and traumatizing his children. She had eventually walked out of the relationship and was at peace, knowing from her recent reading of Christian books that she was not at fault. He was at fault and was actually the hypocrite because he still went to church. Julie's case illustrates how religion acts as a catalyst in the healing of broken spirits.

Without exception, each of my respondents stated in different ways that God was there to help them when they were in need. Their positions of belief and their ambivalences regarding those beliefs varied, as discussed earlier in this chapter. Julie recounts being left on the floor on several occasions, sprawling and helpless. Either her son or another member of the family would eventually come to help her up and back to bed. She adds at the end of the sentence, "God just came to my rescue." When I asked her how that was God, when it was clearly physical help from another human being, she grew very serious, and asked me how I could not see God in the actions of her family. It was as though she was asking me, "Can't you obviously see that God sent these people?"

Nancy was even more explicit in her account of the horrible experience being left for dead. After beating her up and using a *Somali sword* to rip and disfigure her body, the husband went out of the room, locked the door from outside so no one could open it, and left town. She was left sprawling on the floor in a pool of blood with half her intestines on the floor. She could obviously not stand, but pulled herself close to the door and started banging it in the hope that one of the other family members would hear and come to her rescue. She says:

> I knew there was no way I would survive this, I was going to die. I lost consciousness and cannot explain exactly how I ended up in the hospital. I had to undergo a major whole day surgery, which no one thought I would pull through. When I came to, I just thanked God I was alive. I knew that God deeply cared for me to keep me alive.

Later, when talking about her thriving business, she says:

> I think God is there. He provides. I don't know whether these people know it. For instance when I do Tenders,[5] say of diaries,[6] I calculate, and see the costing will be 400, then I decide to make it 600 and I get it. Sometimes I just see the hand of God. I know that God is there.

These are examples of cases where attributions are made to God for help received through other human beings. The recognition of their own helplessness, loss of control in the situation, and lack of explanation for the experiences are driving factors in making such an attribution. The examples also show how religion permeates whole areas of African life (Mbiti 1971, 1991).[7]

5. "Tenders" in Kenya are competitive business bids submitted by various companies that are vying for a project.

6. "Diaries" is here being used to denote yearly recording calendars or journals.

7. Also see Allport's (1951, 3).

I heard similar expressions of God being in control of situations ut-
tered by most respondents. Lillian said, "I begun to pray as I was crying by
the roadside, and a woman saw me and came to see why I was crying," and
later Lillian attributed the woman's help to the intervention of God: "There
was no doubt God had answered my prayer," even though one could argue
that the woman came to her rescue out of general concern for a young
woman crying by the roadside. Among my respondents, attributions to
intervention by a Deity served to restore the woman's self-worth because
they were seen as assurances that God still loved them. God had not left
them alone. At their lowest moment, when they had no hope, when they
cried to God seeking to be heard, God eventually "answered my prayer" or
"pulled me through" (Nancy). From their perception, help was a reminder
that they were still cared for despite their experiences.

Scriptural texts are plausible backgrounds to some of these attributions.[8] These texts are not only important in restoring a lost sense of being
but also in revitalizing the vigor to pick up the pieces and begin anew.
The assurance that they are not alone not only brings about psychological
adjustment but also provides the energy to move on.[9] Might this be an
insight into the question of high functionality of women survivors of violence in Kenya?

The big question that emerges is why is there attribution to a Deity for
things that could normally pass as very human and coincidental? Is it to
mean that all the women are very religious? Before looking at the specific
narratives of the survivors, I wish to state that there are certain conditions
that must be present in the context for religion to be such a powerful agency
for coping: Religion must be *available, compelling* and *efficacious.* McIntosh
discusses availability in terms of building a schema "via encounters with
the environment and can be modified by experience" (1997, 172). Once
the schema has been developed, it becomes the framework from which
situations, and especially stressful ones, are perceived. Pargament and Park
state, "Those who bring an underlying framework of religious beliefs and
practices to crises are more likely to understand and deal with the situation
in religious terms" (1997, 51), pointing to similar notions of availability. I

8. Two such texts are, "Even though I walk through the valley of the shadow of
death, I fear no evil for you are with me. Your rod and your staff, they comfort me" (Ps
23:4); and "God is our refuge and strength, a very present help in trouble. Therefore we
will not fear though the earth should change and though the mountains slip into the
heart of the sea . . ." (Ps 46:1, 2).

9. An example of such a text is, "May the Lord answer you in the day of trouble!
May the name of God of Jacob set you securely on high. May He send you help from
the sanctuary" (Ps 20:1, 2).

have already established religion as readily available in the Kenyan orienting system and therefore a powerful viable personal resource.

Religion must not only be available but also *compelling* for it to be a coping resource. Religion, as Pargament and Park (1997) argue, is especially compelling in situations that are inexplicable and without other natural resources from which to make meaning. In a cultural-religious context such as that of Kenya, religious resources are more compelling than most other available resources in providing meaning for situations beyond normal comprehension. After all, religion for most people in Kenya is a way of life and is an expected recourse.

Discussing the efficacy of religion in coping, both McIntosh (1997) and Pargament and Park (1997) recognize the complexity or development of religiosity as indicative of the level of coping to be expected. For McIntosh, those to whom religion is very important possess a more developed religious schema which facilitates faster cognition, meaning-making and, hence, coping (McIntosh 1997, 178). Greater well-being or healing is associated with faster cognitive processing of traumatic events. Schema theory is most explicit in spelling out the benefits of one's capacity to appraise events quickly, making an internal logical account of them. If the person making the appraisal is a religious person possessing a "cognitive structure that includes ways of thinking about traumatic events," a faster processing of the event is facilitated (McIntosh 1997, 179). The schema may transform the reality of the situation appraised to fit an existing schema, even in the absence of the rationale for which that reality is being shaped (McIntosh 1997, 180). Such an appropriation enables comprehension and accounting for the event, which are in turn associated with better adjusting to aversive events and therefore resulting in better coping skills.

In measuring the efficacy of religion as a coping method then, psychological processes of cognition and meaning-making are important to determining the level of coping achieved: people engage different types and levels of religious resources to adjust to the coping intensity required.

I looked at the data to explore the efficacy of religion as a coping mechanism for survivors. I concluded that the level of belief with which they related to their private God is what made the difference. Consider the following: Nancy, drawing from her brother's "greater" belief, finds some protection from God.

> He was there. You know my brother is very religious. . . . He
> said even when something happened to you he (God) was there.
> That was why the intestines were not even getting infected.

However, Nancy knows she has to do some things, as in following up with the courts herself. She differentiates herself from God and can experience God thus.

Nelly, having a more direct relationship with God, contrasts God with her husband.

> God is a wonderful person. I did not know if I would ever be where I am today. All my kids are going to school, they have food, they have a place to sleep, when they are sick I take them to the hospital, and none of this is from the father. If it is not God I would not even have strength to do my small business and give them such a nice place for them which is even better than their father's right now.

Note that she personifies God and can therefore make a direct comparison with her husband. Her experiences have made her reconstruct, over a long period of time, a highly personalized God with whom she can positively relate. I can only wonder if Nelly's God has in some profound way taken the place of her husband who has failed her.

Neema, from an Islamic faith, similarly demonstrates a highly personalized God who has allowed her freedom to leave her husband when he becomes intolerable. She thus demands that he supports his children.

> I don't want to know who or what God is. He is the creator so why do I want to know beyond that? I know he is the God neither man nor woman. . . . When we were little we thought that God was a man. But when I grew up I don't care. But now I know God is the creator and that is what matters. . . . That is God's secret. Even through these troubles, I have really prayed, and God has assured me that I will get my child back. So I don't need do so much alone, except in the things I am doing to follow up to get back my child.

Irene has a less highly personalized God and draws on what she has heard more than what she knows about God. She states:

> God is the one who knows what he wants with me. (Very helplessly said.) If you are a Christian, you just need to pray hard till God helps you. Yes you can leave him even if you are a Christian. Well you could come to WRAP and I think they can help you.
>
> INT: Where do you think God was when you were going through your bad experience?

(very long silence). I don't really know. But I know God helped me because when I got beaten, I could not even hear or talk and the head was hurting so much I did not know if I would recover. [*From my journal: "almost feels like I am drawing something that is expected of every person—to believe in a God somewhere . . . not a personal conviction."*] I could not even hold the baby. But another woman in the plot would come and help. If my husband finds that I have not washed his clothes, he would just make more noise.

My supposition is that Irene is relying on an image given to her about God, but her relationship to God cannot be said to be mature and may actually be replaced occasionally by an archaic male image, hence the sudden intrusions of references to her husband in a direct question about God.

I could not tell from my data for certain whether all these women could be regarded as staunch adherents of either Christianity or Islam, the two religious traditions dominantly represented in the study. Yet all of them referenced God as being the only way they survived the ordeal on any particular day, the only strength on which they are now drawing, and the hope for their future lives

The presence of religion as an orienting system not only provides an object to which to attribute that which a woman cannot plausibly explain, but also provides a means of offloading[10] from herself the responsibility of being in control of a situation that clearly demands resources beyond her human capability. Offloading empowers her to get up and go on with life. If religion is perceived in this manner, then one does not need to be religious in the sense of strong adherence or a personalized faith to use religion as a coping system and to make religious attributions. The society and socialization itself offers religion as a stable orienting system. A more detailed argument of how religion becomes appropriated and utilized as a personal resource at different levels of religious faith and God representation is discussed below, when I map religion onto my postulated psychosocial framework.

What might differ among the respondents, in terms of turning to and using religion, is the level of intensity, or the position of belief from which they relate to their God. With regard to the position of belief or the quality of relation to God, it is important to appreciate the reality with which the believer relates to such a God (especially one with a highly personalized representation of God). Rizzuto states, referring to this, that we engage

---

10. By using the word "Offloading" I hope to emphasize symbolically the sense of relief that one would experience when she removes a heavy burden off her shoulders.

in "constant dialectic reshaping of our self and object representation to attain psychic balance" (1979, 89). If some of the experiences are beyond the normal tolerance of being maneuvered, "drastic defensive movements" might occur. These may produce symptoms like "persecutory delusions, belief in direct communication with God or of having been given a mission by him, or at a lesser level of disorganization, overwhelming guilt, conversion, religious excitement and the like" (Rizzuto 1979, 89). She goes on to say that, to the adherent, "the conscious religious experience with God will seem intensely real. It will have many qualities of a powerful interpersonal exchange between two people" (Rizzuto 1979, 90). The survivors' statements below illustrate varying intensities of the reality of their God(s) and therefore levels of belief and elicited feelings with which they engage religion in their coping strategies. Nelly's statement reflects such a tangible reality of her God.

> When I think of God, I think of how he was crucified, you know, Jesus. Sometime I have dreams of God coming for me, he brings me water. And you know I am not baptized. When I tell my mother of my dreams she says that God wants me to be baptized. . . . He wants me to be a good example to others. You know in churchwomen's fellowship. . . . Whenever I am present, they even make me like their preacher. I find things coming to me that I do not know where from and I feel a need to just say them. I find I know so much about the Bible even though I am not well educated.

Her special place appointed by God gives her a sense of self and confidence with which she can face life's other perils.

Rose's coping mechanism is her belief in the power of prayer. She also understands that one can pray effectively to God without retaining physical relationship with an abuser.

> Well he [husband] keeps on making me suffer. I am saved and I know God can do anything. My salvation can change his life. So I pray for him till he changes. You don't have to stay there but you can pray for him while you are away because if you stay there you will not even be able to pray well for him when you have no peace. Eventually you will get answers for prayers from wherever you are.

When she eventually calls him back to her house, it is not from fear that God will punish her, but to save her face in the society and traditional expectations. This is evidenced by her later statement that "I would do the same even if I was not saved." One may, however, wonder why God cannot help her with the loss of face in society. My supposition is that societal expectations, within which she is trying to "save face," are simultaneously considered as religious mandates in the traditional sense. She cannot therefore expect God to help her with responsibilities that God expects of her and which she is capable of handling.

From this discussion, it is clear that religion offers the means to cope in two main ways. First, it provides methods for people to preserve what is most important to them. If this first step is not possible, then secondly it provides methods for people to change the significance they preserve by assisting them to give up what they have lost and recreate new significant meanings for themselves (Pargament and Park 1997, 44). McIntosh argues that religion aids in coping by forming congruence with already existing schemata. This congruence, in turn, helps the person to find meaning for the event, which then facilitates a better adjustment to adverse events (McIntosh 1997, 178). Religion may serve to help a person cope and, at the same time, the coping process may reconstruct religion. In this regard, McIntosh states that traumatic events can affect religious beliefs by either reorganizing and strengthening belief systems and prior assumptions, or generating religious doubts. Pargament and Park discuss a similar notion by perceiving religion to be both an independent variable (which affects coping,) and a dependent variable (which is affected by coping) (Pargament and Park 1997, 44).

It is important to note that religion is not the only system that provides for coping. McIntosh states in this regard, "Some probably have other schemas that fulfill the same functions that a religious schema can, in coping" (McIntosh 1997, 179). Pargament and Park clearly refer to the same notion when they say, "However, not all coping is religious, for not all means and ends of coping are sacred in character" (1997, 45). Other coping techniques recognized by psychologists include, physical activities like walking or games, actively researching the issue at hand, or seeking social support.

RELIGION AS A SOURCE OF MEANING-MAKING

Despite the fact that religion, as an orienting system in the Kenyan context, is replete with nuances that disfavor women's experiences, most of my respondents turned to it to find meaning in their experiences. In a way, religion was a lens through which most of the survivors viewed the violence they experienced, and enabled them to form some understanding of it. In a sense, then, religion not only influenced the responses of the survivors, but also became a resource for the survivors' transformational agency.

The turn to religion not only opens the door to a source of help, but also to a wellspring from which to make sense of the experiences that stretch one's conception and capabilities. Religion has historically been considered to have an essential function for providing meaning. All my respondents utilized religion in some way to make meaning of their experiences. In answer to my question of whether God is still involved in her life, Irene asserts, "God has not left me. Since I came here (Nairobi) I have never really been alone. I have never fallen sick. I was even tested for [HIV] AIDS and it is negative!"

Irene's belief that God is still with her, despite her horribly violent experiences, is enough to keep her going. She mentions aspects of God's presence with her, which, although not directly related to the actual violent experience, appear to make up for any abandonment she could have been feeling.

Millicent's example invites a similar interpretation. She states:

> But God was on my side [because] somebody would always tell me that they had met my husband at the *mganga's* (witch's) place. He would never know how I knew it, but God always made sure someone I know would be there at the same time and would come to tell me."

That which could have been coincidental takes on a greater meaning, with God becoming her ally when her husband becomes deceitful. She is satisfied with this explanation and its ensuing alliance with God, and would not be troubled by the possibility that the husband may be seeking the witchcraft more often than she knows, and may even be gone to the other woman on days when no one is there to tell her.

Nancy's long process of coming to terms with what happened to her is a good example of the engagement with the Divinity to make sense of difficult situations. Listen to her engagement:

> Once you believe in Him, your decisions, everything you think about, you think through asking how God will approve it. Yes, I ask why did this happen to me, was it an accident? I read a lot about books, you know like a diamond shines best in darkness. I knew God wanted me to learn something. See? After this happened, my business went down. I wanted to leave for abroad and just move away. I changed my mind. And as if it was not

enough, I then had an accident, and was in ICU for 3 days. I was down. But I tell myself that I have learnt so much from that period than I will have done the rest of my life. Everything was moving like clockwork. If my business did not go down, I would never have known problems. Like I had worked in the bank and said this is not my life. I had ambitions, I wanted to have a house by the time I was 30. I would have taken life for granted. There was something He was trying to show me that He is faithful, he pulled me out of them, I rose up again. I can maintain myself.

Nancy's explanation for not getting infected and dying is that "when something happens to you He [God] is there. That was why the intestines were not even getting infected. . . ."

Nelly connects God's answer to her prayers to stop having disturbing dreams to her beating of her husband's other lover.

Whenever he would beat me, I would just pray for him. Whenever there was a problem, I had to pray because if I didn't it would come to me in the dream. Like the day we fought with the woman, I had been having bad dreams beating her and would pray so hard. After I beat her that day, I never had the dreams any more.

Neema is aware of her mortal limitations and therefore is happy to know that her God is available. She says:

I have no friend. My only friend is God. Allah is my creator and the creator of the whole earth. You see all these things we are bringing here to courts of law and here to FIDA, you tell God and He will answer you immediately. If God does not want to answer immediately, then [He] will not answer. See? It is God who decides if to give you wealth or not. You see since my parents died, I just look up to God to help me, day and night. . . . I don't want to know who or what God is. He is the creator so why do I want to know beyond that? I know he is the God, neither man nor woman.

Marie Fortune states that when people suffer, they ask two main questions: What is the cause or source of suffering, and what is the meaning or purpose of suffering? If the person seeks and finds (rationalizes) the source, meaning or purpose, it softens their pain (Fortune 1995, 292). In like fashion, the psalmist of the Christian Bible is very explicit in many passages that show the intensity with which search for meaning is engaged. The following text is a good example:

My God, My God, why have you forsaken me? Far from my de-
liverance are the words of my groaning. O my God, I cry by day
but you do not answer, and by night, but I have no rest, yet you
are Holy. (Ps 22:1, 2)

The psychological action of appraising a tragic event as the will of
God "allows the individual to find some sense of meaning in an otherwise
incomprehensible situation" (Pargament and Park, 1997, 47). It keeps the
battered woman going and makes the situation purposeful. As Fortune
notes, it helps one regain control of the situation by "incorporating the
experience quickly" (Fortune 1993, 293), an aspect in religious coping
theory that has been claimed to enable faster healing (McIntosh, 1997,
179). If the first step of preserving what is significant is not possible, religion then provides methods for people to change their focus by assisting
them in giving up what they have lost and in creating new understandings for themselves (Pargament and Park, 1997, 45). Making sense of,
and creating new meanings is a two-way process. Religion is drawn on
as a resource, and may give satisfactory explanations, especially for the
woman who takes the position that her belief in religion pertains to a *God*,
a Divine being who cannot be fully comprehended. Then, if she cannot
fully comprehend the situation she finds herself in, it is enough to explain
the situation in some spiritual manner that does not necessarily meet the
natural criteria of comprehension. However, most of the survivors were
not satisfied just to take religious beliefs as they were explained in the
orienting system, and apply the beliefs to their lives. They questioned religion, struggled with areas of its incongruity with their life situations, and,
in some cases, transformed it adequately to be relevant to their lives! For
instance, despite the male image of God (who should reflect the cruelty of
their male husbands,) and a system corrupted with demeaning patriarchal
values (that are unfair, given the women's experiences), the women were
able to draw on the omnipotence of God to transform their lives for justice, against these unfair systems. Despite his many male characteristics,
such a God did not take the representation of a perpetrator. God was a
friend, an ally, a stronghold, a fantasy father!

This perception raises a number of questions. Could it be that attributes from an archaic (pre-Oedipal) father image were being resorted
to, or had never been transformed from the Oedipal direct image of a
loving father? Could these idealized (maybe fantasized) images of God
be replacing the real abusive male figure in the marital relationship as
well? Could it be that, even though the women still held the male image in

idealization, the actual object of idealization had shifted from the physical male in their lives to a fantasized male? These questions demonstrate the individual personalization of each God image and socio-cultural influence, and therefore the futility of attempting to homogenize their varied responses. I attempt to engage these questions in my concluding psycho-social theoretical framework.

A highlight which surfaced from this research is that beneath seemingly hopeless situations for women in the social cultural setting of Kenya, are live, personalized human agencies[11] working to transform their situations. This insight is enormous! Surprisingly, religion may have played the greatest role in bringing about this agency. I am making a bold claim here that there are agencies even within the dominant, seemingly-accepted, patriarchal superiority. In the bid to make sense of their situations, the survivors show a strong creativity for turning what would have been a one-way informational directive relationship with God into a two-way transforming engagement with the Divine. For instance, in making sense of their experiences, the women found no perspective from which their spouses were justified in beating them. Even in the instances where some of the respondents stated that the woman could be disciplined if she was not faithful, or did not cook for the husband, they quickly qualified the statement by saying, "but why not sit down with her and talk to her about it?"(Millicent) or "but you know people react differently!" (Nancy). These clearly reveal the internal psycho-religious conflict the survivor went through in a bid to make sense of why she was being beaten.

In the end, the inability to reconcile the nature of God with the abuse from the partner surfaces in their reasoning. In this way they were also making a statement that God valued them despite the conditional worth with which violence attempted to brand them. Neema's answer reveals someone who has gone through the process of making sense of her worth with God, and who has arrived at some definite conclusion regarding a man beating a woman. She states:

> I am a Muslim. You know Islam law says you should not beat a woman. The woman is a weak sex and can be broken. If you break her she will be broken completely. So you should try to put her weaker bones together and take care of them. The Kadhi[12]

---

11. The term "Human agency" is used to capture the distinctive survival resiliency inbuilt with the human being who on the surface might appear to have accepted their fate but underneath refuses to succumbed to a status quo.

12. A powerful Muslim leader in the local community.

> can give *talaka* (divorce) if he wants on case-by-case of violence,
> even if the man does not want. Normally he will remind the
> man that Islam law does not allow the woman to be abused.

From this position, Neema is able to tell her husband, right from the out-
set of their marriage, that he is never to try and beat or abuse her. Sure
enough, when her first husband beat her, he had to make up by buying her
expensive gold, and when he continued to psychologically abuse her, she
made a decision to leave the marriage. She is at peace with her decision,
especially since she made sure she sought the blessing of the chief Kadhi,
a resource she has sought several times in her marital problems with different relationships.

Four women challenged the claims of forgiveness as held in their
orienting systems. Julie, who comes from a religious tradition that taught
her the need to confess after committing a sin, offers a clear demonstration
of this challenge. She states:

> The worst part is that after he has "thworped" (colloquial for
> beaten) me, left no food and no money in the house, the next
> day he will be confessing to the priest I don't know what. But I
> can't wait to see him stand before the throne of God and answer
> for his behavior!

This is one of those statements that could easily be dismissed and criti-
cized as assuming a passive stance and not taking initiative to deal with
the violence she is facing here and now. Much as this may be the case,
the fact that the orienting system has not deterred Julie from holding her
husband accountable to a higher standard of forgiveness reflects her transformational challenge to the system. If her voice were allowed to speak of
forgiveness in that particular tradition, it would transform the orienting
system, and therefore the church to preaching a message of forgiveness
that calls for true repentance and accountability right here on earth.

Religiously appraising their experiences seemed to give worth to
the respondents' sense of self. Although some of them stayed on in their
abusive relationships and others felt helpless about their situations, making sense of their situations religiously had many positives aspects. None
of the women felt a need to sever their religious identity. For six of the
survivors, religious participation intensified. Three of the women, prior to
their violent experiences, did not express a religious identity, then began
to get involved in faith communities. Two of the women admitted that
their experiences challenged their faith, but wanted it known that they had

not severed these religious affiliations. Five of the women consulted with authority figures in their religions, like pastors. The question that emerges is were the survivors cognitively aware of the discrepancy between the orienting systems and their own making sense of the situations, while expressing their claims, challenges and opinions on religion?. . If so, were they afraid to face the obvious condemnation of "washing their dirty linen in public" ? Or were they afraid of the criticism of their female identity as good wives and mothers? As much as I tried to draw out the answers to these questions, I did not get a satisfactory thematic answer that could explain their operating systems at large. However, my theoretical psycho-religious proposition in Chapter 6 postulates my thinking as informed by the women's narratives regarding these questions.

The survivors of violence continue to reconstruct their sense of self through engaging their beliefs and experiences concerning the Divine. Prior to their traumatic encounters, the sense of self, , was societally pre-scribed through socio-cultural and religious emphases. Some of them may have been living lives that had not required the challenge of their God image or the cultural influences that led to the shaping of that God image. With the experience of traumatic blows to their self-image, (the battering by a spouse) they now stand on the threshold of transforming not only their own sense of self and their God representation, but also the religious-cultural orienting system-the lens through which they view this intimate violence. This continued human encounter with the Divine could lead to a transformation of the orienting system and its agency from the marginal-ized to the center.

THE ROLE OF RELIGION IN THE SURVIVORS' RESPONSE TO INTIMATE VIOLENCE

Closely related to the role of making meaning of their experiences through engaging religion are the ultimate decisions the survivors made after suf-fering intimate violence. In this regard, Pargament and Park state that the religious search for significance is not just a means but also an end (Pargament and Park, 1997, 45). The survivors' reaching out to religion to make sense of their situation was in itself a sign of not *accepting* violence as definitive of their life-long contract. I listened to voices that longed, with hope and intensity, for transformation.

Although all the survivors sought for some transformation in their lives from God, the actual nature of transformation they sought (or found) manifested itself in various ways. Some of the women passively waited on God to do something by handing over everything to God's will. Irene's answer to my question about what she was going to do next is a good example:

> (long silence and second prompting before answer.) I guess all I can now do is to pray to God (long silence). . . . I don't know. I will just have to wait for God's help.

Dorcas's decision about what she was going to do next was "whatever God wills." One might wonder from where this kind of response originated? Biblical texts are one place to look.

> Vindicate me Oh Lord, for I have walked in my integrity, and I have trusted in the Lord without wavering. Examine me Oh Lord and try me. Test my mind and my heart. For your loving kindness is before my eyes and I have walked in your truth. (Ps 26:1, 2)

> Do not fret because of evildoers. Be not be envious towards wrongdoers. For they will wither quickly like the grass . . . Delight yourself in the Lord; and He will give you the desires of your heart. Commit your ways to the Lord, Trust also in Him, and He will do it. (Ps 37:1, 2, 4)

Another example of a text that could enable a survivor of violence to hand over the reins, and sit back is the following:

> Hear my prayer of God Give ear to the words of my mouth. For strangers have risen against me. And violent men have sought my life. They have not set God before them. Behold God is my helper. The Lord is the sustainer of my life. He will recompense the evil to my foes. Destroy them in your faithfulness. (Ps 54:2–5)

As Fortune (1995) rightly notes, such a recognition of suffering discourages the survivor from confronting the real source of her abuse. However, utilizing attribution theory to investigate the response of most intimate violence victims who remain in abusive relationships, one may find that attributing the suffering to the will of God, or as a form of punishment for past sins, may be the victim's way of making sense of her suffering. When current suffering is explained as the will of God and the result of one's own past behavior, one is, in reality, avoiding the acknowledgement that a particular person is indeed responsible for the suffering. Similarly, it may cause the person to give up taking any measures to change her own situation by relinquishing it to God. These attributions may then translate to the victim's decision to stay on in an abusive relationship, either hoping for a miraculous intervention from above, or trying to adjust to the violence as deserved. Fortune challenges Christians to follow Jesus' example of transforming the suffering experience, rather than just explaining it away superstitiously. According to her, suffering at the hand of a spouse in intimate violence should certainly be differentiated from Christ's suffering on the cross, which had a redeeming purpose (Fortune 1995, 294).

Schema theory may interpret such a response as an assimilation of the event of abuse into an already existing schema within the person, a scema that has developed from this witness of prolonged violence. The violence may also be appropriated into a schema of a religious belief that 'nothing happens to a person without a purpose.' The response of the person in the latter view may be evidenced by the person's search for a rational meaning that relates the suffering to the wider world. Such a person may view the suffering as severe, but also deserved. Tolerance in such a relationship now takes on a new shape—either energy is directed toward changing one's behavior (if the belief is that she is the reason for the suffering), or a passive stance is assumed in the belief that the suffering is beyond one's control. These examples illustrate a cognitive account for the religious role in human behavior. They also demonstrate how religion can shape behavior negatively (the abused does nothing to change the intimate violence) to the detriment of one's health. But, as discussed above, the negative aspects of religion should not cloud religion's multitude of positive influences.

Yet this same text from Psalm 54 may be transformed very differently to be empowering to other women, as was the case with a number of my respondents. Julie, for instance, was content to believe that, despite being out of relationship with her husband, she was justified in the eyes of God. She states: "He is the one to be judged for his hypocrisy, not me. I have been faithful and I have tried my best to keep this family together." What we are hearing through Julie is the transformation of her belief that the same God who ordained her marriage as a life-long contract, also understands that she has tried everything to be a good mother and wife, but has not been respected for holding her end of the deal. God will therefore continue to look out for her favorably outside of marriage, giving her the desires of her heart if she continues to be faithful in her Christian walk.

Angela's statement below recognizes the mightiness of God and God's all-powerful status that is beyond her human power.

> Are you forgetting where our help comes from? It is from Him
> who is up there. The Bible says, "Cry to Him and He will surely
> not forsake you."

But she does forget that she still is a significant player in her situation. If anything, God is a "help" to her efforts, and therefore a winning ally. Her response is one that I perceive as resulting from "collaborative coping." She has other allies, such as FIDA, who are physically helping with the process of her court battles, but they take a second place to "Him up there." With this conviction she is ready to take on the task of being an active player in changing her life.

Some of the other women took action by seizing the opportunity that "God had presented to them" to break the cycle. Consider Rose's statement below:

> I may not have fulfilled what I wanted to be a doctor, but God
> has brought me to this school. This is my vision. It is something
> I can personally do and say it is my vision.

Some of the women pointed to the incongruity of their husband's pretentious religiosity. They openly challenged their husbands' credibility before God either directly or through friends and family. Millicent's statement is revealing of such a challenge. She states:

> I asked him how he could go to mass and confession to the
> Father and then beat me in front of the children for no reason.
> It is a shame and that is why I say you cannot mix witchcraft
> and Christianity.

Millicent presents a good example of someone who, even after making what one would call a decision, finds that peace with it does not come immediately and easily. In her earlier engagement, as she challenged the incongruity of her husband's behavior, she seemed to have been making positive progress towards detachment of a self from the instability of her husband. This excerpt, which comes after the first, *seems* like a setback:

> Even now I am out of home, I am not happy because sometimes
> when my children tell me that sometimes there is no food and
> when they ask him for money he says there is nothing. Some-
> times they will look for money themselves, buy some food cook
> and eat and wash the dishes. If he comes and asks if there is food
> they will ask him, did you give any money? He would then be
> quiet. It makes me feel pity on him and I ask them, "Won't you
> make my husband grow so thin?" They say that is his problem
> after all he has money to go and drink right after.

While Julie's peace and comfort are so evident in her face and voice because of the decision she has made, Millicent, having made what, on the surface, looks like a decision similar to Julie's, continues to struggle with issues of societally prescribed identity, and a sense of self that finds expression in union with her husband. They both are drawing on the same religious orientation in making these decisions, but clearly the level of the undercurrent energy defining their sense of self, the alignment of their God images and the role given to them by the society result in significant differences. The difference between these two demonstrates how developmental backgrounds, the psychic formation of a sense of self, and the idealized superego content can be the determining line between how individuals respond to traumatic situations despite drawing on a similar orienting system. Even more specific is how strongly cathected we are to these psychic structures (in other words how strongly is one willing to hold on to them for one's own sense of survival?). Even though on the surface orienting systems may be similar (for instance have the same religious tradition and the same cultural context), the way these systems are handed to us is critical. Experiences, the channel for the orienting systems, and household influences are key.— The importance of the channel through which the text has become part of the religious orienting system cannot be underestimated with regard to ultimate decisions that survivors of violence make. The question is who presented the text, under what circumstance was it presented and if gender sensitivity was anywhere in the consideration as it was interpreted? In short, what was the medium?

Religion is thus ambiguous and multi-faceted in relation to abuse, coping, and transformation, and various questions arise. By referring to a Deity's help or his presence in their suffering, is the person resourcing the strength of the Deity to "walk through" the traumatic situation? Or is the person, in reality, avoiding handling the situation by handing over her emotional and cognitive responsibility to a higher power? What religious schema does the person hold in regard to the phenomena? Delineating these with clarity informs not only the sense of self of the person but also gives an insight into the content of her psychic structures and representations of God.

7

An Interpretive Model for Understanding Survivor Response to Intimate Violence

INTRODUCTION

The purpose of this chapter is to add new perspectives and concepts that have emerged from my critical examinations of the research data within the postulated framework. As a step towards making these perspectives applicable for interventions in intimate violence, I propose some areas for effective management of the situations, and then a model for understanding the socio-cultural and religious context in which the violence is taking place. I begin by summarizing my book claims so far.

In Chapter 4, in an expansion of Kohut's theory of the formation of a cohesive self, I postulated a theoretical framework for understanding female formation of self in collective cultures. I argued that this theoretical framework must incorporate social, cultural, gender, and religious aspects that are not explicit in Kohut's theory. Four major adjustments were made to Kohut's theory, putting forward a perspective from which females' development in collective cultures may be understood. The four adjustments are: (1) gender-specific messages, (2) multi-parent influences, (3) religious influence in the development of a sense of self and (4) on-going interactional communication between psychic structures. In turn, these adjustments affect theoretical postulations of the female development of identity and a sense of self in four ways.

First, gender-specific messages affect the content and nature of maturational pressures by expanding their form from the basic needs of an infant (breast, holding, etc.) to include messages that the child experiences on a daily basis. The phenomenological interpretive approach employed to understand the survivors from their own perspective makes it possible to understand the phenomenon of violence in a contextualized holistic way. Such a methodology calls for the inclusion of other communal influencing factors in understanding the development of a sense of self.

Second, multi-parent influences affect the nature of the idealized imago. In Kohut's theory, the idealized parent imago is primarily premised on the immediate parents. I proposed an added dimension of "multi-parent" imagos which function in a collective society where caretakers beyond the biological parents are involved in the rearing of the child and have, therefore, considerable influence on the person's sense of self.

Third, religion is introduced into Kohut's framework as an influencing agent in the formation of a self right from the beginning of a child's development through adulthood. Major religious influences occur in a person's formation and transformation of her God representation in childhood and her engagement of religious sentiments in life issues through adulthood. This aspect is especially pronounced in a context where religion and all its symbolism are a major part of the orienting system.

Fourth, the psychic structures of the Grandiose self and the idealized imago in Kohut's theory largely develop along independent lines until their integration, which begins in the pre-Oedipal phase and culminates in adulthood. In later works, Kohut mentions a larger amount of interaction of the psychic structures (1978, 441–44; 456–57). In this proposed perspective, I emphasize continual communication and interaction between the primary psychic structures and the newly theorized intermediary structures, thereby influencing and feeding upon each other.

Critically engaging these adjustments to Kohut's theory and their corresponding theoretical influences, I reformulated a contextual and gender-sensitive framework, which implied the possibility of further insights into the female formation of self. Specifically, these are that (1) females found Grandiosity when executing gender roles rather than when pursuing self-achieving endeavors, and (2) specific gendered messages may work in conjunction with multi-parent idealized imagos and religious influences to further form a hierarchy of intermediary psychic structures representing the Deity, the male, and the female, along Kohut's idealized imago's line of development. These may be a possible result of the girl child's conflicted self-mirror, and the gendered aspects of the community.

This formation, I maintain, is likely to occur in a female's development during the idealization of the parent imagos, the transmuting of ideals, and the formation of a moral agency or the super-ego. I have further postulated that these psychic structures are hierarchically aligned depending on the individual's perspective of her place, the male's place, and the Deity's place in society. Grandiosity in gender roles and specific gendered messages in turn influence the values and guiding principles transmuted from the multi-parent imagos into the super-ego.

I use this adjusted theoretical framework as an investigative lens to find out what understandings female survivors of violence in Kenya hold regarding their experiences. Their narratives revealed a number of concepts regarding their development of a sense of self and subsequent response when faced by intimate violence in their lives.

In this chapter, I present an integrated model of intervention in intimate violence in Kenya and draw implications for other broader contexts. In other words, I take the framework postulated in Chapter 4 a couple of steps further to incorporate the women's voices by (1) adjusting the framework as informed by the experiences of Kenyan women and (2) postulating a theoretical framework that addresses a range of female responses to trauma as informed by the survivor's narratives. Emerging concepts from the narratives have provided a basis by which to analytically engage, inform, challenge, and reformulate the theoretical framework, thereby adding the voices and experiences of the survivors to the framework. In a sense, then, this framework for understanding the formation of a sense of self appropriates social, cultural, and gender aspects, as well as religious influence, in the integration of female self-cohesiveness. Such an understanding is essential, since intimate violence cannot be effectively addressed if one does not take into consideration the worldviews, emotions, and psychic mechanisms that emanate from the survivors' sense of self developed and embedded in their context. A number of scholarly contributions will be analytically engaged to strengthen my arguments.

Analytical engagement with the respondents' narratives reveals new and interesting facets to female identity development. The Grandiose self-structure that was postulated as being puffed up by execution of gender roles acquires an added characteristic, that of a Grandiosity acquired through union with a male. In the face of intimate violence especially, this configuration of the Grandiose self has ripple effects to the rest of the theoretical framework that may be compared to Bulhan's work (1985), *Franz Fanon and the Psychology of the Oppressed*, although in a very different context and with different phenomena.

The concept of a highly idealized male imago has been discussed in detail in Chapter 5, and I would like to highlight how such idealization interacted with the Grandiosity of my participants. A profound sense of finding fulfillment in marital or associational relations with a male came across very strongly. Because of idealization of the male imago, many women excused their male partners' behaviors even when it was apparent that they detested their experiences of violence, especially since the very people they held with high expectations brought about their pain. It may be concluded that a strong and powerful hold onto an idealized male imago was present. It appears that the more a female idealized the male figures at a very early age in life, and the more the gender messages spoke to her Grandiosity by fulfilling gender roles, the more she needed to be associated with a male to fulfill her need for Grandiosity in adulthood. Although she might find other Grandiosity fulfillment in executing her female roles of nurture, kindness, love and care, the very character of these roles required her to be in service to, or in relationship to a male. In themselves, the female roles do not command as much Grandiosity and self-achievement as the male roles. They may be idealized because of the importance attached to them through gendered messages, but the essence of these roles depends on their servitude relationship to the males. Such psychological configuration would have the effect of requiring the female to idealize the male figure as superior.

Furthermore, those who are fulfilling these roles (female care-takers), and who have therefore, been mirroring them to the female child, are not treated in the way that would allow their continued reverence and idealization by the child. Instead, the girl experiences an inner conflict between her idealization of imagos and her need for self-Grandiosity. If she does not get praised for her other achievements (which in Kohut's theory would work to make her hold onto a primary narcissistic Grandiosity), there is a likelihood that she will very dearly hold onto the sense of Grandiosity found through being connected to the more superior male figure. Hence, she is likely to hold onto her Grandiosity in later childhood where she finds esteem through association with a male image (a significant physical male, or male-associated characteristics).

Because of this new insight informed by the women's narratives, I rename this second permanent psychic structure pertaining to female development of a sense of self as "male unionized Grandiose self." The structure thus denotes the psychic need for identification with the idealized male to sustain her Grandiosity. This insight has direct implications on the female cohered self. It is a cohered self that substantially differs from Kohut's notion of a healthy cohesive self, which would consist in a well-developed ambition drive emanating from the Grandiose self and a well transmuted moral guide developed via the idealized imagos. Hence, for a female in collective contexts, her central drive is developed on Grandiosity reliant on some male association. Her moral guide, on the other hand, is developed through conflicted idealized imagos (females) that find more praise for execution of gender roles than for their own social standing. I make this observation following Kohut's argument that,

> Form and content of the psychic representation of the idealized parent thus vary with the maturational stage of the child's cognitive apparatus; they are also influenced by environmental factors that affect the choice of internalization and their intensity. (1978, 432)

Furthermore, the significant gender roles (mother and wife) are in some way connected to being in association with a male, thereby enhancing the psychic need to be in identification with a male. Consequently, the cohered sense of self that culminates in adulthood is, for most females, likely to reflect a self organized around gender roles and identification through idealized males rather than a well-developed ambition and moral guide.

THEORETICAL FORMULATIONS REGARDING SURVIVORS' RESPONSE TO VIOLENCE IN KENYA

I sought to understand the various responses by mapping the onset of intimate violence trauma onto the theoretical framework that now has the adjusted aspects from the context. My interpretations of the survivors' responses may be summarized through two general findings from the women's narratives. First, the women's narratives brought about the realization that the alignment, contents, and configuration of the psychic structures do not remain static. The alignment of these intermediary psychic structures can shift depending on one's experiences in life. Hence, while holding constant Kohut's two major permanent structures as modified to the Kenyan context (male unionized Grandiose self and multi-idealized parent imagos), life experiences within specific contexts can adjust the contents or reshape and re-align the psychic structures.Second, the survivors' experience of intimate violence challenged their sense of self, requiring a re-configuration of self, which in turn influenced their range of responses to violence.

In the following discussion I attempt to map onto the theoretical framework the contextual and experiential aspects of females' formation of a sense of self and the understandings held by the survivors regarding violence. I call this framework a "Context- and Gender-Sensitive Theoretical Framework for Understanding Female Formation of a Sense of Self and Response to Intimate violence in Kenya." This framework represents my approach to the three research questions whose answers I summarize in Chapter 8, from my interpretations of the research data. A true testing ground for these formulations would require a longitudinal study, which is beyond the scope of this book.

CONTEXT- AND GENDER-SENSITIVE FRAMEWORK FOR UNDERSTANDING FEMALE IDENTITY FORMATION AND RESPONSE TO INTIMATE VIOLENCE

The psychological cohesiveness of the woman encountering intimate violence faces a greater challenge than that of the average female in Kenya. Her sense of self is in continuous danger of fragmentation for two main reasons, which may be traced through Kohut's two structural psychic lines of developments: the multi-idealized, conflicted mirrors of self imagos that lead to instability, and the traumatic experiences produced by male unionized Grandiosity.

Multi-idealized Conflicted Mirrors of Self Imagos Lead to Instability

The sense of self aligned through the functions of the gendered multi-idealized imagos, and therefore the super-ego, in the Kenyan context is not a stable ground. This is particularly so when one considers that, rather than developing through what Kohut theorizes as normal maturational disappointments of the idealized parent imago, the structure has been established through life experiences by conflicted mirrors of the self (multiple female care takers) and messages that speak to societal expectations of being an acceptable woman. The female is presented with life challenges through education, household roles, division of labor along gender lines, imbalanced opportunities for economic growth, and, eventually, violence in her life.

Violence intensifies any conflicting feelings she may have regarding her God representation, her male imagos, and the ideals held up to her as a woman of worth. Theoretically it would seem that she might constantly question both the ideals that were held up to her as a young child for identity formation and her present experiences of violence inflicted by males whose imagos she has held in high regard and idealized. Simultaneously, she might also be questioning and dialoging with her God imago regarding God's relevance in her life. Violence thus challenges and puts to question the Divine representations she has held. It may be inferred that, as she tries to make meaning of her experiences, her psyche would struggle to reconcile the almost personified Divine and the ideals held up to her.

The resulting God representation is one that is more highly personalized. Her God representation has gone through the rigors of being made sense of and helping with her coping process, and has therefore been reshaped to be most relevant to her life. The survivor's God has had to become very real, be denied, or be made relevant, in contrast to the God of another person who has never gone through a rough time in life requiring her to really seek God in her reality. The resulting God of the survivor of intimate violence (if God has successfully remained in the life of the abused) may most likely continue to have some especially physical male features (Schafer's (1968) immortality of object) but, more importantly, God will also have female attributes of being kind, caring, loving, and forgiving. These can now be positively mirrored in the self-imago, where they would have the likely effect of re-aligning the intermediary psychic structures. In the new alignment of the gendered intermediary psychic structures, God still emerges as the highest in quality and omnipotence. Next in the hierarchy of alignment, however, could either be both male and female. More likely, there will be a psychic placing of the female closer to God because she now possesses characteristics that are God-likened. The male imago may have lost some footing because of his agency as a traumatizing self-object. The power of re-alignment may be evidenced as an elevated self-esteem and restructured sense of self, empowering the survivor to seek alternative fulfilling avenues in spite of any perceived failure in her wifely and motherly roles. As these three psychic structures, namely the deity imago, the male imago and the female imago, continue to transmute and re-internalize their values to the super-ego, the cohesiveness of the person is adjusting positively. The gender roles, for example, may decrease in their nature as "do's and don'ts" and may therefore not hold the power of judgmental obligations. The super-ego may assume its authentic tension-regulating function, if it is not too strongly cathected to the childhood gender role ideals. In this respect, religion is deemed as a powerful agency for transformation.However, if religion does not function as a transformational agency and continues to inform the survivor of her low status in the psychic hierarchy, the survivor may continue to depend totally on God to help her out of the situation and therefore not make any transformational adjustments.

The possibility of realignment of the psychic structures not only changes the configuration of the framework; it also opens a whole realm of possibilities for self-cohesiveness, giving even further insight into the survivors' responses to intimate violence. These responses are best understood after having considered the simultaneous effects of intimate violence, which are taking place in the psychic structures along the second line of development, because the counterpart Grandiose-self line of development is in simultaneous communication with the idealized imagos, and has effects on the level of integration and therefore cohesive adjustment of the person.

Male Unionized Grandiosity Produces Traumatic Experiences

The sense of self, emanating from a male unionized Grandiosity is also in disarray in the case of intimate violence because that significant male from whom the survivor derives unionized Grandiosity has been the source of traumatic painful experiences. The more this happens, the more that "self object" becomes undesirable. Theoretically, it would seem that there ensues a constant struggle to re-organize and re-negotiate the unionizing self-object, which may result in one of three main scenarios.

In the first scenario, strong cathexis to the male unionized Grandiose self may inhibit transformation so that the real life male (source of pain) is repressed, but the survivor continues to relate to him (in real life) as though he were the idealized imago (Diagram 4:2a). Such a configuration may affect the ability of the survivor to accept reality and hold her abusive partner responsible. She may continue to express her dissatisfaction in the relationship and hate the abuse, but find ways to live with it because of her psychic need for this union and/or because few, if any, social options exist for her outside of marriage and motherhood. When the relationship is viewed this way, the practice of finding excuses for the brutality of their partners that reside outside the person himself, like alcohol, friends' influence, and work pressures, is not surprising. The survivor may continue to express feelings of low esteem, depression, ambivalence towards God and achievements, coupled with intruding needs to be in unhealthy relationships with a man. These would inhibit sufficient integration of Grandiosity into the rest of her personality, thereby affecting her general creativity and productivity. Similar sentiments are displayed in Kohut's sample of patients who on the surface may appear cohesive but lack the zest for life. He gives the example of Mr. A whose self-esteem was very vulnerable to simple criticism or absence of praise. Kohut states that though this patient was "a man of considerable intelligence who performed his tasks with skill and creative ability, he was forever in search of approval" especially from men he associated with. Kohut, traces these disturbances to the patient's earlier relationship with the father whom he alternately idealized and trusted with his fantasies and expectations, but who subsequently was a great disappointment to the son.(1978, 482–83).

Kohut also mentions "increasing scope," refinement and deepening of empathic capacity" as outgrowths of therapeutic mobilization of the analysand's "frozen archaic narcissism" (1971, 300), hence classifying faulty empathy to a pathological disturbance. Kohut's perceives empathy as "a tool" limited to its role "of gathering psychological data" (Kohut 1971, 300). Kohut states "if empathy . . . begins to replace the explanatory phases of scientific psychology . . . then we are witnessing a deterioration of scientific standards and sentimentalizing regression to subjectivity . . ." (1971, 301). Though Kohut has in mind the use of empathy in the field of psychology and from the perspective of the analysand, I see, in the Kenyan context, a connection of his postulations in the response of survivors of violence to perpetrators of violence. Kohut states that faulty empathy can be ascribed to the early mother-child relationship especially her absence, withdrawal or coldness (1971, 301). In the case of survivors of violence, I have established that for the female child the female idealized imagos are conflicted mirrors due to the child's lack of admiration for the female caretakers. There is the likelihood of hypercathexis and fixation redirected to the male (the opposite of her conflicted mirror) imago and therefore greater idealization of the male. It may be inferred following this line of thought that the survivors of violence are likely to have unconsciously developed faulty empathy towards their abusers, so that it psychologically distorts their comprehension of the reality of their experiences and supports their non-factual explanations. I suggest that their unrealistic explanations for their abusive male partners' behavior are an unconscious use of faulty empathy towards their abusers. Such faulty empathy is for the benefit of her own narcissistic cohesion.

The second scenario, the survivors' transformation of their failed unionized male figures—may be manifested by their finding other fulfilling activities that fuel their Grandiosity (Diagram 4:2b). These newly found fulfilling engagements might originate as a replacement for the unionized male in the form of male-associated careers and vocations. Strong examples of such a substitution include vocations and professions in areas where the survivor may have experienced successes in the course of her life. When these engagements are a replacement for the psychic need of a unionized male, it would not be surprising to find that they reflect characteristics of traditional male-oriented vocations and careers.

The third scenario—transformation of male unionized self-Grandiosity—may manifest through orientation to socially prescribed female roles that have been redeemed from being inferior by the reconfiguration of the hierarchy of psychic structures. Examples of this manifestation in my sample are the many cases of survivors who found empowerment through their children and turned their energetic investments away from male idealization. Although fulfilling a gender role expectation on the surface, energetic investment in children in this new configuration loses its obligatory nature and takes on a new meaning that drives the individual to want to change her present circumstances. The redemption of female roles is more likely if female attributes of the survivor have now risen in rank to become godly attributes in the re-alignment of psychic structures. In this way the roles would attain a godly status, which in turn reflects on the survivor and has the effect of empowering her. While this status balances the psychic needs, the archaic related imagos (of a male with whom the woman greatly needs a union) may continue to intrude into the arena of the process of new birth of a sense of self, causing guilt, mild occasional depression, or dissatisfaction as part of the process. If a new private, highly personalized and reconstructed God representation (in the idealized objects hierarchy) approximates the image continuing to be offered by the society (religious orienting system), then such an image may become well-integrated into the self-Grandiosity structure (Diagram 4:2c). This modified God representation has the effect of creating a positive reflection of God's attributes to the woman's self through her sense of a personal relationship with the god image, thereby providing an impetus for self-esteem. Such re-configuration enables the female to be more confident and believe in herself or be hopeful of a change of situation.

In any case, the resulting cohesive self, portraying a modified self-image through God representation, or the turn to male careers and/or empowerment through redeemed female roles, falls within a spectrum of a fairly integrated sense of self. To apply Kohut's words specifically to this situation, the "infantile Grandiosity [that previously depended on female union with a male] becomes gradually built [or redirected] into the ambitions and purposes of the personality and lends not only vigor to a person's mature strivings but also a sustaining positive feeling of the right to success" (1971, 299). A possible diagramming of such a sense of self of my survivor sample in Kenya, though, would show a continuum that allows great integration of sense of achievement and moral guidance in the median and, on either side, varying levels of occasional intrusions of guilt and depressive moods on one hand and tension-generating structures of a narcissistically held super-ego on the other. This representation recognizes the fact that it is part of being human not to always be in high spirits, however well integrated we are. We have moments of mild depressive intrusions and of guilt tensions from a sense of temporary failure to reach our ideals. Kohut recognizes this human way of being in his statement that,

> Under favorable circumstances, the neutralized forces emanating from the narcissistic self . . . become integrated into the web of our ego as a healthy enjoyment of our own activities and successes and as an adaptively useful sense of disappointment tinged with anger and shame over our failures and shortcomings. (1978, 440)

A constricted self in my theoretical framework would present itself in two main ways: (1) an insufficient integration of Grandiosity structure, which may manifest as lack of self-motivation, ambition and creativity; persistent guilt and depression; and a general failure to thrive with Kohutian empathy or creativity in her given circumstances, and (2) a non-transmuted super-ego, which continues to function as a tension-generating, judgmental and legalistic psychic agency. These may be caused by a strong psychic need or cathexis to a unionized male Grandiosity or by traumatic maturational pressure characterized by very discriminative gendered messages leading to a chronically injured narcissistic self.

In Diagram 4, I have attempted to illustrate the above theoretical adjustments and likely responses by female survivors to intimate violence. It generally illustrates the possible avenues that a female in a collective context would take to regain cohesion from a threat to the fragmentation of self, posed by intimate violence.

DIAGRAM 4

Intrusions of Archaic grandiosity | Well integrated self | Tension - regulating super-ego

Values transmuted to super-ego

Highly personalized image of God mirroring female values creates positive sense of self & replaces need for male identification

GOD
- Omnipotent
- Caring, loving
-Nurturing
-Kind

FEMALE

MALE
- Physical power
-Violent, unkind
-Social status

Reflection of self through God

-Vocations
- Careers
-Religious morals

Repression of real male –lives with ideal male

Male attributes still a function of the self, though she values female

Male idealization too ingrained to find clear sense of self

TRANSFROMATION

←— **TRAUMATIC INTIMATE VIOLENCE** —→

Grandiose self- by fulfilling gender roles

You are admirable, because your attributes & gender roles are similar to God's characteristics.

Idealized multi-parent imago

Gendered Maturational Pressures

I = YOU

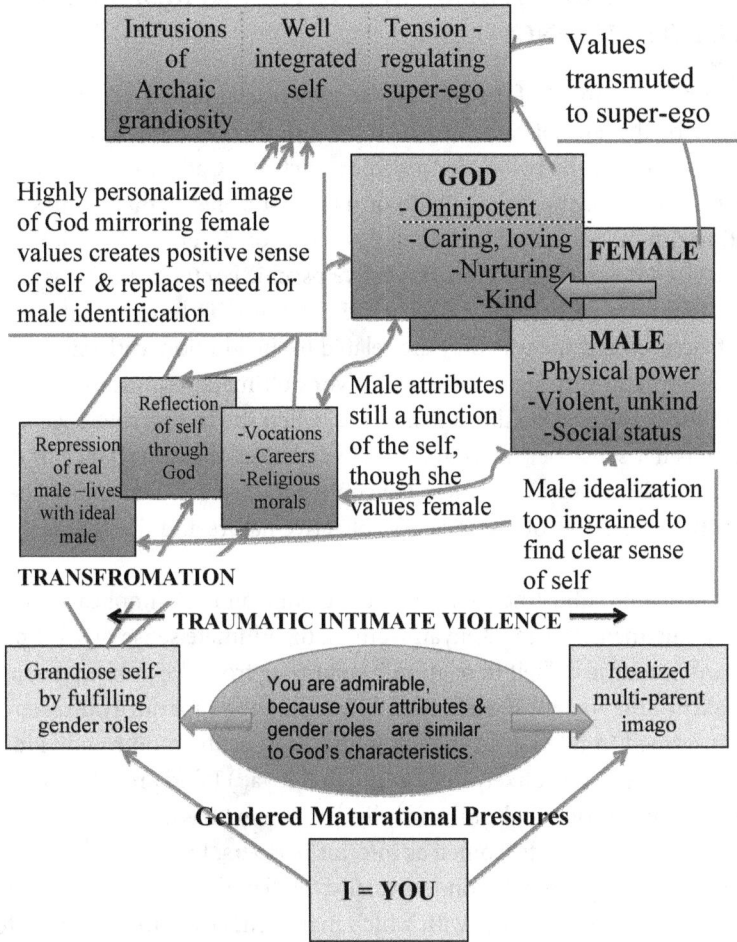

DIAGRAM 4: Gender and Context Sensitive Theoretical Framework for Understanding Female Survivors Response to Intimate Violence

It should be borne in mind, however, that the transformations proposed above depend largely on the level of cathexis, which the survivors, through developmental formation of a sense of self, attach to the psychic structures. The following section on cathexis will aid in understanding the responses of the survivors interviewed for this book.

IMPORTANCE OF CATHEXIS IN RELATION TO RESPONSE TO INTIMATE VIOLENCE

A major determinant of the response to violence, as discussed above, appears to be the level of cathexis which the girl, then woman, has, over the years, invested in the two major psychic structures. Cathexis, in this work may be defined as the strong libido or narcissistic energy that defines the relationship of the female with the self-objects of either idealized imagos or the Grandiose self and their respective psychic contents. Cathexis is of utmost importance because it is what ultimately establishes the contents of the structures and the way they are related to. In addition, cathexis to the psychic structures determines the survivor's ultimate response, irrespective of the configuration that a female has, when she faces a challenge that threatens her sense of self, as in intimate violence. The importance of the role that cathexis plays in the Kenyan contexts is clearer when approached from the perspective of the society's collective nature and the subsequent sense of self.

Given the adjustments to Kohut's theory and the implications of those adjustments for the Kenyan woman, the ultimate sense of self I put forward is a sense of "self in relation,"[1] stemming from the profound communality of the society. Even though I recognize the superiority of a sense of self formed in relation to the other and its benefits to both individual and society, (as is most likely to be found in Kenya,[2]) I find problematic the way the Kenyan socio-cultural and religious context has called on females to form a self that posits women as inferior partners. I recognize the self's vulnerability to fragmentation, especially the female sense of self, given the unhealthy strong energy with which many females in Kenya assign to gender roles and expectations. The gendered facets that make the females

---

1. Where great emphasis is placed on individuation and differentiation, with very clear boundaries in the formation of a psychologically mature self, a self in relation is one that allows permeability of boundaries. Feshbach et al. (1996) acknowledge that such a self is not necessarily poorly integrated, as indicated in their statement that "Loss of self boundaries need not necessarily be maladaptive; it may entail a widening of self to include others" (271). I recognize that a "self in relation" is a phrase widely used in some psychological literatures, such as that of the Stone Center in Wellesley, MA. I am not attempting to engage these other theoretical formulations.

2. A sense of self in relation fulfills a human need to be in relation. In most African contexts, as already discussed in Chapter 3, such a sense of self acts to unite communities, gives relevance to families and defines the responsibility of adults to children and vice versa.

form selves that are highly vulnerable to fragmentation and abuse need to be addressed.

To demonstrate these gendered facets that I conceive as problematic, I would like to take a closer analytical look at the notion of cathexis. If either or both the idealized imagos and the male unionized Grandiose self are related to with high levels of cathexis, a pathological psychic configuration similar to that theorized by Kohut is likely to occur. According to Kohut, the child retains these self-objects in their archaic forms if the maturational pressures are traumatic. The female who has had a traumatic challenge as a child through realization of her place and obligations in society may, as I have argued, invest enormous energy towards these objects, resulting in a strong cathexis that may take one of three forms.

The first possibility of strong cathexis is that three hierarchical idealized multi-parent imagos—of God, of male, and of female—are retained in their archaic forms of stereotypes. God is therefore supernatural, omnipotent, unquestioned, judgmental, removed and un-engaging. The male is strong and of high status, is intelligent and rational, makes a great leader, and has the right to impose discipline. The female is good if she is conforming, nurturing, obedient, and submissive. When integrated into the super-ego in their primary form, these traits become do's and don'ts that cannot be questioned. The super-ego structure increases psychic tension in the face of the female experience of violence rather than promoting tension-regulating or tension-reducing functions.

The second possibility of strong cathexis is that, in conversation with the above stereotypes of male and female, the male unionized Grandiose self continues to be related to in its archaic form. Hence, if a significant male is inflicting intimate violence, the female may repress the real male figure and continue to relate with the "archaic idealized imago." When there is such retention of an archaic Grandiosity, the structure, according to Kohut, cannot be sufficiently integrated into the rest of her personality. The self is therefore characterized by occasional intrusions of Grandiosity that are short-lived because they are not continuous with the sense of self, and her fairly-well integrated sense of self in relation may be adversely affected, disempowering her agency. This view of psychological dynamics in the self-structure may explain the tendency of some women to stay in abusive relationships or to keep going back even when they cognitively know they have the resources to leave the relationship.

The third possibility resulting from strong cathexis is that if cathexis to either or both psychic structures of the female survivor is not narcissistically fixed, a traumatic experience may present an opportunity to constructively engage and creatively modify her psychic apparatus in the light of her praxis so that her hierarchical structures of God, man, and woman are re-aligned. She might replace the Grandiosity of the male unionized Grandiose self by re-directing her energy to careers, vocations, and self-development. She might personalize her Deity to be more relevant to her experience, thereby being empowered in that respect using her religion to become an agent of transformation.

For most of the women survivors I interviewed, the factor of cathexis can be seen as significant in two major ways (see Diagram 4). In the first instance, it seems to have robbed some of them of their newly found power attained through engaging the Divine in constantly transforming encounters. Although able to re-organize their God representations to a highly personalized omnipotent God, who is more like them in characteristics, the counter-influence established by strong cathexis seemed to bear greater weight. Such counter-influence may be perceived as a deep-seated psychic indoctrination regarding what it means in the society to be a woman of worth in relation to her role as a wife and mother and the idealized male imago. For those whose cathexis to these roles was intensive, even when they had seemingly broken from the cycle of violence, all but two of them experienced intrusions of guilt, deflated sense of worth, and anxiety around possible fragmentation of the sense of self if they were to be detached from their roles of mother and wife. Ultimately, for the majority of the women, their transformational reconstruction of their God-representation did not necessarily work towards actually breaking the cycles of violence. Rose exemplifies this kind of survivor: although empowered by her new-found role as a community worker, she is still tied down in some way to intrusions of guilt and shame over leaving her husband and the unfair disapproval from the community. Hence, she ends up going back to the village to bring him to Nairobi, so she can care for him in her house, despite her hard feelings concerning the mistreatment she receives from him. Jackie may also fit within this category in that, despite knowing that she does not deserve the life of abuse she is living, she finds it difficult and futile to break off and begin anew. She has, instead, decided to try to develop herself educationally while continuing with her struggles with violence in her life. The women began to integrate the archaic idealized imagos and their contents into the super-ego, but the process fell short because of their strong cathexis of the archaic imagos. We may interpret the situation as one where the idealized objects (in this case, their content that is associated with their gender roles) are therefore related to narcissistically, continuing to fulfill the need for security and moral uprightness.

The second instance in which strong cathexis can be seen as having manifested itself was in the strong need to find self-definition through a male figure even if the God image emerged as a great representative of the self, but the woman had a strong cathexis to the Grandiose self that is unionized with the male imago. Millicent, who at the time of the interview was out of the abusive relationship, expressed feelings of disillusionment at being separated from her husband and her role as a mother. She consciously seems to be grateful that he initiated her move from home, thus taking the burden she would have been carrying of having left home herself. Yet most of her energy seems to be invested in regret at not being home and not being like other women who are able to be with their husbands. The pull from such cathexis may be so great that it negatively redirects the energy that could have been used towards her newfound reflection in finding other ways to fulfill the self, like careers or vocations or family. These women sought over and over again to be reunited with either their male figures or replacements.

For some of the women in my sample, that very longing for transformation was a source of inner conflict as it brought forth contradicting voices within themselves. Millicent, caught in the dilemma of disturbance and simultaneously feeling relief at being separated from her abusive husband at his own demand, said, "You know even God knows you cannot completely leave your husband"—an understanding I believe may be premised on Gen 3:16b.[3] The issue of cathexis is therefore fundamental to understanding the configuration and responses of women in Kenya to intimate violence.

INTERPRETIVE MODEL OF INTERVENTION IN INTIMATE VIOLENCE AND THE IMPLICATIONS FOR WIDER CONTEXTS

Having mapped some insights from the research onto a theoretical framework, I now proceed to highlight effective areas of intervention as derived from the framework, and to propose principles of constructing an interpretive model for understanding and intervening with victims of intimate violence, respectively. I highlight three areas as critical to effective intervention in intimate violence. These areas point either to efforts that transform systems that sustain intimate violence (pre-emptive) or to empowerment of individual survivors to enable them positively to recreate their sense of self (restorative and transformative). I argue that the gendered aspects of

---

3. "Yet your desire will be for your husband, And he will rule over you."

the society that influence female formation of a self in the collective context constrain the females by demanding strong psychic investment in them by being heavily packaged with undue sacredness, identity requirements, and obligatory dimensions. Non-conformity towards them threatens stability of the female sense of self.

I also discuss in this section the benefits of both the proposed theoretical framework of understanding survivors of intimate violence and the model of intervention for wider contexts. This section emphasizes the importance of formulating theoretical frameworks that are contextualized and informed by the praxis of survivors in addressing the issue of intimate violence.

Effective Areas of Intervention

The above theoretical framework helps reveal areas that would make intervention most effective. These can be grouped into two broad areas: pre-emptive intervention and restorative intervention.

Pre-Emptive Interventional Areas

Pre-emptive interventions are measures that can be employed to prevent both the occurrence of intimate violence and the formation of selves that are vulnerable to becoming resigned to abuse. While I acknowledge deranged personalities as being among the causes of violence that have been identified by established research and literature, I locate the root cause of abuse, and the tolerance of it, in the social cultural systemic configurations of the society. It is in these systems that gender messages pervasively influence the female to construct an inferior self-image, and it is these systems that work to present gender roles as sacred ancestral obligations and principled norms. From the weight assigned to these gender expectations, a powerful cathexis emerges as the females respond to them. Hence, the socio-cultural milieu would be a fundamental place to begin any form of transformation. Addressing the systems would also be tackling directly the notion of gender relations, which, as demonstrated in this book are seen as a determining factor for the formation of a sense of self by a girl child developing in a collective society. In turn, the nature of maturational pressures would be affected with regard to female images and gender messages presented to her.

Restorative Intervention

Restorative intervention refers to the need to continue working with both individual survivors of violence, and the perpetrators, to bring transformation in the society. My comments refer to work that can be done directly with the survivors. Areas that seem to be effective targets are those revealed by the survivors themselves in the narratives, as well as their implications for the psycho-social and religious framework for understanding survivors.

One such area of effectiveness is to find ways, on an individual level, to re-align gendered psychic structures. Religion was found to be a strong transformational agency, which can be very empowering. A healthy realignment not only redeems the roles that are generally relegated to females, but also feeds the woman's Grandiosity through these roles, and therefore supports the construction of a more stabilized sense of self rather than one that is constantly striving to be "fed" by the male union. It helps release the energy invested in finding self through a male unionized Grandiosity, enabling this energy to be available to the rest of the personality and therefore to creativity. Angela, discussed in various places earlier, is a good example of a survivor who seems to have modified the psychic structure's alignment of God, male and female, presented by the society to be one where she describes herself as a child of God. That mirroring enables her to decide to continue being married to her husband for the sake of providing for her children and her place as a married woman in the society. Simulteanously, the mirroring empowers her to psychologically block out his abuse and his unfaithfulness such that they do not affect her. She is now empowered and can confidently say, "He [husband] has no idea who he is playing with, a child of God!"

Working with individuals to aid them in finding personalized images of God that are empowering is critical. Caroll Saussy's (1991) arguments regarding the image of God and its correlates of self-esteem demonstrate the power the image of God has on the sense of self. Although Saussy argues that the God image needs to be transformed to a female "God/dess," which I do not perceive to be a necessity, even for the Kenyan woman she is completely correct, in holding that the God representation having some female characteristics has a great deal to do with the woman's self-esteem and therefore integration to the Grandiose self structure. She states:

> When women image in exclusively male terms, they relate to God (that is male Deity) as "like the other but not like me." The symbols used of this Jewish and Christian male Deity or God are

> most often symbols of power and authority: Father, Lord, Ruler,
> and King. When women image Deity in female terms, however,
> they relate to Goddess as "like me." Symbols that speak of the
> Goddess are also powerful symbols but are more likely represen-
> tatives of nurturing and relational power and are perhaps more
> serene: Earth Mother, Life Giver, Comforter, Wisdom. (1991, 17)

My major departure from Saussy is that the whole image does not
have to be transformed to a "Goddess"; the enablement of female characteristics to Godly reflection is just as good. When we look at the most
popular terms used to refer to God in traditional Kenya, such as *Murungu,*
Mwene-inya,[4] *and Ngai,*[5] they are not gendered. These terms refer to mys-
terious forces, nature, and blessings like rain. Newer terms like *Mwathani,*
meaning "Lord," have more of the colonial connotations. These terms
present a traumatic disruption to the image of God (as the colonial image
of a male Deity) and are currently being used in the orienting system. It
is a perpetration on the male counterpart like that which has been perpetrated on the female. If a survivor as an individual, however, came to
a female construction of her image during her metamorphic process, her
reconstructed female image of a Deity must be respected. Saussy recognizes this in her statement that,

> Replacing the male imagery with the female images is not a
> long term solution. Genuinely inclusive imagery is the only true
> solution. In the meantime women need a transitional space in
> which they are able to claim the source of female beauty and
> power of Deity. (1991, 17)

Allowing women, especially those struggling with congruency of
their spiritual beliefs and life experiences, to populate that "transitional
space" with characteristics of a Deity that draws from both male and female would be a powerful transformational tool. The power is especially
strong with regard to the redemptive quality of traditionally female characteristics that have historically reflected inferiority.

My other departure from Saussy regarding building self-esteem for
the woman in Kenya is that the interpretation of God must remain that
God is an omnipotent God, a Divinity to look up to, and lean on when
necessary, to challenge sometimes, and to draw strength from, just as the
woman would relate to a friend, companion, father, mother, a sibling, or a
close aunt. Saussy states:

4. Meaning "The Almighty."
5. Meaning "Rain."

> Religious faith does not contribute to self-esteem unless it grows
> out of and along with faith in one's abilities, in one's intrinsic
> worth, in one's capacity for intimacy, out of and along with faith
> in oneself. Religious faith that is built on faith in oneself pro-
> vides powerful motivation to join the struggle to liberate anyone
> who is not free to enjoy such fullness of faith. (1991, 14)

Much as Saussy is right about the positive correlation between faith in religion and faith in oneself, that correlation does not resonate for many women in Kenya. Her statements above presume that the women, in their own power, can claim a "faith in themselves." The masses of these women have grown up in very difficult circumstances of both psychological and physical abuse, not to mention poverty and a sense of life based on survival just for a day at a time. The onset of intimate violence, whether as a wit-ness to it, or as a persoanl experience in marital relations, is a cut onto an already bleeding wound. Where would they begin to have faith in them-selves? Their life is in sharp contrast to Saussy's life. She mentions that she is very grateful for having a loving husband, educational opportunities, a successful career, and a secure family life—all of these are conditions that she sets out as necessary for self-esteem (1991, 18).

What I found in the women I interviewed was not the presence of these conditions but the capacity and potential to develop them through their faith in an omnipotent Deity. I agree that if their relation with such a Deity boosts their self-Grandiosity and therefore their self-esteem, they become empowered to believe in themselves and make decisions they can live with. However, they need the Deity to be omnipotent. Most of the women I interviewed have actually maintained their God representation as omnipotent. This transformation of the God representation might explain why not even one of the survivors renounced the influence, relevance, and adoration of God despite having had horrible experiences. It is in the in-terest of such women that we should begin the process of transforming the orienting religious and cultural system so that it can offer a Deity that can be integrated and/or approximated by the privatized God representation without leaving bruise marks.

Towards an Interpretive Model for Intervention in Intimate Violence

The need to intervene is unquestionable. The previous observations and the consideration that intimate violence is not just a traumatic situation, but an experience that raises deep issues regarding self-worth and sense of self for the survivor is paramount. It is important that aspects of intervention be developed from understandings informed by the socio-cultural and religious context, and by the views of the survivors themselves. Three main areas promise the greatest efficacy I draw them from the context and gender-sensitive theoretical framework presented above.

First, the earliest point of intervention is obviously the redirection of maturational frustration of the baby up to latency, so that the formation of the two major psychic structures is normalized. This intervention would include measures that present the maternal caregivers for the child to be desirable objects of idealization so that they mirror satisfactory self-images. Practical measures of transforming this aspect of the orienting system must involve drastically changing how we women treat one another to reflect respect irrespective of whether we are maids or career women. Balanced out with an equally male idealized imago, this intervention would ensure that the child does not need to grow up thinking she has to be in union with a male to be important. It would allow a normalized cathected Grandiose self in which positive elements from male and female experience are united rather than a self in which one is prized over the other.

Second, eradication of gender-discriminative policies, traditions, and religious values would give all children and young people, male and female alike, a chance to utilize their opportunities and to believe in their capabilities. This measure would permit well-balanced structures that allow self-Grandiosity and values from multi-idealized imagos that are not necessarily gendered with differential values attached to them.

Third, and most important, is the transformation of the orienting systems, both socio-cultural and religious. I tag this as the most important area because the first two would slowly but surely sort themselves out if this one major area were to be effectively addressed. It is the orienting system that feeds the multi-parent imagos with their low self-esteem that is in turn mirrored to the girl child. The orienting system is responsible for discriminative policies in education, economies and household units; it is the justifier for violence against women; it is the supplier of the imagery of a male closer to God than the female, and so on.

Current interventions are directed mainly toward those who are experiencing violence and who can gain the courage to seek help. While these interventions are necessary as they address individual situations, there is an urgent need to address the systems in a systematic structural manner. The interpretive model presented below has been constructed using a systemic approach that takes into consideration the three proposed areas of intervention presented above. The model is one that can be used by community agencies on a broad environment as well as on an individual therapeutic intervention level. Both the communal agency and the individual levels would need to consider the narrower psycho-social process of an individual, as well as the expanded systemic context in which the person has developed a sense of self. The model's efficacy is grounded in its versatility and its adaptability to varying contexts. I now proceed to offer the guiding principles towards developing of a model of understanding and intervening against intimate violence in a given context, framed as a five-step process.

Step 1: Test universal theories against context.

This first step is premised on the need for anyone hoping to do intervention work with intimate violence, to familiarize oneself with the orienting theoretical framework of a given community before applying any theoretical approaches. The challenge posed here is to first test that theoretical framework being adapted for intervention against the context to determine its applicability. Relevant questions to consider in testing the grounds include the following:

- What aspects in the context would change the theoretical base?
- Do these aspects change the whole theoretical thinking, or can the theory still be used with some adjustment?
- Does the context totally challenge the whole base of the theory?
- What aspects of the theory coincide with aspects in the socio-cultural context where it is being employed?
- What labels are put on the people using this theoretical framework?

Answers to these questions help determine the applicability of the theoretical framework that one is bringing in attempt to intervene or understand intimate violence in a given context.

Step 2: Engage the systems.

A brief pilot study will clearly reveal the features of the orienting system. This is a critical step in that it gives insight to the deeper personal and usually secretive processes that are ongoing within the persons in that context. Larry Graham's (1992) psycho-systematic approach to providing care is an excellent resource on how to work with individuals from a systemic approach. Several questions need to be asked. What are the orienting systems in the culture in terms of social systems and religious, cultural, and traditional beliefs? What are their media? What are the important cultural institutions, and how do these function in the traditions and actual real-life situations? How are mediators of these institutions situated with regard to worldviews, and how is this position reflected in the ongoing formation of God representation for those they minister to? Are there aspects in the orienting systems that are "liberative" and that can be used as transformative agents?

Step 3. Create space for the players to have a major role in strategizing intervention.

It is critical to acknowledge that the responses of survivors are deeply embedded in their psychological structures and may or may not be changed through intervention. The importance of this measure is to honor that place deep within them that yearns for transformation of their lives. It entails a move from mere application of theories to an engagement with real lives, trusting that through their voices they will guide what needs to be done. It means entering their space through listening to them—to their fears, their inspirations and aspirations, their directing forces. Overlooking this step may lead to an engagement of systems suggested above but a failure to pinpoint aspects of these systems that influence the survivors' thinking and self-formation.

Step 4. Empower survivors by allowing relations that strengthen the mirroring of a positive self-image.

In Kohut's framework, the self-psychologically trained analyst is privileged to enter the inner world of the survivor, and is therefore in a position to discern the operating mechanisms and use these to mirror positive aspects that strengthen the survivor's self-image. Outside a situation as narrowly structured as the therapeutic consulting room, the expanded theoretical framework presented in this book provides non-specific "shoulds" and "should nots." In the Kenyan situation, for instance, empowerment should not be measured in any competition with the male. The male imago has already failed the survivor fundamentally. If the woman is determined to have a very strong narcissistic cathexis with the archaic male unionized Grandiose self, and yet the male imago she is holding onto has failed her, is there any other significant male symbolism that can be used? If so, it may provide a good transitional space as she moves to a more stable self-image that is not so strongly cathected. For example, one alternative may be the survivor's capability in areas that are associated with masculinity. It could be her own conjured image of God as an anchor and partner in her strivings to achieve that in turn uplifts her self-image. As this stage is engaged in, the therapist must realize that this is already shattered ground, and therefore proceed with caution. This stage depends strongly on the therapist's skills to draw out the operating mechanism from the survivor using the theoretical model.

The model's efficacy at this stage can be increased by following two general guidelines: (1) Seek embedded gender roles in the society and determine how they manifest in the person's sense of self. If stringent gender roles already populate the psychic structures, to speak against them is to fight a losing battle because one is up against not only a set of beliefs but a deeply rooted part of self. (2) Join the roles in an empowering way but at the same time try to objectify them outside of the self, so that they are related to as objects that can be part of the person's integration instead of standing as archaic cathected objects that define the self. In this way, a role like that of mother or wife will be an important role. The role will make the woman proud of what she is doing, but it will not necessarily define her whole psychic and social life to the extent that she cannot do anything outside of these roles to define her humanity. Such roles can be used to reflect God's characteristics, but at the same time go beyond these to reflect other characteristics that are desirable as sacred and that afford transformative possibilities for women. If, for instance, these roles were to be taken away (as in the case of a divorce), the ideal would be to have the loss of roles become not a threat of self-fragmentation but rather a sad part of the self that can be normally grieved, leaving the entity functional and ready to regain cohesion after grieving. These psychoanalytical interventions coincide with Kohut's objectives towards specific changes in the narcissistic realms that can be achieved through relinquishment of aspects of the idealized imago and through gradual building of "infantile Grandiosity" into "ambition and purpose of the personality" (1971, 299).

Step 5. Initiate necessary transformation in the orienting systems.

Transformation will allow the marginalized populations within that context to bud and bloom in their creativity, providing the basis for a greater transformation to take place as it nurtures a space for the survivors and families one is working with to feel at peace with their ongoing transformation. This step involves a larger part of the society in the process of transformation, so that the burden is not on those directly working with survivors of violence. In a similar manner, it involves transformation of the perpetrators as well. This perspective comes from Larry Graham's (1992) work, *Care of Persons, Care of Worlds.* Graham illuminates the interactional nature of personal development whereby systems not only

define persons, but persons define and contribute to the ongoing formation of systems. Hence, personhood is a function of development through
interaction with a variety of systems and subsystems, of which the person
is also a subsystem of sorts. Persons both reflect the characteristics of systems, and transgress and subvert them. In my view, the survivor in her
response to violence, not only draws worldviews and ideologies from the
orienting system but also contributes to it by being a statistic, an example,
or a confirmation of the existing system, thereby adding to its transformation or continuity.

Writing from the perspective of a pastoral psychotherapist, Graham
asserts that any caring of persons must involve a systemic approach that
locates the person within the family, community, and other systems that
contribute to the definition of his/her being. In a similar way, it becomes
necessary to transform those systems to enable transformation of its
members. Graham's views exactly mirror the model of intervention being
proposed here. A survivor cannot be regarded apart from the systems that
define her, her family, community of faith, social community, and friends.
Any intervention work with her must also address the system around her.
When both the systems and the individual self-structure are addressed,
her transformational agency has a better chance of working smoothly, as
it finds confirmation and encouragement in the larger systems orienting
her life. What such transformation would look like is discussed further in
the concluding chapter.

I am proposing a shift of paradigm—from intervention merely informed by symptoms and direct application of methods that have worked
elsewhere to curb intimate violence, to intervention grounded in the socio-cultural and religious context. The interventions are grounded on systemic structural transformations. With regard to a sense of self anchored
in family, for instance, a model that seeks to interpret self-formation that
is contextualized has a greater chance of being effective in that it does not
burden the survivor with the guilt for choices she has made that may very
well be embedded in her sense of self. Such a model would look critically
at the dynamics of the socio-cultural and religious environment in the
community where the violence takes place. These dynamics would aid the
understanding of the formation of the self for a female and a male in that
particular context. In turn, the understanding would give insight into why
persons within or originating from that community would be likely to respond to violence in ways that are unique to the context. If these responses
are determined to be unhealthy, then an interventional model that seeks to

address the contextual dynamics would be employed. The benefits of this kind of model are four-fold. I will elaborate.

First, the intervention model is based on a theoretical framework that provides a point of reference from which to begin understanding deep human processes that are at work in the realms of the psyche and the core of the self. I use the word "begin" because I acknowledge that what I have proposed is basically theoretical. A theoretical framework cannot account in totality for all human processes and behaviors, which are very complex and often unpredictable. The framework at hand has been developed from emerging concepts of a sizeable number of narratives, but these cannot be said to be representative of every single experience of violence that takes place. Human experience is in itself highly subjective and therefore varied, irrespective of similarity in phenomena. Yet a theoretical framework has the strength of being adaptable and adjustable, of being able to be critiqued and applied to suit the context in general, and then the individual in particular for whom the intervention strategy is being developed can be helped. It provides a space within which conversations about the nature and course of intimate violence are taking place, thereby allowing the possibility to perceive concepts and issues that would normally not be perceived by mere observation. With respect to the highly personalized, often hidden processes with which survivors of intimate violence make meaning and therefore respond, intervention through an interpretive framework is a powerful and essential tool.

Second, the model aims to deal with the contextual root problem instead of the surface symptoms. Treating symptoms alone will never cure or bring holistic healing to the disease, because treatment simply gives a temporary relief that does not change the hearts of the players involved. The model recognizes that players go beyond the survivor and the perpetrator to the larger system that includes the family, extended kinship, the community and its cultural beliefs, and the religious communities of faith. On the other hand the root problem will be addressed, time will certainly be needed, , but the intervention would ultimately be more efficient and transformative. Sensitization regarding the ills of violence needs to be addressed through educational, religious and health entities, and are among the excellent examples of how to address intimate violence. Similarly, individual attention to the survivors and their families, an effort to recognize the survivors' capabilities beyond the home into the society, and addressing the issue of unequal educational opportunities, (and other gender-based social "norms" which foster status and, therefore, esteem) would increase the success of the intervention endeavor.

Third, the model recognizes that although the symptomatic presentation of violence may look similar, certain nuances may point to huge differences that could distinguish between effective and non-effective intervention. For instance, the absence of apologies in what is deemed as the honeymoon phase of the cycle of violence points to the belief (by most Kenyan men,) that what they are doing is normal and denotes a 'right' they have over their women. That alone points to one real issue that needs addressing, the fact that he beats her and it is wrong. It points to the fact that we recognize the need of making laws against intimate violence, (thereby creating channels of recourse and justice), this measure alone will not eradicate violence. Until both survivor and perpetrator know that the man has no right to hit his wife, the abused wife may never make use of a readily available intervention strategy.

Fourth, the model helps shed light on what aspects of intervention are not effective in a certain community and why they are not effective. For instance, pressuring the survivor to "see the better way" of breaking away from her relationships, possibly giving over her role of rearing children and becoming free of the abuse, may indeed be asking her to walk away from her sense of self in the Kenyan context. This result may not necessarily pertain to another context, where the formation of the self is prioritized in a different manner for the man and the woman, or where there are more or different social options for females responding to violence.

The greatest appeal of both the theoretical framework and the implications of the proposed model is that they are interpretive, freeing the model to be used to theorize similar frameworks for other certain contexts. Its strength is anchored in the fact that while it focuses on the contextual dynamics, it simultaneously acknowledges the subjective individual differences and their operating psychic structures and self-identity in that particular context. Hence it is not only versatile in its adaptability but also specific in applicability. It offers potential effectiveness for use on other social, traumatic issues beyond intimate violence.

In this chapter I have discussed the new perspectives and insights added to the framework postulated in chapter 4, by incorporating the voices, experiences and inferences derived from my analysis of the narratives from the survivors of violence. I have also offered interpretive modeled steps for making these perspectives applicable in a collective context like Kenyan. I now seek in the next chapter, to discuss how I have addressed the research question stated at the beginning, and used to navigate this study, as well as offer areas for further research.

8

Conclusion

INTRODUCTION

In this chapter I revisit the three research questions posed at the beginning of the book to show how these have been addressed. In the initial section of this chapter, I answer the three questions by discussing insights that have deepened the understanding of female development of a sense of self in Kenya, the survivors' understandings of their experiences, and their range of response to intimate violence. These insights include both theoretical conceptualizations and experiential derivations from the survivors' narratives. In the last part of the chapter, I present my final thoughts and point to possible areas of further study.

ANSWERING THE RESEARCH QUESTIONS

Research Question 1: How does the female in Kenya form a sense of self, given her socio-cultural and religious context?

The answer to this first question lies in consideration of the theoretical formulations discussed in Chapter 7, of the context, and of the survivors' narratives. I have made the argument that females in Kenya form a sense of self that is organized around wifely and maternal roles, as well as a sense of self unionized in Grandiosity with the male. They assume great influence on the psychic development of females because they are sanctioned as sacred by the religious orienting systems. Inadvertently, they strongly influence the female's formation of self from very early in life, so that she builds her identity or place and worldview in the society from this sense of self.

Two female gender roles are notably important in the formation of a sense of self. The girl child is constantly reminded that it is important to be a mother and to be a wife. Her play, her admonitions or praise, her pride all are based on these two adult female roles. When she exhibits characteristics that point to a future of being a good mother and good wife, she is praised. This puffs up her Grandiosity. In the course of her development, she notes the differential aspects of what the boy child is praised for: being a protector, or tough, being smart, being skilled in school work and in the use of hand tools, being celebrated as the future provider of the family. I have submitted that this is the beginning of the girl's admiration of the male "characteristics" and female gender roles.

Noting that both female roles are achievable through relation to a significant male works to idealize the male and leads to establishing a relationship with a male so as to continue finding her fulfillment of Grandiosity. By adolescence and adulthood, these aspects of gender that have been nurtured in her whole life have become a part of her psychological development, piloting the very establishment of her identity or place in the community. Hence, being a mother and a wife defines her sense of self, her relationships with the other, and her world view.

Research Question 2: How does the survivor of violence understand the phenomenon of intimate violence from her subjective viewpoint and her place in the community?

The answer to this second question emerges from insights derived from the understandings expressed by the survivors themselves within their contexts. These insights include the survivors' own understanding about what constitutes violence, why they experience the violence, their feelings towards violence, and their experience of God during episodes and recovery from violence. I came to these understandings through the various psycho-social and religious concepts that emerged from the study.

According to the survivors, violence occurred only when the man physically beat them. It was expressed by the words *kupiga* (to beat) or *utatandikwa* (colloquial for "you will be thoroughly beaten"). Nelly was several times locked out of the house and at one time had her daughter thrown out of the house as well, but she did not describe that as violence. When a woman experienced slaps as opposed to an actual beating, she did not necessarily characterize it as violence but referred to it as "discipline," or justified it by citing the man's stress from work, finances, and other frustrations. This practice may explain why a woman like Nelly will answer, when asked what she thinks about intimate violence, "it is not always the man who is bad, even the woman."

The women had different explanations for why they experienced violence from their male partners. According to Jane, it is "because of affairs." She goes on to say, "In the past we used to go to church together, then I realized that he did not want us to travel together. Then he would make up trips that were really lies." Nelly, like Jane, traces the violence in her life to mainly "after the other woman came to his life. I think the fights intensified because I would tell him that the other woman was much older than him," which speaks, I believe, to the challenged ego of his manhood. Jane says, "Many men think that the only way a woman can be good is to be beaten . . . because a man should not beat you all the time," which indicates that she believes that there are times that a woman can be "justly" beaten.

Yet as pointed out in the discussion of the various concepts, every woman I interviewed offered an alternative to even what they thought were instances of 'acceptable violence' expressed by citing circumstances, which they thought they were "justly being beaten." Hence, none of the women thought that violence was acceptable. Many found ways to live with it, especially by learning to not ask questions or not to stand for their rights even when they knew they had a right not to be beaten. Many condoned unthinkable acts of violence for long periods before looking for help or breaking from the cycle.

The most cited reason for staying in violent situations was for "the sake of my children," so that they would have a father, or so that they could attend good schools, or so that they would not think badly of their mothers. As discussed under the concept of "children as empowerment," children were also the reason that some of the women finally broke the cycle of violence or found a reason to keep living. Also notable is that their understanding of God or Biblical teachings required them as women to be *mtu wa kunyenyekea* (a submissive person). In Neema's case, the woman has to be *mjinga* (foolish). She said,

> If both the man and the woman are smart, that brings trouble, but if the woman is foolish, then it is okay. You see if both are smart, by the time the man talks, the woman has already figured him. One needs to be foolish, mainly the woman.

While Neema's statement does not necessarily mean that she has a low opinion of women as foolish, she knows that unless the woman acts as if she is foolish, there is going to be violence. Similar sentiments were expressed unanimously in the group interview of Catherine, Linet, Eva, and Leah. Their notion was that as women, even if they knew that their partners were doing something wrong, it was safer not to mention it because it would only invite beating. Leah reported that that is how she had managed to stay on in her relationship. Millicent says that is how she had managed to stay on in her marriage until she was forced out of her home. Nelly says, "So I stopped listening to these things [about his infidelity] because I wanted to make a home and for my kids to have a father." These are all clearly women who know that violence is not right but who have to weigh their value for marriage, family life and children against standing for their rights.

None of my participants indicated an understanding of violence as being mandated by God or inflicted as punishment from God. I have already mentioned in discussing the religious concepts that God was expressed as a helper through other people's interventions, a comforter, a source of hope for a better future, and a contrast to their abusive partners. In reflecting on their partner's violent behavior, the survivors located the cause of violence outside of their partner's selfhood (as discussed in the male idealization concept) and in many cases attributed it to the possession of a bad spirit that was definitely the opposite of God.

Research Question 3: What effect do the sense of self and understandings held on intimate violence have on the survivors' response to violence in their own lives?

It is clear from the foregoing discussion that the formation of a sense of self and therefore understanding of intimate violence have substantial bearing on survivors' response to violence. The understandings of violence expressed by the survivors, as well as their insights into their formation of a sense of self, were very helpful in comprehending their operating systems and their consequent response to intimate violence.

In all instances, it was evident that survivors turned to religious coping as a way of making meaning of their experiences through theological engagement. I have stated that the likely explanation of why all my informants turned to religion is because it was readily available in the orienting system. Most people in Kenya would readily have a religious schema with which to comprehend difficult circumstances in their lives that may not have other explanations. From Pargament and Park's perspective, people use religion as a coping device to maximize what is important to them by attempting to "preserve, maintain or transform the things that people care about most deeply" (1997, 44). I submit that the survivors' use of religion to cope with violence may be to preserve identity or place in the community, which I have theorized as being most important in their lives. While acknowledging that coping was an important way in which the survivors responded to violence in their lives, I also recognize that whichever way the survivors responded was also informed by deeper psychic operative mechanisms better understood from self-psychological interpretation of the data. These mechanisms are the focus of this work and have been the basis of my arguments. I therefore perceive the range of response of the survivor from psychoanalytical, specifically self-psychological interpretations as discussed in chapter 7.

Two main responses were manifested by the survivors, within which there is a range of sub-categorical responses. The first response was to break away from the cycle of violence, either voluntarily or as a forced circumstance. The characteristics of women who left abusive relationships varied. Some of the women in this category interpretively displayed greater and transformed self-understanding. Their status as women in the society was characterized by respect for females in general and for self; enhanced esteem, and confidence. As I have theorized in Chapter 7, these would most likely be women whose religious beliefs and engagement with their God representation had led them to transform their own image to approximate to Godly characteristics. Some of these women were able to sever any strong cathexis to male idealization and were able to believe in their own capabilities of raising families or getting into healthy relationships. These women were able to re-direct their energies to careers and educational opportunities, and also to take pride in their gender roles from a less defining perspective. Nancy and Julie are excellent examples of women in this sub-category.

Others within this first response category continued to have powerful intrusive guilt feelings and instabilities about being out of their marital relationship, even though it was abusive. Thus, even though they may have succeeded in approximating their self-reflections to Godly characteristics, their cathexis to archaic self-objects was so narcissistic that breaking from these would not be easy. Millicent, who continues to wonder why she cannot live with her husband like other women, and who constantly keeps thinking of the well-being of her abusive husband and wishing she could get back home and continue to take care of him, is a good example of women in this sub-category. She clearly states that her husband's beatings are beyond tolerance, yet she is ready to give excuses of stress, alcohol, and possession by evil spirits as influencing factors of his abusive tendencies. Annastasia could also fall in this category. She is grateful that she is no longer living in the abusive relationship with her husband, but is also re-gretful that the decision was his and not hers. Her pattern of choosing who she goes to for help when in crisis, and who decides for her if she should fight in court for her children, as well as her constant blame of husband's promiscuous and irresponsible behavior to the sister-in-law, all reflect her idealization of the male and her own inferior sense of self as a woman in the community. Despite her husband's failings, she continues to look for other male relationships to fulfill her deep-seated need to be in union with a male. Other women who were out of the relationship showed varied levels of self-definition that were removed from their self-objects. Most of these women were out of their relationship under forced circumstances and many of them, including Faima, Linet and Jane, continued to struggle with the reality that they were not in their rightful places as wives to their abusive husbands. Some, like Nelly, showed great strides to developing an empowering God representation and therefore self-empowerment.

The second response category of women is those who chose to con-tinue living in abusive relationships. Again, there is a range of findings that can be clustered into sub-categories. Some women who chose to stay on in the relationship did so in a subversive manner, making the statement that they continued to defy violence and did not just accept it as a way of life. Angela does this by letting the husband move out of the home (as was his wish) but by denying him divorce. In this way, she is able to continue to hold her place of prestige in the family, thereby commanding respect; getting the husband's financial support of the children's education; and becoming free of violence by threatening further severe court action if he ever laid a hand on her. Her statement that "he does not know whom he is playing around with, a child of God," suggests a transformed self-image that closely approximates God's image. Rose is yet another good example of this category. She has apparently achieved great success in community work, and in self-reflection is closer to God than her husband, as he had abandoned his family for more than 15 years. Yet she cannot live at peace as long as she is vulnerable to people's talk about her abandoning the hus-band in the village. So she brings him to Nairobi and can now pursue her vocations in peace. Nelly may also be a classic example of one who has replaced a need to be in union with a male by her relationship with a male God, and her ability to take on male responsibilities in the family and community. Both these women have concluded, through their understanding of God, that God would understand if they were to divorce their husbands. Hence, negative religious coping is apparently not a factor here. If anything, religion has empowered them to raise their self-esteem and self-image to come to these conclusions, even though they choose to remain in the relationships. Their staying on is more to fulfill a deep-seated psychic need than it is a religious sanction.

Jackie could also fall in this subcategory. She decides to continue living in the abusive relationship, but as a step toward breaking the cycle, she tries to find ways to pursue further education that could allow her to earn more money. Her narrative, however, reflects more of a struggle with the question of what her status and identity in society would be if she walked out of this relationship. Despite the apparent fact that she is currently the one supporting the family financially, she seems to be burdened with uncertainty as to whether she would really be able to hold her family together financially. Interpretively this may reflect a strong cathexis to male idealization and Grandiosity found in union with a male.

A few other women did not show that much transformational change had taken place, whether they had stayed on in the abusive relationship or had been forced out. Yet they did not express acceptance of the violence. Irene and Faima are good examples of this sub-category. It is notable that neither seems to have a well-developed or established God representation. It may be concluded that their traumatic experience of violence is yet so new that they are just in the initial stages of engaging theological dilemmas that would reformulate their God representations.

In summary, then, the range of responses to intimate violence displayed by the survivors of violence clearly points to the use of religion as a coping device. Further psychoanalytic interpretation of the coping methods, however, reveals deeper psychic states and manipulations, including various levels of survivors' cathexis to childhood self-objects, varying theological engagement and development of God representations, and simultaneous transformation of the sense of self in relation to a reformulated God representation.

CONCLUSION AND AREAS FOR FURTHER STUDY

Clearly, in Kenya the understandings of intimate violence held by survivors are influenced by multiple factors traceable to socio-cultural traditions, mores, and values and contextual religious interpretations as well as the survivors' personal appropriations of these through life experiences and the formation of the self. Clearly, also, these understandings are not static. Every experiential encounter of the dominant patriarchal context, whether through academic discourse or through direct and indirect experience of violence, challenges these understandings, which are then reappropriated and transformed or adjusted by the survivor. Corresponding to these dynamic understandings are varying forms of response to violence rather than a clear cut decision of remaining in or moving out of the violent relationship. Both the articulated and lived-out responses of the survivors in this study demonstrate the complexity of the ongoing subjective transformation of the survivors' internal sense of self as she tries to appropriate and wrestle with the ever-emerging images and emotions that the trauma of violence elicits.

I hypothesized, at the inception of this study, that the high functionality of women living in violence is a façade that serves to maintain her identity and value in the society. While on the surface the survivor's functionality approximates that of a woman who has not experienced the trauma of intimate violence, I have demonstrated in the foregoing chapters that this functionality is not only a façade, but also a fundamental psychic necessity, essential for fulfilling maternal and wifely roles while the sense of self is under constant threat of fragmentation. Using a theoretical framework that adapts aspects of Kohut's theory, I have discussed how such a sense of self comes into being through the development of specific psychic structures. My discussion of the female formation of a sense of self, however, departs from Kohut's framework in very specific fundamental ways that reflect socio-cultural, gender biased systems, and religion, within collective contexts using Kenya as a case study.

I have critically engaged the data collected from the survivors' narratives and distilled from them five themes that I have discussed analytically at length. These themes are (1) a sense of self found in union with an idealized male image, (2) a sense of self anchored in gender roles, (3) the powerful role of children in determining a woman's response to violence, (4) a mechanical self-righting functionalism, and (5) use of religion as a resource for empowerment to cope with, make meaning of, and to transform the sense of self and identity.

These five themes affect the nature and contents of the two Kohutian psychic structures in that the psychic structures on one hand are characterized by a Grandiosity of the self in union with a male, and on the other hand exist in relation to idealized objects that are both gendered and aligned in hierarchies. The psychic structures are shaped by contents arising from constant messages of both the socio-cultural and religious orienting systems. Both psychic structures are narcissistically cathected at various levels to fulfill the primary need for a solid sense of self.

Regarding the question of cohesiveness, I have illustrated that females have the potential to form a cohesive sense of self that exists in relation. However, the socio-cultural and religious aspects of the society call on females to form selves that are based on gender-related roles, leading to a female sense of self that is, for the most part, highly vulnerable to fragmentation. Even when cohesive, such a sense of self is bound to experience occasional intrusions of primary Grandiosity in union with a male object on the one hand, and by a tension-generating super-ego, institutionalized by gender roles, on the other. Thus the level of cohesiveness and vulnerability to such intrusions depends largely on the cathexis with which the individual attaches to self-objects of Grandiosity and idealized images. Cathexis, in turn, is determined by the nature and intensity of aspects of socio-cultural and religious influences on the formation of a sense of self, including cultural gender messages, the level of esteem of multiple caregivers, and the woman's own privately developing God representation.

The cohesiveness of the survivor of intimate violence faces an even greater challenge. Her sense of self is continually in danger of fragmenting for two reasons. First, the sense of self, gained through the unionized male, is in perpetual disarray because of relentless and powerful disillusionments by a man who also functions as a part of her *self*. Second, the sense of self aligned through the functions of the super-ego is also unstable because of transformational conflicts as the survivor confronts the incongruence between the ideals held up to her and the experiential reality of violence now unfolding in her life.

In my critical engagement of these factors, I have argued that the survivors of intimate violence should not be perceived as having *accepted* their fate. The commonplace façade normally interpreted as acceptance masks an ever-present defiant energy. This energy can be seen in various directions. First it challenges the aspects of the patriarchal domination as they present in the socio-cultural and religious orienting systems. Secondly, there is ongoing private but powerful engagement with, reshaping of, negotiating with and transforming of the Divine representation and the self. Third, is the adjusting the contents and status of the psychic structures and therefore the cathexis invested in them.

Indeed, I suggest that the seemingly normal functionality of the survivors be viewed instead as an expression of their ongoing struggle to seek transformation either directly or as an undercurrent. This shift of paradigm on how to understand survivors of violence results from insights gained through examining their perspectives on the phenomenon of violence. These insights led to my postulation of a theoretical framework that can be used to understand victims of violence and, at the same time, to highlight critical areas for effective intervention. I proposed a model that is founded on an interpretive process grounded in the specifics of a given socio-cultural context.

I mentioned in the introductory chapter the process of transformation that I myself underwent during the data-collection and analysis process. I would now like to describe that process. I originally proposed that my research be an attempt to understand violence from the "victim's" perspective. However, I now realize that by the mere use of the term "victim" I was "other-ing" the survivors, making them objects of study apart from me. I was creating a distance premised on the assumption that if I were in their shoes, my response to violence would definitely differ from theirs. I struggled with the current use in Kenya of the word "survivors" to refer to women in violence because, from my perspective, a survivor was one who had discarded the cycle of violence and moved on. I could not conceive how a woman who continued to live in a violent situation could be called a survivor. I also noted in my journal how the various representatives of organizations working with women in violence in Kenya responded to the term "survivors of violence" instead of "victims of violence." As I consider my journal reflections, I see that the transformation to conceptualizing these women as survivors did not come through hearing all the explanations I was given by these organizations. It came through listening to the women's narratives and realizing, as they recounted their experiences, that their lives were characterized by human complexities. I cannot tell the exact point at which the transformation occurred, but a note in my journal states that "these women are true survivors in the literal sense of the word." Even when a respondent indicated that she continued to live with her abusive partner, she found ways to challenge his behavior, to engage in everyday discourse regarding the aspects of her community that she found incongruent with her own understanding of what it means to be human, and to engage the Divine in fashioning epistemological convictions that empowered her to move on. This realization that the women were indeed survivors was immensely powerful. I came to realize that a helpless victim could in no way do what these women were doing.

My transformation is not only reflected in moving away from the term "victims" in my book, but also in a change that occurred in the central core of my "self." This change placed me in an empathic position as a researcher. Henceforth, "I" was "she" and "she" was "I." I was no longer protected in my own privileged world where there is no physical violence. I, as a woman, belong in the same socio-cultural and religious context that creates victims who become survivors, and I continue to deal with structural and emotional challenges similar to hers even though not specifically in violence. This insight provides powerful support for the argument that discriminating structures in gender, race and class need to be destabilized in a population by un-anchoring the structures themselves to minimize intimate violence and other social ills. My thinking in this direction is evident in the proposed model of intervention in intimate violence as informed by the concepts emerging from the women's praxis (as discussed in chapter 7). The question I would like to conclude with, which forms my challenge for further research, is, "What would transformation of structures into those that do not allow intimate violence look like?"

I conclude this work by suggesting areas for further inquiry through briefly describing how such a transformation might look. In doing so, I would like to acknowledge Professor Amina Mama, whose opening remarks at a general staff and faculty conversation regarding transformation at the University of Cape Town, South Africa (May 2005) confirmed my own advocacy for transformation of structures that perpetuate intimate violence in Kenya. Much work is being done which directly addresses the interpersonal relations between men and women in the workplace and in the home. Important as this is, lasting measures need to be taken to address the systems and structures that surround these interpersonal relations.

With respect to socio-cultural structures, a starting point would be an examination of the traditional beliefs and moral values that stereotype persons along gender lines. These beliefs and values influence the messages we subtly, but powerfully, send to our children as they grow up in our homes and communities. These messages affect one's sensitivity to interpretation of, and the importance to certain traditional rites of passage, which in themselves are wonderful ideologies that should be utilized to recreate loving and respecting communities; they transmit mores and values through our myths, proverbs, sayings, names, and lyrics; they give discriminative access to educational opportunities; and, of course, sadly they result in the disparities these systems present.

Similarly, the religious orienting system must be seriously considered. When we divorce our intervention strategies from the religious beliefs of those on whose behalf we are intervening, we miss an opportunity to address an integral part of the self before us. Such a self is formed through building a God-representation from our cultural and familial contexts early in life and through eventual engagement with this Divine representation. By excluding consideration of the religious orienting system, we are in effect addressing only a small portion of the person before us. It is therefore important to acknowledge that religion plays a very important role in the formation of a self, in the strategies employed in making meaning of and coping with crisis, and in the ultimate decisions made by the survivors.

Transformation of the system may include incorporating gender sensitivity training into pastoral care programs and theological schools' curricula, thereby creating spaces for the marginalized to inform the academic conceptualization of religion. It may also call for communities of faith to be open to constructive criticism of text studies that allow the sifting of the cultural from the inspired Word, and teach those in authority to be sensitive to scriptural interpretive ideologies passed down through our communities of faith, especially regarding politicized text passages. Transformation may require those concerned to question traditional values that were held sacred in the traditional religions and that are now integrated into contemporary religious traditions, looking for how these values may coincide with gender-based values and perceptions.

These transformational measures go beyond the numerical values of looking at, for example, how many women are in what positions or how many girls are enrolled in higher education, or whether percentages of women in the mainstream professions are increasing. While statistics are important in demonstrating that strides are being made to lift the status of women by incorporating them in what traditionally have been male-dominated arenas, they more often than not may indicate token or only partial compromises. An increased percentage of women in the legal profession in the last decade compared to the one before it may, for example, be used to support a claim that because women are in these professions, they therefore have the opportunity for development. This explanation, however, does not address the question of *how* these women got into the positions they are now holding. Did they have to put up a fight at home and in the larger society? Did they have to doubly prove their capability relative to what the men in the professions had to do? Does the society look at the figures and conclude that women were *let in* (allowed in), which would still connote the perception that this profession is not really their ground? Do the women feel at home in these professions? While in some instances, being in these positions may affect female self structure positively by building self-esteem and re-directing formerly frozen energies into new and fulfilling careers, being in such a position may in some other cases become a source of anxiety emanating from guilt (intruding from the woman's unconscious,) for "neglecting" important gender roles. Again the intensity of cathexis to self-objects is a determining factor.

These questions clearly show the need to move beyond statistical reductionism to intrinsic values of transformation that would allow discourses that relate to all in the society. Included in that examination should be the feelings of men, who in various conversations regarding gender empowerment, voiced perceptions of being the "endangered species."

In brief, true transformation in addressing the issue of gender violence in any culture must engage methodologies that are grounded in interpersonal relationships, and self-structures, as these emerge from socio-cultural and religious contexts.

Appendix 1

RESEARCH GUIDING QUESTIONS

NB: These are guide questions with the first one in each section being the major one asked. The sub-questions below it are to be used, as a guide for what respondents may not cover in their answers and for those needing a more structured approach.

I tried to classify the questions in sections that regard: Personality/Identity; Relationships and views of the other; Place of self within a community; Role within the family; Self-actualization/fulfillment; Theological reflection and self within that theological framework; Views of self within domestic violence relationship; and a few questions in each cluster aimed at speaking to the inner person in the respondent.

1. Tell me all you can about yourself.
- How would you describe yourself as a person, a woman, a wife?
- What memories do you hold growing up as a girl?
- Which of your parents would you say you are close to and why?
- What was most important for you in your relationships within your family of origin?
- Who was your role model and why?

2. Tell me how you met your husband and your decision to begin a family.
- Was marriage something you planned or did it just come about?
- Do you have children, and if so were they part of your marriage plan?
- What has it been like to care for them?

- What is most precious in your marriage right now?

3. What would you consider the most important role in your life at present?

- When did you start viewing this role as a priority in your life?

- How did you assume this role?

- Is this role different from that which you hold in your immediate family?

- Has this priority role changed over the years since your marriage, or has it always been the same?

- Have you ever thought of giving up this role? When and why?

4. Do you consider yourself an ambitious person?

- What are some aspirations you have dreamed of achieving in your life both at present and in your younger years?

- Would you say that these aspirations have changed over time and, if so, in what ways?

- Have you achieved any of these aspirations?

5. Are you a member of any group?

- What is your role in this group?

- How is this group significant in your life?

- Do you have any other friends or people that you associate with outside of this group?

- How do these people affect/influence you as a person in your life?

6. I will mention some words and I would like you to just say out loud the first two or three words that come to your head in association with what I say:

   Peace; children; marriage; girls; intimate violence; anger.

7. What do you feel/think about intimate violence?

- What are your general opinions about intimate violence?

- Do you think it is okay for a woman to be beaten at any time? If so what circumstances?

- Do you think it is okay for a woman to retaliate if beaten?

- Why do you think there is intimate violence?
- Do you think that the prevalence of intimate violence is exaggerated beyond reality?

8. What would you do with a woman who sought your help because her husband is beating her?

- What advice would you give her?
- What would you advise her if she stated she was planning to leave the relationship?
- What do you think your community of faith should tell such a woman?
- Do you think anyone should do anything about intimate violence? What?

9. Have you faced violence in your marriage?
   If so:

- How often does this occur?
- Do you have any ideas why this happens to you?
- Does it affect your daily functioning? In what ways?
- Does it affect your relationship with your husband?
- Have you ever sought shelter to get away from the beating? If so, what factors made you go back to the relationship?
- Would you have gone back if you did not have children?
- Are there any signs that warn you that a beating is coming your way?
- Give me a brief scenario of what happens from the time of a beating to the time when you make up.
- How do you deal with the emotions involved in the violence?
- Have you ever sought for help? Where?
- Are you aware of anywhere else where there might be a source for help?
- Would you like me to make some referrals for places you may get confidential help?
   If not:

- What would you do if you faced violence in your marriage relationship?

10. What do you think about God?

- What characteristic do you think that God has?
- Do you believe in God?
- In what ways does God affect your life?
- What do you think is God's will for you?
- In times of agony, say, like that of violence, what kinds of thoughts go on in your mind?
- Are these thoughts different from those that would go in your mind say when you have faced a disaster like losing a loved one, or losing a job, or having a member in the family that is seriously ill?

11. Would you be interested in seeing a counselor or pastoral care person to discuss your issues of intimate violence?

Appendix 2

Table 2: General Demographics of Participants

(see 210–11)

NAME	Age Grp.	Education	Religion	Child	Marital type
Survivor					
Millicent	41–50	Up to grd. 8	Christian- Adh.	Yes	T. Marriage
Rose	41–50	Up to grd. 8	Christian- Adh.	Yes	T. Marriage
Faima	31–40	Up to grd. 8	Muslim	Yes	Mus. Rites
Irene	18–30	Up to grd. 8	Christian Nom.	Yes	Live in
Catherine (grp.)	18–30	Up to grd. 8	Belief—No affli.	Yes	T. Marriage
Linet (grp)	31–40	Up to grd. 8	Belief—No affli.	Yes	T. Marriage
Eva (grp)	18–30	Up to grd. 8	Christian Nom.	Yes	Live in
Leah (grp)	18–30	Up to grd. 8	Christian Nom.	Yes	Live in
Jane	31–40	High S.	Christian Nom.	Yes	Chr. Rites
Dorcas	18–30	High S.	Christian Nom.	Yes	Chr. Rites
Jackie	18–30	High S.	Christian Nom.	Yes	T. Marriage
Doreen (grp)	18–30	High S.	Christian Nom.	Yes	Live in
Lillian	31–40	C. College	Christian Nom.	Yes	Chr. Rites
Angela	31–40	C. College	Christian Nom.	Yes	Chr. Rites
Nelly	18–30	C. College	Christian Nom.	Yes	T. Marriage
Neema	31–40	C. College	Muslim	Yes	Mus. Rites
Annastasia	18–30	C. College	Christian- Adh.	Yes	T. Marriage
Julie	31–40	Univ. Grad.	Christian- Adh.	Yes	Chr. Rites
Nancy	41–50	Univ. Grad.	Christian- Adh.	Yes	Live in
Deviant S.					
Freda	18–30	Upto grd. 8	Christian Nom.	Yes	Live in
Carol	41–50	Univ. Grad.	Christian Adh.	Yes	Chr. Rites
Winnie	41–50	Univ. Grad.	Christian Adh.	No	Single
Sophie	31–40	C. College	Christian- Nom.	Yes	Chr. Rites
TOTAL	**23**				

Key:

Marital Relationships:

Traditional marriage (T. marriage)—recognized by extended family, traditional rites observed.

Muslim Marriage (Mus. Rites)—Islamic rites and requirements for marriage met

Christian Marriage (Chr. Rites)—Christian rites and requirements met.

Current Marital Status				Ethnic Group	Econ. Status	
In-Rel.	O-Rel-C	O-Rel-F	Single		Orig. Family	Current
		X		Lake Nilote	Low	L. Employ
X				Lake Nilote	Low	Ctty. Work.
		X		Cushite	middle	Small. Business
		X		Agr. Bantu	Low	No income
X				Agr. Bantu	Low	Small. Business
		X		Plain Nilote	Low	Small. Business
		X		Coast Bantu	Middle	Small. Business
X				Lake Nilote	Low	Small. Business
		X		Agr. Bantu	Middle	Low middle
		X		Agr. Bantu	Low	No income
X				Lake Nilote	Middle	Low middle
		X		Agr. Bantu	Low	Small. Business
X				Plain Nilote	Middle	Low middle
X				Agr. Bantu	High	High Middle
	X			Lake Nilote	Low	Small Business
	X			Swahili	Middle	No income
		X		Lake Nilote	Middle	Small Business
	X			Lake Nilote	High	Low middle
	X			Agr. Bantu	High	High Middle
	X			Plain Nilote	Low	L. Employ
X				Agr. Bantu	High	Graduate Student
			X	Agr. Bantu	High	High middle
X				Swahili	Middle	Low middle

Live In—No rites observed, generally known as 'come we stay.' Perceive selves as man & wife.

In Rel.—currently in abusive relationship

Out Rel. C.—Out of abusive relationship by choice

Out Rel. F—Out of abusive relationship under forced "fateful" circumstances

Appendix 3

DEFINITIONS OF TERMS

Archaic: In self-psychology, the term refers to the unchanged state of self-objects. When a self-object is held in its archaic form, it is related to with narcissistic instinctual energy, producing feelings similar to those of infant Grandiosity. In a sense, the presence of archaic self-objects in the adult psyche denotes lack of healthy differentiation development. In Kohut's words, such "adult personality and its mature functions are impoverished because they are deprived of energies that are invested in the ancient structures" (1971, 3).

Cathexis: Strong instinctual energy directed towards an object or self-object. Cathexis is the need to hold on to primary perfectionism now invested in the Grandiose self and the idealized parent imago. "Cathexis" is a conceptual term used by Kohut to refer to the instinctual energy in which the person relates to the self-objects of love, i.e. the Grandiose self and the idealized parent imago.

Cohesive self: A unified, consistent, solid, organized and inter-related self. "Cohesive self" is used by Kohut to refer to the integration of two major forms of narcissism into the personality (1978, 445). It refers to the homeostasis, or sustained balance, of the ego ideal (the super-ego), the ego, and the narcissistic self (Grandiose self) structures. According to Kohut, the cohesive self is the inner balance achieved by the interplay of these psychic structures, which "determine the characteristic flavor of personality, and is thus more than the building blocks or attributes of personality . . ." (1978, 443). It thus refers to the optimal transformations of narcissistic self and narcissistic idealization (1978, 446).

Differentiation: A normal, psychological human development process of separating oneself as an entity from another. According to Kohut,

212

differentiation is brought about by the mother's necessarily imperfect ministrations causing psychic tensions. The baby's psyche tries to deal with these frustrations in Kohut's perspective by "building up new systems of perfection" namely *narcissistic self* [Grandiose self] and *idealized parent imago* (1978, 430). Hence, differentiation is the gradual process of moving away from primary narcissism. Differentiation is an important developmental process in psychoanalysis and self-psychology for later development of important psychic structures that shape individual drive for achievement and transmutation of moral ideals in adulthood.

Ego ambitions: Self-aspirations, dreams, desire, or hopes. In self-psychology, ego ambitions are a function of a well-tamed Grandiosity, which comes about as a child realizes that the world does not always revolve around oneself and that he or she has some shortcomings. Such realizations function as natural checks that subdue the feelings of Grandiosity and simultaneously foster the beginning of a drive for achievement in the individual. Ego ideals are directly derived from a system of infantile Grandiose fantasies (1978, 437).

Grandiose self: A high-flying, flamboyant feeling about oneself resulting in the feeling that the world revolves around oneself. It is a "stage in development where everything pleasant, good and perfect is regarded as a rudimentary part of self" (1978, 430). In Kohut's words, it corresponds to Freud's "purified pleasure ego" (1971, 27). Kohut states that he uses the term Grandiose self to "designate Grandiose and exhibitionistic structure, which is the counterpart of idealized parent imago," (1971, 26) because, while the energy invested in the idealized imago is directed to a self-object outside of the self, the energy invested in the Grandiose self is in the self. In infancy, though, both psychic structures achieve similar end results because they are narcissistically related to. Kohut uses the term "Grandiose self" instead of "narcissistic self," stating that it has "greater evocative power" (1971, 26). He further states that "under optimal developmental conditions, the exhibitionism and Grandiosity of the archaic Grandiose self are gradually tamed, and the whole structure ultimately becomes integrated into the adult personality and supplies the instinctual fuel for our ego-ambitions . . ." (1971, 27).

Idealized Imago/Image: According to Kohut, idealization may be described as an aspect of narcissism (1978, 431). The idealized image is a highly-regarded representation, figure or reflection of an object. In self-psychology, "idealized parent imago" refers to the baby's "attempts to maintain the original perfection and omnipotence by imbuing the rudimentary you, the adult, with absolute perfection and power" (1978, 431). The idealized parent imago is best understood as a self-object. It is one of the two psychic structures that form in the baby's attempts to deal with maturational frustrations of losing primary narcissism and in the course of an infant's differentiation from the mother.

Identity: Following Erik Erikson, "identity" is the individuation that makes one stand unique in personality and yet whole, in the sameness and continuity achieved by the approximation of the inner drives and the outer social approval or confirmation of these drives. It is the fulfillment or belonging found in what Erikson describes as letting go of the safe hold on childhood and reaching out to adulthood. The quality of this process, according to Erikson, depends on the "reliability of those he must let go of and reception of those receiving him" (1964, 89). Erikson recognizes that the sense of identity, although negotiated in adolescence and adulthood, is nurtured very early in life. He states, "The self-images cultivated during *all the childhood stages* thus gradually prepare the sense of identity . . ." (1964, 94). For Erikson, successful identity formation depends on successful resolution of each epigenetic crisis, which serves as a building block to the next stage and which culminates in adolescence. In this book I expand the use of the term identity for understanding females in the Kenyan context by making the argument that the formation of female identity is reliant on the psychological formation of a sense of self. In other words, aspects of identity formation of females in Kenya may be traced to the social, cultural, and religious environment that nurtures the developing child and engenders a sense of self in that child. I base my view on the observation that, in the majority of African cultures, the individual finds his/her identity by finding a place for the self within the whole, namely, the community.

Narcissism: Narcissism in self psychology is a healthy investment in the self. Narcissism is not necessarily pathological. Kohut states that narcissism may be understood as an investment in the self, although an observer in the social field may assess it differently (1978, 429). Narcissism is an infant's psychological way of being, so that the baby experiences the mother and her ministrations not as an independent object, but within a view of the world in which the I = you differentiation has not yet been established (1978, 430). It is a necessary stage in infancy from which the infant forms self-objects which he/she can relate to with certain control to exert feelings "that preserve a part of the original experience [of an infant's world of] perfection" (1971, 27). Kohut states that narcissism "is not defined by the target of the instinctual investment . . . but by the nature of the quality of the instinctual charge" (1971, 26). For instance, when a child invests other people with narcissistic energy, the child experiences the other as a self-object, therefore expecting to exert control over the object as an adult would have control over his own body (1971, 27).

Religion: Acknowledging the wide use of the term and definitions of religions, I have narrowed the use of religion in this book to depict African religiosity, specifically, descriptive characteristics of African religiosity and the subsequent appropriation of indigenous African beliefs and ideologies in the people's embrace of other world religions in Kenya. John Mbiti describes religion as a pervasive reality in the lives of people in the African context—a lens through which the African seeks to comprehend, both intellectually and spiritually, the world and his/her place in it. He views religion as an intricate weaving of all aspects of being human: "religion is found in all areas of human life" (Mbiti 1991, 10). Consistent with Mbiti's perspective that religion permeates all spheres of life, the practice of religious rites and expectations in individual behavior expresses a socially-engendered inner belief in the existence of a Deity that could be related to with some special significance. Yet the daily practice and observance of religion of religious rites has a reciprocal effect of confirming, developing, and strengthening that inner reality.

Sense of Self: In this book the term "sense of self" is used as conceptually understood in Heinz Kohut's perspective of the formation of a cohesive self. I expand Kohut's self psychological understanding of a cohesive self based on the optimal development and integration into personality of individual psychic structures, to include the broader African communal perspective. Hence, development of a sense of self in many African contexts is a function of the internalized social, cultural, and religious demands placed on the individual's aspirations to belong to the community. I make the argument that the need to belong in the community and the aspects that nurture the child's sense of how to develop as one who belongs are internalized from the very early stage of infancy and continue to unfold through the structural development of the psyche. The female sense of self in particular is thus pre-consciously formed through internalization of social messages aligned to society's pre-conceived definition of what it means to be a female.

Super-ego: The psychic structure that can be equated to an internal legal force or agency. According to Kohut, the formation of a super-ego is a direct function of the gradual object loss of the idealized parent imago. He states, "every shortcoming detected in the idealized parent leads to a corresponding internal preservation of the externally lost quality of the object" (1978, 433). The super-ego is regarded as the "vehicle of the ego ideal" because its formation is a result of phase specific introjections of the idealized qualities, specifically unavoidable disappointments of the parent imago (1978, 434). The fact that "the original narcissism has passed through a cherished object before its re-internalization . . . account for the unique emotional importance of our standards, values, and ideals . . ." (1978, 434). Our ideals, first reflected in our idealized parent imago, then introjected into the super-ego, become our moral guide and leader (1978, 437).

Bibliography

Akintunde, D., and H. Labeodan, eds. 2002. *Women and the Culture of Violence in Traditional Africa*. Ibadan: Sefer.

Adams, C., and M. Fortune, eds. 1995. *Violence against Women and Children: A Christian Theological Sourcebook*. New York: Continuum.

Allport, G. 1973. *The Individual and His Religion*. New York: Macmillan.

———. 1996. The religious context of prejudice. *Journal of Scientific Study of Religion* 5:447–57.

Armstrong, A. 1998. *Culture and choice: Lessons from survivors of domestic violence in Zimbabwe*. Harare: Violence against Women in Zimbabwe Research Project.

Bahemuka, J. 1992. Social changes and women's attitudes toward marriage in East Africa. In *The Will to Arise: Women, Tradition and the Church in Africa*, ed . A. Oduyoye and M. Kanyoro, 119–94. New York: Orbis.

Bardwick, J. M. 1971. *Psychology of Women: A Study of Bio-cultural Conflicts*. New York: Harper & Row.

Barnett, O., Miller-Perin, C., and Perrin, R. 2011. *Family Violence across the Lifespan*. Thousand Oaks, CA: Sage.

Barth, K. 1980. The Revelation of God as the Abolition of Religion. In *Christianity and other religions*, ed. J. Hick and B. Hebblethwaite, 32–51. Philadelphia: Fortress.

Batson, C. D., P. Schoenrade, and W. L. Ventis. 1993. *Religion and the Individual: A Social-Psychological Perspective*. New York: Oxford University Press.

Beers, W. 1992. Self psychology, Narcissism and Gender: Male Narcissism, Women and Sacrifice. In *Women and Sacrifice: Male Narcissism and the Psychology of Religion*. Detroit: Wayne University Press.

Belenky, M. F., and others. 1986. *Women's Ways of Knowing: The Development of Self, Voice, and Mind*. New York: Basic.

Blau, G., M. Dall, and L. Anderson. 1993. In *Family Violence: Prevention and Treatment*, ed. R. Hampton, T. Gullota, et al.,. Thousand Oaks, CA: Sage.

Brown, L. 1994. *Subversive Dialogues: Theories in Feminist Thought*. New York: Basic.

Bula, O., and C. Lunda, eds. 1993. *Reports on a Seminar: Living without Violence*. Nairobi: N.C.C.K.

Bulhan, H. 1985. *Frantz Fanon and the Psychology of the Oppressed*. New York: Plenum.

Butler, J. 1990. *Gender Trouble: Feminism and the Subversion of Identity*. New York: Routledge.

Cooper-White, P. 1995. *The Cry of Tamar: Violence against Women and the Church's Response*. Minneapolis: Fortress.

Counts, D. A., and others, eds. 1999. *To Have and to Hit: Cultural Perspective on Wife Beating.* Urbana: University of Illinois Press.

Creswell, J. W. 1998. *Qualitative Inquiry and Research Design: Choosing among Five Traditions.* Thousand Oaks, CA: Sage.

Dixon, S. L. 1999. *Augustine: The Scattered and Gathered Self.* St. Louis: Chalice.

Downs, D. A. 1996. *More than Victims: Battered Women, the Syndrome Society, and the Law.* Chicago: University of Chicago Press.

Eisikovitz, Z., and E. Buchbinder. 2000. *Locked in a Violent Embrace: Understanding and Intervening in Domestic Violence.* Thousand Oaks, CA: Sage.

Erikson, E. 1959. *Identity and the Life Cycle: Selected Papers*, Vol 1. No. 1 Monograph 1. New York: W. W. Norton.

———. 1963. In *Childhood and Society,* Second Edition. New York: W. W. Norton.

———. 1964. *Insight and Responsibility: Lectures on the Ethical Implications of Psycho-Analytic Insight.* New York: W. W. Norton.

———. 1968. *Identity: Youth and Crisis.* New York: W. W. Norton.

Feshbach, S., B. Weiner, and A. Bohart. 1996. *Personality.* Lexington: D. C. Heath.

Fiorenza, E. S., and M. S. Copeland, eds. 1994. *Violence against Women.* New York: Orbis.

Fortune, M. 2001. Religious Issues and Violence against Women. In *The Sourcebook on Violence against Women* ed. C. M. Renzetti et al. Thousand Oaks, CA: Sage Publications.

Fortune, M. 1995. The transformation of suffering: A biblical and theological perspective. In *Family violence and religion: An interfaith resource guide.* Compiled by staff of Volcano Press, B. Ogawa (foreword). Thousand Oaks, CA: Volcano.

Fortune, M., and D. Hormann. 1981. *Family Violence: A Workshop Manual for Clergy and Other Service Providers.* Rockville, MD: National Clearing House on Domestic Violence.

Fowler, J. 1981. *Stages of Faith: The Psychology of Human Development and the Quest for Meaning.* San Francisco: Harper Collins.

Freud, S. 1910. *The Psychopathology of Everyday Life: Letters, Drafts and Notes to Wilheim Fliess.* Garden City: Doubleday.

———. 1914. *On Narcissism: An Introduction.* London: Hogarth.

———. 1961. *Civilization and its Discontents,* trans. J. Strachey. New York: Norton.

———. 1962. *Totem and Taboo,* trans. J. Strachey. New York: Norton.

———. 1964. *Future of an Illusion.* Garden City: Anchor Books.

———. 1990. *The Standard Edition: New Introductory Lectures on Psychoanalysis,* ed. and trans. J. Strachey. New York: Norton.

Gatobu, A. 2003. *Domestic Violence: A Challenge for Pastoral Care of Victims and their Families.* Nairobi: Faith Institute of Counselling.

Geertz, C. 1973. Religion as a Cultural System. In *The Interpretation of Cultures.* New York: Basic.

Gelles, R., J. S. Milner, and J. L. Crouch. 1993. Physical Child Abuse. In *Family Violence: Prevention and Treatment,* ed. R. Hampton et al. Thousand Oaks, CA: Sage.

Gilligan, C. 1979. Woman's Place in a Man's Life Cycle. *Harvard Educational Review* 49(4) 431–46.

Glenberg, A. M. 1996. *Learning from Data: An Introduction to Statistical Reasoning.* 2nd ed. New Jersey: Lawrence Erlbaum Associates.

Goetting, A. 1999. *Getting Out: Life Stories of Women Who Left Abusive Men*. New York: Columbia University Press.

Gondolf, E. 1993. Male Batterers. In *Family Violence: Prevention and Treatment*, ed. R. Hampton et al. Thousand Oaks, CA: Sage.

Graham, L. K. 1992. *Care of Persons, Care of Worlds: A Psychosystems Approach to Pastoral Care and Counseling*. Nashville: Abingdon.

Granadason, A. 1993. *No Longer a Secret: The Church and Violence Against Women*. Geneva: WCC.

Green, D. 1999. *Gender Violence in Africa: Africa Women's Responses*. New York: St Martin's.

Greenberg, J. R., and A. M. Stephen. 1983. *Object Relations in Psychoanalytic Theory*. Cambridge: Harvard University Press.

Gyekye, K. 1997. Person and Community. In *Tradition and Modernity: Philosophical Reflections on the African Experience*. New York: Oxford University Press.

Hampton R. and others, eds. 1993. *Family Violence: Prevention and Treatment*. Thousand Oaks, CA: Sage.

Herman, J. 1994. *Trauma and Recovery: From Domestic Abuse to Political Terror*. London: Pandora.

Hinga, T. 1994. Violence against Women: A Challenge to the Church. In *Pastoral Care in African Christianity: Challenging Essays in Pastoral Theology*, ed. D. Waruta and H. Kinoti, 117–33. Nairobi: Acton Printers.

Hood, R. W. 1996. *The Psychology of Religion: An Empirical Approach*. New York: Guilford.

Horton, A., and J. Williamson, eds. 1989. *Abuse and Religion: When Praying Isn't Enough*. Lexington, MA: Lexington.

Hunter, R. 1990. *Dictionary of Pastoral Care and Counseling*. Nashville: Abingdon.

Husserl, E. 1975. *The Paris Lectures*, trans. P. Koestenbaum. 2nd ed. The Hague: Martinus Nijhoff.

Jonte-Pace, D., and W. B. Parsons, eds. 2001. *Religion and Psychology: Mapping the Terrain: Contemporary Dialogues, Future Prospects*. New York: Routledge.

Joseph, S., R. Williams, and W. Yule, eds. 1997. *Understanding Post Traumatic Stress: A Psycho-social Perspective on PTSD and Treatment*. London: Wiley.

Kariuki, Njenga. 2003. Methods and Theories in Religious Studies. Unpublished.

Keller, E. F. 1978. Gender and Science. In *Discovering Reality: Feminist Perspectives on Epistemology, Metaphysics, Ethodology & Philosophy of Science*, ed. S. Harding and M. Mintikka, 187–205. London: Reidel.

Kibwana, K. 1996. *Law and the Status of Women in Kenya*. Nairobi: Clairpress.

Klein, E. 1997. *Ending Domestic Violence: Changing Public Perception/Halting the Epidemic*. Thousand Oaks, CA: Sage.

Kohut, H. 1971. *The Analysis of the Self: A Systematic Approach to the Psychoanalytic Treatment of Narcissistic Personality Disorders. The Psychoanalytic Study of the Child, Monograph no. 4*. New York: International Universities Press.

———. 1978. Forms and Transformations of Narcissism. In *The Search for the Self: Selected Writings of Heinz Kohut: 1950–1978*, vol. 1, 427–60, ed. P. H. Ornstein. New York: International Universities Press.

———. 1978. The Psychoanalytic Treatment of Narcissistic Personality Disorders: Outline of a Systematic Approach. In *The Search for the Self: Selected Writings of*

Heinz Kohut: 1950–1978, vol. 1, 477–509, ed. P. H. Ornstein. New York: International Universities Press.

———. 1979. The two analyses of Mr. Z. *International Journal of Psychoanalysis* 60:3–27

Kung, H. 1993. *Christianity and world religions: Paths of dialogue with Islam, Hinduism and Buddhism,* trans. P. Heinegg. Maryknoll, New York: Orbis Books.

Magesa, L. 1997. *African religions: The moral traditions of abundant life.* New York: Orbis Books.

Mbiti, J. S. 1969. *African religions and philosophy.* Nairobi: East African Educational Publishers.

———. 1975. *Introduction to African religions.* Oxford: Heinemann International.

———. 1991. *Introduction to African religions.* 2d ed. Oxford: Heinemann International.

McIntosh, D. N. 1997. Religion-as-Schema: With implications for the relationship between coping and religion. In *The psychology of religion: Theoretical approaches,* ed. B. Spilka and D. McIntosh. Boulder, CO: Westview Press.

Milner, J., and J. Crouch. 1993. Physical child abuse. In *Family violence: Prevention and treatment,* ed. R. Hampton et al. Thousand Oaks, CA: Sage.

Moustakas, C. 1994. *Phenomenological research methods.* Thousand Oaks, CA: Sage.

Mucherera, T. 2001. *Pastoral Care From a Third World Perspective: A Pastoral Theology of Care from an Urban Contemporary Shona in Zimbabwe* New York: Peter Lang.

Nasimiyu-Wasike, A. 1994. Domestic violence against women: A cry for life in wholeness. In *Pastoral care in African Christianity: Challenging essays in pastoral theology,* 103–16, ed. D. Waruta and H. Kinoti. Nairobi: Acton Printers.

Nasimiyu-Wasike, A., and D. Waruta, eds. 2000. *Mission in African Christianity: Critical essays in missiology.* Nairobi: Acton Publishers.

NiCarthy, G. 1995. Building self-esteem: Overcoming barriers to recovery. In *Family violence and religion.* B. Ogawa (foreword). Volcano, CA: Volcano Press.

Obeyesekere, G. 1981. *Medusa's hair: An essay on personal symbols and religious experience.* Chicago: University of Chicago Press.

Oduyoye, M. A. 1986. *Hearing and knowing: Theological reflections on Christianity in Africa.* Maryknoll, New York: Orbis Books.

Oduyoye, M. A. 2001. *Introducing African women's theology.* England: Sheffield Academic Press Ltd.

Ogawa, B. 1995. *Family violence and religion: An interfaith resource guide,* foreword. Compiled by staff of Volcano Press. California: Volcano Press.

Pargament, K. I., and C. L. Park. 1997. In times of stress: The religion coping connection. In *The psychology of religion: Theoretical approaches,* ed. B. Spilka and D. McIntosh. Boulder, CO: Westview Press.

Parsons, T. 1964. The superego and the theory of social systems. In *Social structure and personality,* 17–33. London: Collier MacMillan.

Pedersen, P., ed. 1999. *Multiculturalism as a fourth force.* Castleton: Hamilton.

Proudfoot, W., and P. Shaver. 1997. Attribution theory and the psychology of religion. In *The Psychology of Religion: Theoretical Approaches,* ed. B. Spilka and D. McIntosh. Boulder CO: Westview Press.

Renzetti, C., Edelson, J., and Bergen R. 2011. *Sourcebook on Violence Against Women,* Second Edition. Thousand Oaks: Sage.

Roberts, A. R. 1998. *Battered women and their families: Intervention strategies and treatment programs.* New York: Springer.

Robinson, S. 1999. A rough kind of justice: Battered women are beginning to speak out against a troubling tradition of domestic violence. *Time.com,* vol. 153, no. 18 (May 10).

Rogers, C. 1959. A theory of therapy, personality and interpersonal relationships, as developed in the client-centered framework. In *Psychology: A study of science,* vol. 3, ed. S. Koch. New York: McGraw-Hill.

Roy, M., ed. 1997. *Battered women: A psychological study on domestic violence.* New York: Van Nostrand Reinhold.

Rizzuto, A. 1979. *The birth of a living God: A psychoanalytic study.* Chicago: University of Chicago Press.

Rubin, A., and E. Babbie. 1997. *Research methods for social work.* 3d ed. Pacific Grove, CA: Brooks/Cole.

Saunders-Robinson, M. A., 1995. Battered women: An African American perspective. In *Family violence and religion: An interfaith resource guide,* compiled by the staff of Volcano Press. California: Volcano Press.

Saussy, C. 1991. *God images and self esteem: Empowering women in a patriarchal society.* Lousiville: Westminster/ John Knox Press.

Scalia, J. 2002. *Intimate violence: Attacks upon psychic interiority.* New York: Columbia University Press.

Schafer, R. 1968. *Aspects of internalization.* New York: International University Press.

Schleiermacher, F. 1969. Romanticism. In *Attitudes towards other religions: Some Christian interpretations,* 49–69, ed. C. Owen. Notre Dame: University of Notre Dame Press.

Seligman, M.E. P. 1990. *Learned helplessness.* New York: Knopf.

Shaikh, S. S. 1996. Battered women in Muslim communities in the Western Cape: Religious constructions of gender, marriage sexuality and violence. Masters Thesis, University of Cape Town.

———. 1997. Exegetical Violence: *Nushuz* in Qur'anic Gender. *Journal of Islamic Studies* 17:49–73.

———. 2003. Transforming feminisms: Islam, women, and gender justice. In *Progressive Muslims: On justice, gender and pluralism,* ed. O. Safi. Oxford: Oneworld.

Shweder, R. A., and N. C. Much. 1987. Determinations of meaning: Discourse and moral socialization. *In Moral development through social interaction,* ed. W. Kurtiness and J. Gerwitz. New York: Wiley.

Sipe, B., and E. Hall. 1996. *I am not your victim: Anatomy of domestic violence.* Thousand Oaks, CA: Sage.

Spilka, B., and D. McIntosh, eds. 1997. *Psychology of religion: Theoretical approaches.* Boulder, CO: Westview press.

Stacy, W., and A. Shupe. 1983. *The family secret: Domestic violence in America.* Boston: Beacon Press.

Stanfield, J. H. III, ed. 1993. *Race and ethnicity in research methods.* Newbury Park, CA: Sage.

Stets, J. E. 1988. *Domestic violence and control.* New York: Springer-Verlag.

Sundermeier, T. 1998. *The individual and community in African traditional religions,* Hamburg: Lit Verlag.

Taylor, M.C., ed. 1998. *Critical terms for religious studies.* Chicago: University of Chicago Press.

United Nations Documents. 1993. *Monitoring the implementation of the Nairobi for-ward-looking strategies for the advancement of women: draft report* 1993, 03, 24 Doc. E/CN.6/ 1993/ L.1/ Add.2

———. 1999. *Violence against women in the family: Report of the special rapporteur on violence against women, its causes and consequences.* Radhika Coomaraswamy, submitted in accordance with Commission on Human Rights Resolution 1995/85. 1999,03,10. E/CN.4/sub.2/RES/1999/68

———. 2000. *Traditional practices affecting the health of women and the girl child.* 2000,11,23. E/CN.4/sub.2/RES/2000/10

Walker, L. 1979. *The battered woman.* New York: Harper & Row.

———. 1984. *The battered woman syndrome.* New York: Springer.

Winnicott, D. 1953. Transitional objects and transitional phenomena. *The International Journal of Psychoanalysis* 35:

———. 2000. Transitional objects and transitional phenomena. In *Identity : a reader* 150–62. ed. Paul du Gay, et al. Thousand Oaks, CA : SAGE Publications in associa-tion with The Open University.

Women and Law in South African Trust, ed. 2001. *Gender violence: The invisible strug-gle: Responses to the justice delivery system in Zambia.* Lusaka, Zambia: Women and Law in South African Trust.

Wundt, W. 1998. Excerpt from Grundiss der psychologie (Outline of psychology) (1897–1902). In *Readings in the history and systems of psychology.* 2d ed., ed. F. Brenan. New Jersey: Prentice Hall.

Wulff, D. M. 1997. *Psychology of religion: Classic and contemporary.* 2d ed. New York: Wiley.

———. 2001. Psychology of religion: An overview. In *Religion and psychology: Map-ping the terrain: Contemporary dialogues, future prospects,* ed. D. Jonte-Pace and W. B. Parsons. New York: Routledge.

www.ingramcontent.com/pod-product-compliance
Lightning Source LLC
Chambersburg PA
CBHW070407270326
41926CB00014B/2740